DXHM.

D1284369

Hawai'i:
The Royal Isles

Crown of Hawaii. No. 252

Hawai'i:
The Royal Isles

Roger G. Rose

with
an introductory essay
by

Adrienne L. Kaeppler

Photographs by
Seth Joel

Bernice P. Bishop Museum Special Publication 67

BISHOP MUSEUM PRESS
Honolulu, Hawai'i

Hawai'i: The Royal Isles
was developed and organized by
Bernice Pauahi Bishop Museum
and made possible with support from the
National Endowment for the Humanities
and
United Airlines

Copyright © 1980 by Bernice Pauahi Bishop Museum
All Rights Reserved
Library of Congress Catalog Card No. 80-65718
ISSN 0067-6179
ISBN 0-910240-27-2

Contents

Foreword   Edward C. Creutz   vii

Preface   Richard J. Ferris   ix

Acknowledgments   Roger G. Rose, Adrienne L. Kaeppler, and Mary Lee Weaver   x

The Persistence of Tradition   Adrienne L. Kaeppler   53

   Origin of the Islands, The Gods, and Men: Tradition   54

   Origin of the Islands and Men: Science   55

   Aspects of Hawaiian Tradition: Persistence and Change   57

The Exhibition   Roger G. Rose   157

   Visions of Hawai'i   157

   The Gods Were Many   162

      Images of Deity   162

      Arrival of the First Missionaries   167

   The Life of the Land   171

      "A Fine Handsome Sett of People"   171

      Calabashes and Kings   177

      The *Hula*   185

   Symbols of Sovereignty   191

      Featherwork   191

      Chiefly Ornaments   196

      The Kamehameha Dynasty   199

      The Kalākaua Dynasty   206

   Contemporary Reflections of the Past   215

Kings and Queens of Hawai'i   218

Glossary   219

Bibliography   221

Photo Credits   223

Illustrations:

   Map of Hawai'i   xii

   Color plates   1-52

   Black and white photographs   63-156

Hawai'i: The Royal Isles

Itinerary	*Dates*
Art Insititute of Chicago	September 6, 1980-October 19, 1980
Denver Art Museum	December 3, 1980-January 18, 1981
Natural History Museum of Los Angeles County	February 20, 1981-April 26, 1981
Seattle Art Museum	June 3, 1981-July 26, 1981
The Fine Arts Museums of San Francisco M. H. de Young Memorial Museum	September 26, 1981-December 6, 1981
Cooper-Hewitt Museum, New York	March 9, 1982-May 9, 1982
Museum of Fine Arts, Boston	June 3, 1982-August 8, 1982

National Museum of Natural History—
    National Museum of Man,
    Smithsonian Institution, Washington, D.C.
	September 15, 1982-November 1, 1982

Bernice P. Bishop Museum, Honolulu	December 19, 1982-March 1, 1983

Foreword

We at Bishop Museum are particularly fortunate to be immersed in a unique cultural mélange, but one in which the undertones of Hawaiian historical experience are always present. The Polynesian people, in their purposeful wanderings throughout the Pacific, developed techniques for living, playing, fighting, praying, and beautifying their surroundings with no knowledge of concurrent civilizations to their east or west. This powerful civilization, influenced by none of those that are more familiar to us through our standard courses in "World History," has much to tell us and much for us to admire.

With the influx into their isolated world of Europeans, Americans, and Asians that began two centuries ago, the Hawaiian people had to adjust to different living styles and values. Their response to these external pressures and also their resistance to change, owing to the strength of past traditions ingrained by total cultural self-sufficiency and preserved through chants and the remarkably expressive *hula*, are what this exhibition is all about.

There is a deep message here: that human experience accumulated and preserved for some fifty generations may give way to new influences. But this will happen slowly, since the process is moderated by strong traditions that even today, in the case of the Hawaiians, continue to tell us much about their ancestral period.

Thus, Bishop Museum has, with the greatest of enthusiasm and pleasure, created this exhibition to bring to many people an important and fascinating story that will be new to the majority of those who see it.

An exhibition with this significance can never be the work of just a few people. In this case, the two principal creators are Roger G. Rose and Adrienne L. Kaeppler of the Department of Anthropology at Bishop Museum. Many others of the staff contributed their best, and some should be mentioned: Cynthia A. Timberlake, Museum Librarian; David B. Kemble, Chairman of the Department of Exhibits; and Mary Lee Weaver, Special Exhibitions Coordinator.

The essential funding was provided by a grant from the National Endowment for the Humanities and by generous gifts from United Airlines. Particularly pleasant was the continuous backing provided by Governor George R. Ariyoshi of the State of Hawaii, who recognized from the start that the exhibition would be an important cultural statement on behalf of those who have Hawaiian blood in their hearts and whose roots are less than well known in many mainland states.

Thus, Bishop Museum is thoroughly proud to offer this pleasurable and educational Hawaiian experience, with the cooperation of the several participating museums, to a large segment of the public.

EDWARD C. CREUTZ
Director, B. P. Bishop Museum

Honolulu, Hawai'i
February, 1980

Preface

When Hawai'i became the 50th state in 1959, the culture of a unique Oceanic world became the newest part of our national heritage. Through the exhibition HAWAI'I: THE ROYAL ISLES, Hawai'i is offering its fellow Americans a rare view of the treasures from its persisting traditions.

HAWAI'I: THE ROYAL ISLES, organized by Bernice P. Bishop Museum in Honolulu, is a comprehensive exhibition of the richness and scope of Hawaiian culture, past and present.

The exhibition shows us the emblems, featherwork, and adornments of Hawai'i's royal dynasties. It displays the arts and crafts of life in Hawai'i as it evolved from ancient chiefdoms through royal monarchies and into our time. A continuous thread of inspiration and creativity links Hawai'i's Polynesian ancestral origins of more than a thousand years ago with today's modern statehood.

It is a great privilege for United Airlines to join with the National Endowment for the Humanities in sponsoring HAWAI'I: THE ROYAL ISLES and to present this distinctive part of our heritage to mainland America.

RICHARD J. FERRIS
Chairman, United Airlines

Chicago, Illinois
February, 1980

Acknowledgments

HAWAI'I: THE ROYAL ISLES is a milestone for Bishop Museum. This is the first time most of the objects will be leaving Bishop Museum and the Hawaiian Islands and many Mainland visitors will have their first opportunity to enjoy the unique beauty of Hawaiian treasures. This is also the first time that an exhibition of Hawaiian artifacts focuses on Hawaiian culture and values in order to explicate traditions that have both persisted and changed.

An exhibition of this scope and importance can only be realized through the inspiration, interest, and hard work of many people. We thank all of those individuals and institutions who have given of their expertise and time to all aspects of the project from its conception and throughout the tour of the exhibition.

We especially want to thank the lenders who have so generously shared their objects for the three years of the exhibition. Our deepest appreciation to: Mrs. George R. Ariyoshi; Daughters of Hawai'i, Queen Emma Summer Palace; Hawai'i State Archives; Hale Nauā III, Society of Hawaiian Artists; Dennis Kana'e Keawe; Lyman House Memorial Museum; Drs. Ben and A. Jess Shenson; and The Kamehameha Schools, with the kind cooperation of Mr. and Mrs. John Dominis Holt.

Bishop Museum's curatorial staff has once again shown the highest professional standards throughout the various stages of the exhibition. We appreciate the contributions of Dr. Yosihiko H. Sinoto, Chairman of the Department of Anthropology; Lynn Davis of the Photo Archives; Elizabeth Tatar, Ethnomusicologist; and John Cotton Wright, Historian. A special heartfelt thanks goes to Cynthia Timberlake, Librarian, under whose direction the works of art on paper have become an important part of this exhibition. Special appreciation is also given to Editor Genevieve A. Highland and Associate Editor Sadie J. Doyle for the expertise and patience they have imparted to the preparation of this catalog.

Many of the beautiful photographs in this catalog are the excellent work of Seth Joel, who shares our warmest gratitude to Bishop Museum photographers Benjamin Patnoi, Lynne Gilliland, and photography assistant Joseph C. Cordle, Jr.

A myriad of curatorial and logistical details were handled expertly by the staff of the Ethnology Division. We are indebted to the tireless dedication of Dora D. Jacroux, Ann Marshall, Betty J. Long, Linnea Brown, and Laura Carter. We are grateful for the thorough research of the competent staff of the Bishop Museum Library, Marguerite K. Ashford, Janet G. Ness, and Janet Short, and to Debra Sullivan of the Photo Archives. David Kemble, John McLaughlin, and Toni Maiava of the Exhibits Department have given much time and creative talent to the installation plans of the exhibition. A special thanks is extended to those staff members whose typing talents have been fully appreciated throughout the project, Marge Tamaye, Dorothy Hoxie, and Patience Bacon.

Pacific Regional Conservation Center deserves many plaudits for the excellent conservation and preparation of the objects in the exhibition. We thank Dr. Anthony E. A. Werner, Chairman and Chief Conservator, and his able staff, Mary Wood Lee, William Phippen, Natalie Firnhaber, Robert Du Meer, and Janet Begg for their special touch. We are also grateful for the National Science Foundation's support of the bark cloth conservation project which has enabled us to include examples from the Museum's bark cloth collection. Pacific Regional Conservation Center is also responsible for the fine shipping crate design, manufacture, and packing, with the aid of Hisao Goto, Exhibit Preparator, and his staff.

There have been many individuals outstide Bishop Museum who have been helpful and supportive of "Hawai'i: the Royal Isles." We thank the host museums and their staffs who ultimately are responsible for breathing life into the exhibition. Our deepest appreciation to Dr. Evan M. Maurer, Curator of Primitive Art, Art Institute of Chicago, for his superlative advice and aid in the initial installation. Many management questions were generously answered by Sam Farmer and Lee Lambert of Battelle, Pacific Northwest Laboratories. We are grateful for the specialized knowledge and advice of the following individuals: Peter Morse for the Lahainaluna material; Irving Jenkins and Roger Skolman for wood identification; Paulette Kahalepuna for feather identification; and Harriet O'Sullivan, our educational consultant. Jimmy Sur, of Palace Upholstery; Rhoda Komura of the Honolulu Academy of Arts; Dorothy B. Weight, *volunteer extraordinaire;* and the Department of Fashion Design and Merchandising at the University of Hawai'i contributed significantly to special conservation and installation efforts. We are most appreciative to Nina Wright, Karen Hughes, and Susan Bloom of Ruder & Finn, Inc. for their constant support, expertise, and encouragement.

We are indebted to the Bishop Museum Board of Trustees and the Administration for their unending support of the project. And, finally, we are most grateful to our generous sponsors for this exhibition, the National Endowment for the Humanities and United Airlines.

ROGER G. ROSE
Senior Project Co-director

ADRIENNE L. KAEPPLER
Project Co-director

MARY LEE WEAVER
Project Coordinator

B. P. Bishop Museum
Honolulu, Hawai'i
February, 1980

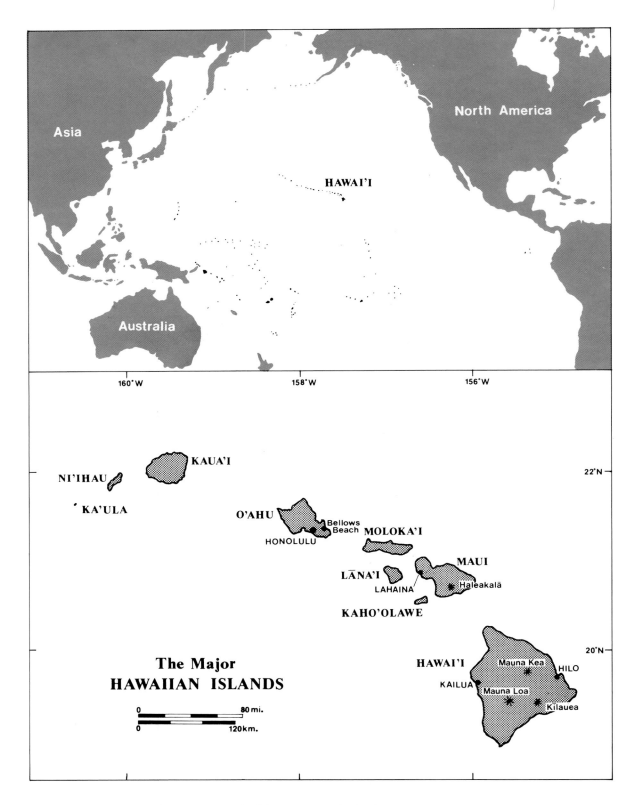

Asia

North America

HAWAI'I

Australia

160°W · 158°W · 156°W

KAUA'I

NI'IHAU

' KA'ULA

22°N

O'AHU

Bellows
Beach

HONOLULU

MOLOKA'I

MAUI

LĀNA'I

Haleakalā

LAHAINA

KAHO'OLAWE

**The Major
HAWAIIAN ISLANDS**

0   80 mi.

0   120km.

HAWAI'I

Mauna Kea

HILO

KAILUA

Mauna Loa

Kilauea

20°N

The major Hawaiian Islands lie 20°-22° north of the equator in the Pacific
Ocean and comprise the southernmost portion of the approximately
2,000-mile-long Hawaiian archipelago, shown in the upper half of the map in
relation to North America to the east and Asia to the west. (Drawn by Eric
Komori, Bishop Museum.)

I   The Death of Cook, by George Carter, c. 1783. No. 1

II   Honolulu Harbor, unknown photographer, c. 1856. No. 13

III   Kīlauea, Day Scene, by Titian Ramsay Peale, 1842. No. 16

IV   An Offering before Captain Cook, 1779, by John Webber. No. 22

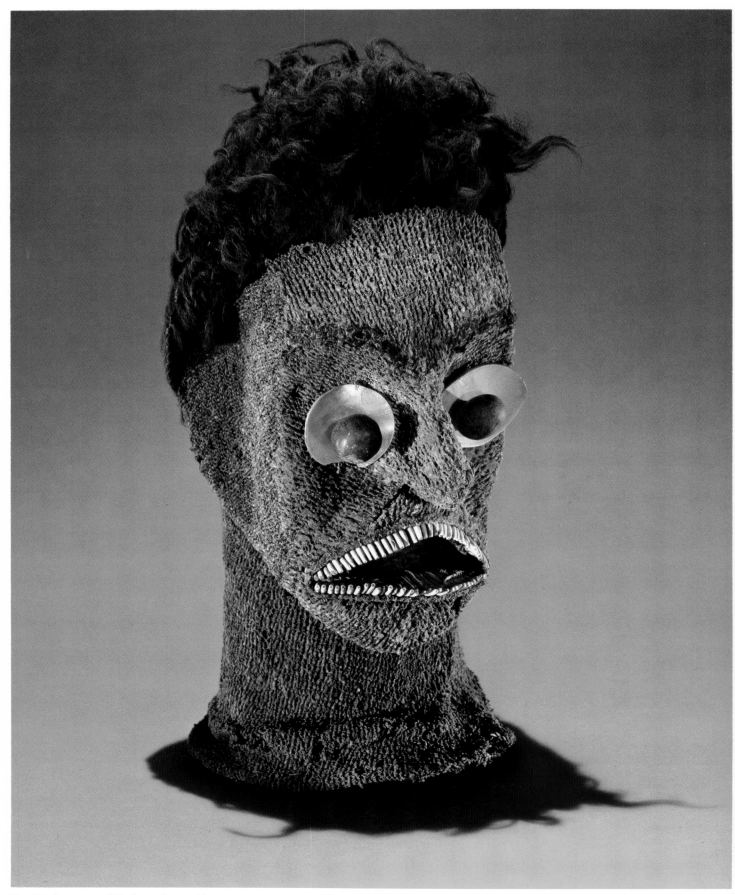

V   Feather-covered Basketry Image. No. 24

VI   Wooden Image, claimed by King Kalākaua t
Kūka'ilimoku, War God of Kamehameha I. No

5

VII   Wooden Image. No. 26

VIII   Wooden Image,
said to be a God of Rain. No. 27

IX   Wooden Image, from Forbes Cave. No. 29

XI   Stone Image. No. 37

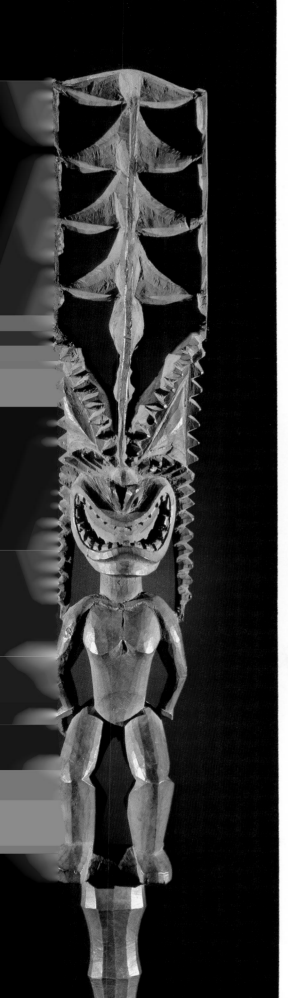

ÎLES SANDWICH: BAPTÊME DU PREMIER MINISTRE DU ROI, À BORD DE L'URANIE.

XII   ''Îles Sandwich: Baptême du Premier Ministre du Roi . . .,''
1819, by Crépin after sketches of Arago. No. 49

X   Wooden Image, from Forbes Cave. No. 30

9

XIII "The Lei Maker," by Theodore Wores, 1902. No. 65

XIV   Fernstem Hat. No. 91

XV   Covered Poi Bowl. No. 101

11

12

XVII   Medicine Bowl,
used by Kamehameha I. No. 122

XVIII   Ivory Medicine Pounder,
used by Kamehameha I. No. 123

"Calabash of the Winds." No. 119

XIX "Hawaiian Child and the Poi Bowl," by Theodore Wores, 1901. No. 140

XX   Double Gourd Drum, used by Kamehameha Court. No. 150

XXI   Coconut Dance Rattles. No. 153

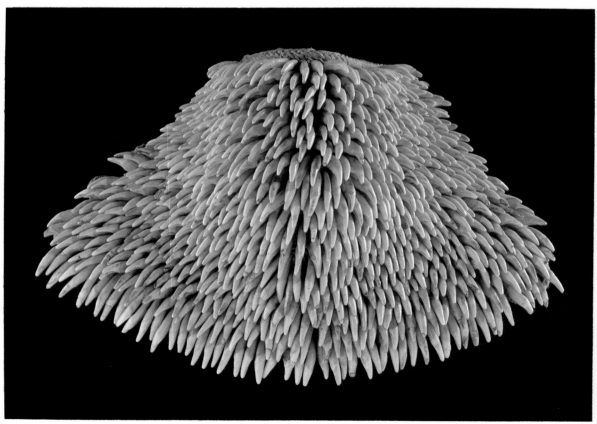

XXII   Dog Tooth Anklet. No. 161

16

XXIII *'Ukulele,* made by David Mahelona. No. 164

XXIV   Boki and Liliha, 1824, by John Hayter. No. 165

XXV   Man from the Sandwich Islands with Feathered Helmet,
Helmet Band, and Cape, by John Webber, c. 1780. No. 167

XXVI   Feather Helmet of King Kaumuali'i. No. 168

20

XXVII   Joy Cloak. No. 170

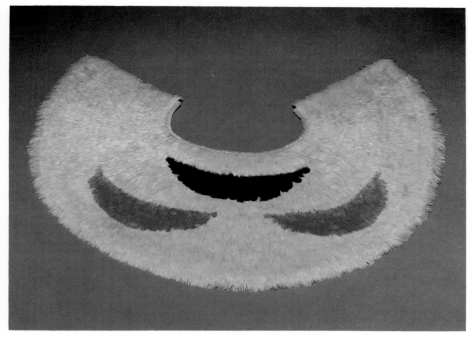

XXXI   Revivalist Period Cape. No. 177

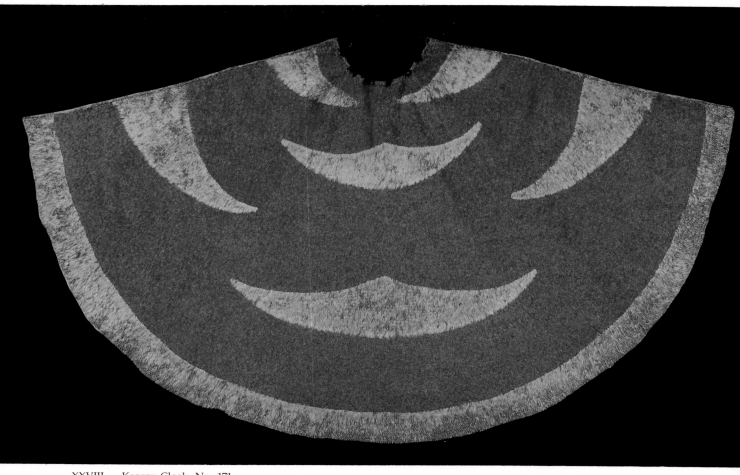

XXVIII   Kearny Cloak. No. 171

XXIX   Kaumualiʻi Cape. No. 173

XXXII   Feather Lei, Nos. 183, 180, 182, 179, 178, 181 (left to right)

25

XXXIII Feather Lei from
Princess Ka'iulani. No. 181

XXXV Feather Hat Lei. No. 184

XIV Feather Lei, detail. No. 179

27

XXXVI   Feather Hat Lei. No. 185

XXXVII   Feather Hat Lei. No. 186

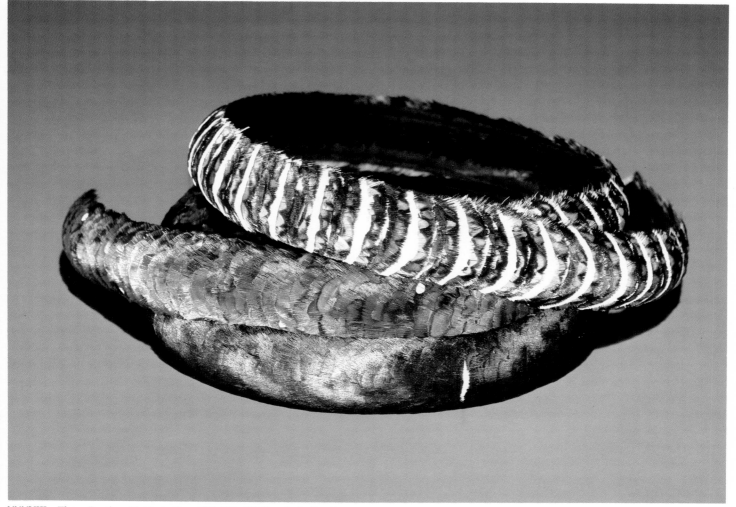

XXXVIII   Three Feather Hat Lei. Nos. 187, 188, 189 (top to bottom)

XXXIX   Hook Pendant on Human Hair Necklace. No. 197

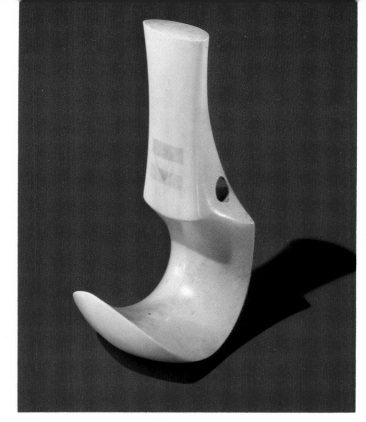

XL Hook Pendant of Imported
Elephant Ivory. No. 199

XLI Hook Pendant on Bead Necklace. No. 203

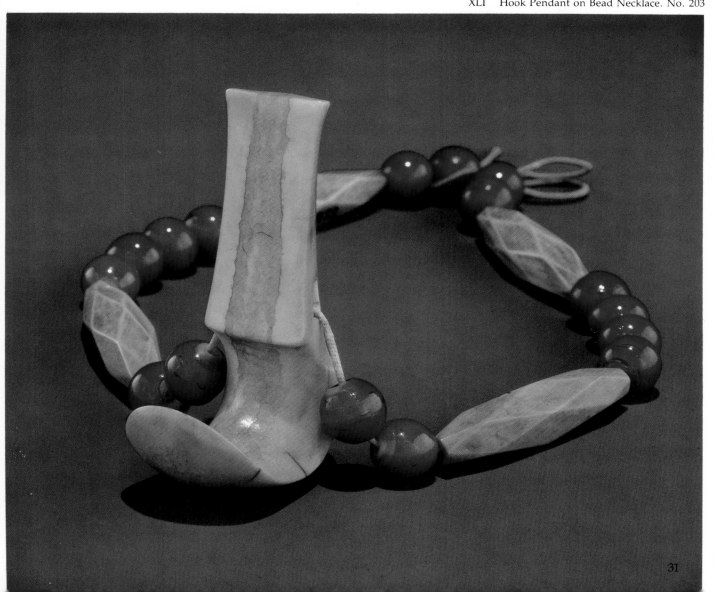

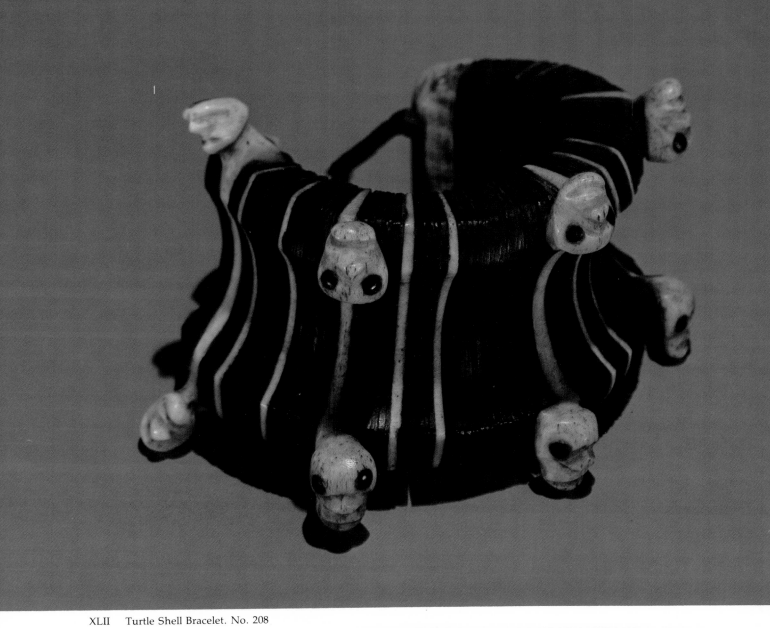

XLII   Turtle Shell Bracelet. No. 208

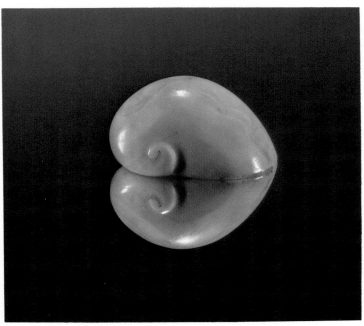

XLIII   Ivory Wristlet. No. 210

XLIV   King Kamehameha I (?1758-1819), unknown artist. No. 214

XLV   King Kamehameha II (c. 1797-1824), unknown artist.   No. 215

34

XLVI   Miniature Bust
of Kamehameha II, 1825. No. 219

XLVII   Silver Teapot given to
Ka'ahumanu in 1825. No. 220

XLVIII   King Kamehameha III (1813-1854), unknown artist. No. 221

XLIX   Throne of Kamehameha III, 1847. No. 223

LI   King Kamehameha IV (1834-1863), by William Cogswell.   No. 231

L   The Kamehameha Royal Family,
unknown photographer, c. 1852. No. 228

LV   State Sword of Kamehameha IV. No. 240

LII   Prince of Hawai'i (1858-1862), by Enoch Wood Perry.   No. 233

LIV   Silver Christening Cup, detail. No. 234

LIII   Silver Christening Cup given by Queen Victoria to the
Prince of Hawai'i, 1862. No. 234

LVIII   King Lunalilo (1835-1874) as a Young Man, unknown artist. No. 248

LVII   Gold and Coral Jewelry Set, worn by
Princess Bernice Pauahi Bishop. No. 247

VI   King Kamehameha V (1830-1872),
by William Cogswell. No. 241

LIX   King David Kalākaua (1836-1891), by William Cogswell.   No. 251

LXI   Royal Scepter, detail. No. 253

LX   Royal Scepter. No. 253

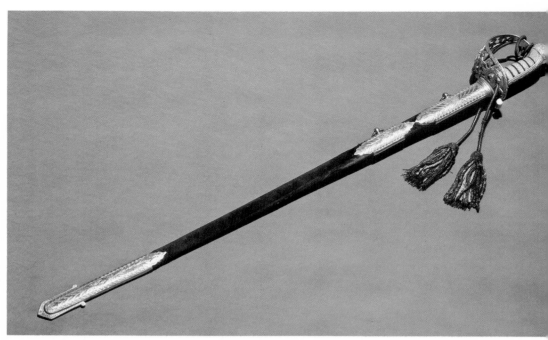

LXII   Sword of State. No. 254

LXIII   Ring of State. No. 255

LXIV   Hawaiian Coat of Arms. No. 256

LXVI   Court Uniform of C. P. Iaukea, made for
Queen Victoria's Jubilee, 1887. No. 273

LXVII   Coronation Gown Worn by Princess Lili'uokalani, 1883. No. 278

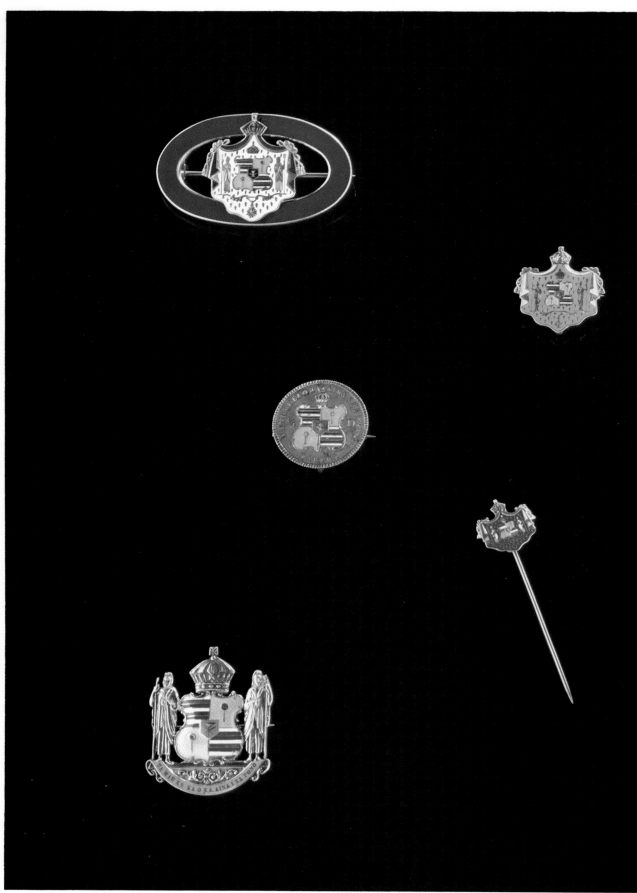

LXV   Royal Order of Kamehameha I, Knights Commander. No. 257

The Persistence of Tradition
Adrienne L. Kaeppler

Mai kapae i ke a'o a ka makua,
aia he ola malaila.

Do not ignore the teachings of a parent,
for there is life in them.

Hawaiian proverb
(Handy and Pukui, 1958, p.194)

Tales related as prose or poetry by parents or ancestors constitute the preferred Hawaiian method of acquiring knowledge of the past. Concepts or details about specific events or people passed through the oral tradition carry great influence in the daily lives of Hawaiians, while books or written history are but a minor modern supplement. Traditions relate the intimate relationships of Hawaiians with the gods and their environment. Historical epics recount concepts of creation, and narratives indicate how people cared for each other and how chiefs and people interacted. Those with specialized knowledge passed on their skills in arts and crafts, music and dance, to selected individuals who, in turn, elaborated or simplified them, and passed them on again. Life was lived and knowledge passed on, just as in every other culture—ordinary and unromantic to the people who live it.

How different was an outsider's view, based on the published journals of Captain Cook and other explorers that depicted, in words and engravings, the sights they encountered in the late 18th and early 19th centuries in Hawai'i. The accounts of whalers and merchants who later plied the Pacific added to the romantic European and American vision of the Pacific islands and their peoples. Historical events that occurred in the Pacific were imaginatively portrayed in paintings and engravings. Famous poems such as Samuel Taylor Coleridge's *The Rime of the Ancient Mariner* told of the mystical experiences to be found, and Herman Melville's romantic novels added to the mythology that represented most of the world's conception of the Pacific islands. Subsequent ideas that have been widely disseminated throughout the world through motion pictures, radio, and television, have largely built upon the original erroneous conceptions, and have done little to dispel the myths.

An Austrian song, "Eine Insel aus Träumen Geboren," suggests that Hawai'i is an island born of dreams. Images conjured up of little brown girls, little grass shacks, fish with difficult-to-pronounce names, endless beaches of pristine white sands, and the wind whispering through palm trees under balmy night skies are American versions of this erroneous vision derived from Hollywood and the popular songs of the 1920's and 1930's. This image is not only superficial, but is receding like the sound of the waves that once graced "Hawaii Calls," the popular radio program that was beamed to rapt audiences in the mainland United States and elsewhere. European and American visions of Hawai'i and the Hawaiians have been a mixture of the concept of the noble savage, and of happy, carefree natives who sing and dance but do little else. The fading of this vision is owing to a recent interest in Hawaiian culture that is based more in truth than in fantasy, and to the development of cultural movements throughout America and the world that attempt to separate the genuine from the spurious.

It is surprising to many to find that traditional Hawaiian world views, philosophies, arts, and crafts still flourish in Hawai'i in spite of the overlay of 19th and 20th century European and American value systems, a competitive money economy, and an introduced Christian God. Even before the recent resurgence of Hawaiian tradition, there were many visible elements of Hawaiian culture that had never died. The persistence of tradition is a more appropriate vision of Hawai'i, from both within and without. This theme, which will be explored here, demonstrates that Hawaiian values have not fossilized; they are living forces for inspiration and creation that form a continuous link between the Hawai'i of today and of yesterday.

Hawaiian culture and values have evolved during the past two centuries and are now part of life in a multicultural society. Hawaiian objects and the persons who made and used them are particularly relevant in an examination of changing and persisting Hawaiian values during the two centuries since 1778, when Captain Cook first visited the Hawaiian Islands and made their existence known to the Western world. The overall theme of the strength and persistence of tradition will be explored through several continua of objects, beginning with indigenous forms and following their development over time to their modern interpretations and uses. In this way it is hoped to explicate Hawaiian values in connection with technological and aesthetic achievements, as found in and symbolized by featherwork, wood carving, music, bark cloth, clothing, and ornaments. Objects and people will be related to their religious and social context and to the evolution of the Hawaiian sociopolitical system, from fractious chiefdoms, through a dynastic monarchy of the European variety, to statehood.

In this introduction some of the concepts about the origin of the Hawaiians and the Hawaiian Islands will be related from the points of view of tradition and of science, and a short overview of some of the concepts and principles by which Hawaiians organized their lives will set the stage for an appreciation of the objects and their histories which follow. It is hoped that this volume will be a step toward furthering our understanding of the Hawaiian experience past and present. However, as Rubellite Kawena Johnson has recently noted, "the patient analysis of Hawaiian traditions and literature for the ethical components of the ancient values which may truly enhance and bring vitality to the culture of today and tomorrow is a job for humanities scholars without intruding in those matters which are the purview, primarily, of the Hawaiian ethnic group" (Johnson, 1979, p. 8). Some things remain strictly the province of Hawaiians and are shared only among themselves. No doubt they will not be written down, for that is not the Hawaiian way. Such traditions will continue to be passed down orally and, I trust, they will not be ignored, for "there is life in them."

On the 21st anniversary of Hawaiian statehood, it is appropriate and timely that at least some aspects of Hawaiian culture be given their rightful place in the appreciation of the varied achievements of the pre-European inhabitants of the United States.

Origin of the Islands, the Gods, and Men: Tradition

Wakea son of Kahiko-lua-mea,
Papa, called Papa-giving-birth-to-islands, was his wife,
Eastern Kahiki, western Kahiki were born,
The regions below were born,
The regions above were born,
Hawaii was born,
The firstborn child was the island *Hawaii*
Of Wakea together with Kane,
And Papa in the person of Walinu'u as wife.
Papa became pregnant with the island,
Sick with the foetus she bore,
Great *Maui* was born, an island . . .
Papa was in heavy travail with the island Kanaloa
    (*Kahoolawe*) . . .
A child born to Papa.
Papa left and returned to Tahiti,
Went back to Tahiti at Kapakapakaua,
Wakea stayed, lived with Kaula as wife,
Lanai-kaula was born,
The firstborn of that wife.
Wakea sought a new wife and found Hina,
Hina lived as wife to Wakea,
Hina became pregnant with the island of *Molokai*,
The island of Molokai was a child of Hina.
The messenger of Kaula (Laukaula) told
Of Wakea's living with another woman;
Papa was raging with jealousy,
Papa returned from Tahiti
Bitter against her husband Wakea,
Lived with Lua, a new husband,
Oahu son of Lua was born,
Oahu of Lua, an island child,
A child of Lua's youth.
She lived again with Wakea,
Conceived by him,
Became pregnant with the island *Kauai*,
The island Kama-wae-lua-lani was born,
Ni'ihau was an afterbirth,
Lehua a boundary,
Kaula the last
Of the *low reef islands* of Lono . . .[1]

Wākea, personification of the sky father, and Papa, the earth mother, according to this tradition, gave birth to the individual islands of the Hawaiian chain, starting with the largest in the east and moving westward to the low reef islands. This tradition, in addition to offering an explanation of how the islands came to be and telling of the origin of Wākea and Papa in Tahiti, is also illuminating because of the underlying conceptualization that it reveals of the intimate relationships among the gods, man, and the physical environment. Wākea and Papa not only gave birth to the islands, but are the ancestors of the Hawaiian

---

[1]Beckwith, 1970, pp. 301-302, based on Fornander, 1916, pp. 12-14.

people. Traditional texts, perpetuated in the oral tradition for many generations, told how chiefs and people were related to their forefathers, as well as all things in the universe, and thereby established a claim upon the care of the spirits that animated the material world.

Indeed, the origins of the world and all things in it were set out in detail in the first section of a chant called the *Kumulipo* (beginning in-deep-darkness).

At the time when the earth became hot
At the time when the heavens turned about
At the time when the sun was darkened
To cause the moon to shine
The time of the rise of the Pleiades
The slime, this was the source of the earth
The source of the darkness that made darkness
The source of the night that made night
The intense darkness, the deep darkness
Darkness of the sun, darkness of the night
   Nothing but night.

The night gave birth
Born was Kumulipo in the night, a male
Born was Po'ele in the night, a female
Born was a coral polyp, born was the coral, came forth
Born was the grub that digs and heaps up the earth,
   came forth
Born was his [child] an earthworm, came forth
Born was the starfish, his child the small starfish came
   forth
Born was the sea cucumber, his child the small sea
   cucumber came forth
Born was the sea urchin, the sea urchin [tribe]
Born was the short-spiked sea urchin, came forth
Born was the smooth sea urchin, his child the
   long-spiked came forth
Born was the ring-shaped sea urchin, his child the
   thin-spiked came forth
Born was the barnacle, his child the pearl oyster came
   forth
Born was the mother-of-pearl, his child the oyster came
   forth
Born was the mussel, his child the hermit crab came forth
Born was the big limpet, his child the small limpet came
   forth
Born was the cowry, his child the small cowry came forth
Born was the naka shellfish, the rock oyster his child
   came forth
Born was the drupa, shellfish, his child the bitter white
   shellfish came forth
Born was the conch shell, his child the small conch shell
   came forth
Born was the nerita shellfish, the sand-burrowing
   shellfish his child came forth
Born was the fresh water shellfish, his child the small
   fresh water shellfish came forth
Born was man for the narrow stream, the woman for the
   broad stream
Born was the Ekaha moss living in the sea
Guarded by the Ekahakaha fern living on land
Darkness slips into light
Earth and water are the food of the plant

The god enters, man cannot enter
Man for the narrow stream, woman for the broad stream
Born was the tough seagrass living in the sea
Guarded by the tough landgrass living on land

    . . . .

     Refrain

Man for the narrow stream, woman for the broad stream
Born was the hairy seaweed living in the sea
Guarded by the hairy pandanus vine living on land
Darkness slips into light
Earth and water are the food of the plant
The god enters, man cannot enter
The man with the water gourd, he is a god
Water that causes the withered vine to flourish
Causes the plant top to develop freely
Multiplying in the passing time
The long night slips along
Fruitful, very fruitful
Spreading here, spreading there
Spreading this way, spreading that way
Propping up earth, holding up the sky
The time passes, this night of Kumulipo
   Still it is night[2]

Other creatures then come upon the earth and with the coming of gods and men, day begins. La'ila'i, a woman, Ki'i, a man, Kāne, a god, and Kanaloa, a god, are the first to be born, and after some generations Haumea, a goddess, bears a number of children to the god Kanaloa. Later she takes a husband among men and becomes the goddess of childbirth. Gods and men, personifications of the forces of nature, mated and created and finally, through Wākea and Papa the Hawaiian Islands were formed and populated.

According to the Hawaiian view, man is a product of nature and the gods.

Origin of the Islands and Men: Science

According to geologists, the Hawaiian Islands are the peaks of a great range of volcanic mountains that stretches for 2,000 miles across the North Pacific Ocean, rising from the bottom of the sea to 32,000 feet at the highest point. This mainly submerged mountain chain rises above the sea to expose eight large islands and some fifty islets. The closest land to the east is California, 2,400 miles distant. It is the same distance to Japan from the western end of the Hawaiian chain. Some 2,000 miles north lie the Aleutian Islands and to

---

[2]Beckwith, 1972, pp. 58-60

the south are the scattered islands of Polynesia. Geographically, Hawai'i is the world's most isolated land mass.

The islets in the northwest part of the Hawaiian chain are sandy reefs near sea level and some enclose a shallow lagoon. One of these islets in atoll form is Midway, a United States Naval installation that played an important role in World War II. The middle section of the Hawaiian chain is composed of volcanic pinnacles which stand on extensive submerged platforms, suggesting that the islands were once much larger and have been worn away by erosion. A United States Coast Guard station is located in this central part of the Hawaiian chain on French Frigate Shoals. The largest islands in this part of the chain are Necker Island and Nihoa Island, which were occasionally used by the prehistoric inhabitants of the eight main Hawaiian Islands that lie to the southeast. In addition to the large islands of Ni'ihau, Kaua'i, O'ahu, Moloka'i, Lana'i, Maui, Kaho'olawe, and Hawai'i, the Hawaiians visited many of the small islets, such as Kaula, Lehua, Moku Manu, Manana, and Molokini. Although the chain of islands is 2,000 miles long, the land area is 6,442 square miles—comparable in size to Connecticut (4,899 square miles) or New Jersey (7,522 square miles).

The movement of the floor of the Pacific over a volcanic hot spot appears to be responsible for the creation of the Hawaiian Islands. Moving westward about 5 inches per year over the outpouring lava at the hot spot, the volcanic activity, sending fluid lava in submarine and aerial eruptions, created the islands one by one during the past 35 million years. On the island of Hawai'i this process continues with volcanic eruptions at Halema'uma'u and on the slopes of Mauna Loa. In contrast to the birth order of Papa's offspring, geologically the island of Hawai'i is the youngest of the island chain.

For millions of years wind and water eroded the hardened volcanic outpourings to shape the islands as we know them today. During these millennia winds, ocean currents, and birds carried living organisms to the islands which established themselves by evolutionary mechanisms as the ancestors of the endemic species of plants, insects, and land snails characteristic of Hawai'i in prehistoric times. In addition, there were wide-ranging sea birds and migratory birds that visited the islands regularly, and at least 15 immigrant stocks of land birds somehow found their way to the islands to evolve 78 species and subspecies of native Hawaiian birds—all of which became vitally important when man finally reached this last outpost of the Pacific voyagers.

According to physical anthropologists, the Hawaiians as Polynesians are part of the widespread Mongoloid division of mankind, traceable ultimately to Asia. Branches of the early generalized Mongoloid populations expanded into Southeast Asia and Indonesia probably 6,000 years ago. The ancestors of the Polynesians appear to have belonged to this stock and to have had a separate origin from the Papuans and Australian Aboriginals, who belonged to the Australoid division of mankind.

About 3000 B.C. or before, the ancestors of peoples who eventually became Polynesians began to move in small groups into the Melanesian area. These ancestral voyagers were part of a cultural group who migrated from island to island and eventually inhabited many coastal areas from New Guinea to Fiji. Moving into Tonga and Samoa, they adapted their culture to slightly different conditions of land and sea. Over the centuries, they evolved cultural forms which developed into what we now call Polynesian. It must be emphasized that it was not Polynesians who migrated from the Asian area, but members of an ancestral Oceanic cultural group who became Polynesians in their newly discovered island homes by evolving new cultural forms from the prototypes they brought with them. The process of adapting their cultural and social forms to these new environmental and living conditions is what made them Polynesians.

Characteristic of these people were a high degree of seamanship, developed canoes, pottery with distinctive ornamentation, an economy based on shellfishing, marine fishing, raising pigs and fowls, which they brought with them, and cultivation of plants that they brought, such as coconut, taro, yam, and breadfruit. The primary tool was the adz made of stone or shell. These were untanged and quadrangular, lenticular, or plano-convex in cross section. Stone, shell, and obsidian were also used for other tools such as knives, scrapers, and pounders and there were other characteristic cultural forms. From this cultural complex, about 1500 B.C. in Tonga and 1000 B.C. in Samoa, was developed what we know as Polynesian culture.

After the people had lived some time in this West Polynesian area, the next major migration period is thought to have begun about 100 B.C. Small groups of settlers moved into areas of the Marquesas Islands, Society Islands (Tahiti), and eventually to the many islands of Polynesia and evolved a type of culture known as East Polynesian. The first settlers in these areas again adapted the cultures they brought with them to evolve new characteristics distinctive, at least in their later stages, of each island group.

Although the homeland of the first migrants to Hawai'i cannot be precisely pinpointed, the earliest migrants probably came from the Marquesas Islands arriving by A.D. 600, while later influences appear to have come from the Society Islands. It is not specifically important in this context whether the earliest migrants came from the Marquesas Islands or the Society Islands—but only that the culture they brought with them was clearly East Polynesian in character.

One of the distinctive elements of Hawaiian culture is the Hawaiian language. Although closely related to southeast Marquesan and to Tahitian, the Hawaiian language is not mutually intelligible with either. In a comparison of 202 basic words, it was found that Hawai'i shared 76 percent of them with Tahiti and 70 percent with the Marquesas Islands. This linguistic association is consistent with the archaeological evidence and suggests that an early settlement of East Polynesians, possibly from the Marquesas, was overlain by a second influence from Tahiti and fused into a single linguistic form that eventually evolved to become a separate language—Hawaiian.

According to traditions and genealogical reckoning, new influences appear to have been introduced from Tahiti about the 12th century. The distinctive Hawaiian forms of material culture then begin to appear in archaeological contexts. These seem to be the result of evolution—developed from a variety of forms brought by groups of East Polynesian migrants. Shortly after, the sporadic two-way ocean-going voyages between Hawai'i and the East Polynesian homeland ceased and Hawai'i was isolated from significant cultural contact with other groups for 500 years, when Europeans entered the scene. During this 500 years were evolved the religious, social, and artistic traditions with which we will here be concerned.

Aspects of Hawaiian Tradition: Persistence and Change

Man is a product of nature and the gods. This concept was a guiding force in the daily life of the Hawaiians and their relationships with the gods and the environment. Using the materials and resources of their natural surroundings, under the guidance of the gods, men fashioned irrigation systems and fishponds to make better use of their total environment, structures for the worship of the gods and for their own shelter, and intricate and brilliant objects for use and decoration. These structures and objects are manifestations of social relationships between men, between man and the gods, and between man and nature. Changes in similar kinds of objects over time are visual representations of changes in social relationships.

Changes in status, rank, prestige, and power are reflected in objects and the ways in which they were made and used. And, even more important, from an examination of such objects the underlying concepts that persisted and changed can be followed.

Changes in structures and objects are readily observable in an analysis of prehistoric Hawai'i. Indeed, change is inevitable and observable in all cultures. These changes may be the result of internal evolution that occurred relatively slowly, or they may be the result of new ideas coming in from the outside, rapid at first, and then fusion and evolutionary change again take over. Such was the case in prehistoric Hawai'i. The original cultural traits brought by the ancestors of the Hawaiians from East Polynesia changed slowly by evolving new forms in response to new conditions. With the influx of new ideas and concepts thought to have come from Tahiti in about the 12th century, change was rapid for a time. A fusion of the two cultural styles occurred and evolutionary change again took over. With the coming of Europeans at the end of the 18th century, another series of rapid changes took place, in many ways more profound than the Tahitian overlay. A fusion of the two cultural styles again occurred and evolution from this second fusion still goes on.

Changes are easiest to observe by examining dated structures and objects. From an analysis of such material things we can go further to suggest changes that occurred in social relationships as well as in the society that produced them. But change may be only superficial and may even hide underlying concepts that persisted over time and evolved only slowly. Such concepts are invaluable for the cultural identity of specific groups in a multicultural society. Objects can illustrate the persistence and change of Hawaiian concepts and their intermixture with influences from the Western world and Orient. Yet they also illustrate the persistence of Hawaiian values, evolved to have meaning in a modern world.

The persistence of Hawaiian traditions, of moral and aesthetic values, are embodied in individual Hawaiian men and women today. These values of the past have evolved and changed, yet continue. It is hoped that these values can be seen and admired, appreciated and even understood by examining the objects in this exhibition, not as isolated art objects—although works of art they certainly are—but as objects that express the social and cultural conditions and traditions of the Hawaiian people yesterday and today.

Hawaiian life was unified by strong spiritual beliefs intertwined with a stratified social system which included gods, priests, chiefs, and the people in general.

Gods were invisible spirits that were often symbolized by natural objects such as stones or shell, or fashioned in the form of human or animal images in wood, stone, feathers attached to basketry bases, and even such unusual materials as sea urchin spines. These images and objects, however, were not the gods themselves, but served as dwelling places for their spirits and were given power through prayers and offerings. The pantheon of gods included state gods, *akua*, who looked after the welfare of all Hawaiians and were often worshiped in open air structures, *heiau*. A large and important group of gods, often called *'aumākua*, included gods of a family or personal nature and others that were concerned with sorcery, crafts, or special functions. *'Unihipili* were familiar spirits that were created by deification and became associated with a relic of the dead person, such as bones or hair.

These gods and spirits were part of a dynamic religious setting interwoven with all aspects of life. Concepts associated with these gods helped to explain the unexplainable, to reduce anxiety and fear, and served as a means of social control. The natural and supernatural, the human and superhuman, were inextricably intermixed. Set within a dramatic landscape and incorporated with a hierarchical social and political system, Hawaiian religion depended upon the observance of restrictions associated with *mana* and *kapu*. *Mana* was conceived as a supernatural quality of divine sanctity. The possession of *mana* carried with it power, authority, and prestige. *Kapu* were prohibitions which safeguarded *mana*. Some *kapu* were the prerogatives of individuals of specified ancestry, such as the offspring of full brother and sister matings. In the presence of such an individual, all of lesser prestige must prostrate themselves. Temporary *kapu* or prohibitions could be placed on certain foods or on the access to certain areas of land or sea by *kāhuna*, priests who were authorized to do so by individuals of *kapu* status. The Hawaiian *kapu* "system" included such restrictions as prohibiting men and women from eating together. Certain foods, usually those used as sacrifices to the gods, such as pork, were denied to women. Some individuals had so much *mana* that their presence was dangerous to those who carried little or no *mana*.

The various *kapu* comprised a developed system of prohibitions and regulations which governed human behavior in relation to the gods and the *ali'i*, or chiefs. If *kapu* were not heeded, or even broken unintentionally, the gods and spirits were displeased and calamity brought by nature might result. Rapport with the gods and spirits had to be continually maintained. A special priestly group of *kāhuna* specialized in keeping peace with myriad gods and spirits on the state level, while the head of the family took care of interaction with the gods for his relatives.

The social system can be characterized as a series of rank-oriented groups of individuals, related and unrelated, organized into chiefdoms. These chiefdoms might be thought of as a group of pyramids. At the apex of each was an *ali'i nui*, a paramount chief, known, at least in later times, as *mō'ī*. Below the paramount chief were lesser chiefs and retainers. Commoners, *maka'āinana*, made up the base. Sacred individuals at various steps in the pyramid had prestige and/or power depending on the closeness of blood and social rank of their parents. Prestige and power often did not coincide, and *ali'i* with the highest prestige were not necessarily close to the paramount chief in power. The distinction between *ali'i*, nobility or chiefs, and *maka'āinana*, nonchiefs, was basic and served to separate an aristocracy from the people in general. There were graduations of rank within the *ali'i*, and there was a separated group of "inferiors" called *kauwā*, a hereditary group from which human sacrifices were usually drawn.

Although the binding force that held the blocks of the pyramids together was the religious system based on *mana* and *kapu*, the resulting societal order was primarily a political system centered on power. Shifts in power owing to death, marriage, or warfare, sometimes loosened the binder and the blocks were reorganized into slightly altered pyramids.

A large unit of land was called a *moku*, or district. *Moku* literally means island, but an island might consist of several autonomous "islands," or *moku*. Hawai'i island, for example, was divided into six *moku*. The head of a *moku* was an *ali'i 'ai moku* and there might be several of these under a paramount chief. *Moku* were divided into *ahupua'a*, each of which was under a lesser chief or *konohiki*, and varied in size from a few hundred to more than 100,000 acres. Ideally an *ahupua'a* ran from the sea to the mountains, enabling the inhabitants to have access to the varied products of land and sea. *Ahupua'a* were divided into *'ili*, each with its own name and known boundaries. Ideally, *'ili*, too, ran from the sea to the mountains, or an *'ili* consisted of sections comprising pieces of land at the seashore, in the lowlands, and in the mountains.

In historic times, an *'ili* was inhabited by an *'ohana*, extended family, which was entitled to a share of the produce. When communal labor was desirable, such as building a house, harvesting certain kinds of fiber, or community fishing, all of the *'ohana* took part—as they did in celebrations and ceremonies. Nearly every day there would be sharing of foods and other useful articles. *'Ohana* also usually shared a religious shrine and a cave or sand dune for burials.

Hawaiians were extremely sophisticated in their knowledge and use of the sea, for their lives were largely dependent on it. The sea was a great highway, not only between islands, but also between localities on the same island. Two types of canoes were used; the single outrigger canoe was particularly useful for fishing and for short trips, while large double canoes were used for interisland travel. But, perhaps more important, the sea was also the main source of protein in the Hawaiian diet and a complex fishing technology was developed. A fisherman's knowledge included not only the techniques of the manufacture and use of fishing equipment, but also methods of capture, habitats of the various fish, seasons of spawning and movement, and the responses of the fish to attempts at capture. Interrelationships of fish, birds, land, sun, moon, and sky with the sea were intimately known—knowledge that was necessary, not only to catch fish, but to assure their ample supply as well.

Elaborate fishponds were constructed in coastal and inland environments making possible a continual supply of fish during the spawning season when catching fish in the sea was prohibited. The most spectacular of these ponds consisted of huge walls built on reefs enclosing as much as 500 acres of water. Although built by communal work, many of the fish from these ponds were reserved for the chiefs. Inland ponds, many of which were quite small, were a useful source of fish for those who did not possess the specialized equipment and knowledge of fishermen.

In the 19th century, the economy was based on marine exploitation and agriculture with distribution or sharing of resources from these two activities among the extended family, *'ohana*. Kinsmen living inland furnished land crops such as taro and bananas, and the raw materials for bark cloth and fibers to their relatives living near the sea, who, in turn, supplied those inland with fish, shellfish, seaweed, and salt. The *'ohana* as a group gave tribute to the chiefs in the form of food, mats, bowls, and feathers. These helped to support aristocratic taste in food and decorative objects as well as ornaments and clothing. In turn, the chief protected his people from devastation by war and gave tribute to the gods, who then blessed the people with good crops and good fishing and the cycle of sharing began once again.

Marriage as a formal institution was largely determined by one's rank in the society and often included more than one mate. Unions among *maka'ainana* were based on choice and convenience—the young persons simply asked permission of their elders, and one of the young people went to live with the family of the other. In marriages of chiefs, however, it was socially necessary to marry a close relative in order to produce chil-

dren of the highest possible rank. A suitable partner for a chief of highest rank was his own sister, half-sister, or niece—while lesser chiefs usually married more distant relatives. After a child was born to a high-ranking union, both husband and wife could take second partners of their own choice. Children of the senior partner would become the new rulers, while children of other partners would become executive officers, ministers, and supporters of the new chiefs of exalted lineage.

Child rearing was in many ways a community responsibility rather than simply the duty of the immediate family. Children were free to go where they wished and often traveled in groups, older children caring for the younger ones, sometimes traveling considerable distances to visit. When it was time to eat, children were invited to eat wherever they were and sleepy children were allowed to sleep at any home in the community. It was customary to give the firstborn child to the grandparents, who were wise teachers, and thus the parents were freed for the heavier work. Children were taught to listen without unnecessary comment or movement and they had to wait for a convenient time to ask "why" or "how." It was rude to beg for things—for food was shared and property belonged to others. A child was rarely struck, although his knee might be tapped by vexed adults as a warning to take heed or pay attention. Children were considered treasures and a source of joy, especially to grandparents, who considered them as *lei* to adorn their old age.

The practice of medicine was under the jurisdiction of trained specialists, known as *kāhuna lapa'au*, who were recruited as children and apprenticed to a local medical expert. Medical practice was based largely on herbal lore and massage. Knowledge, however, came not only from observation and practice, but from consultation with the gods. The gods knew without error what the ailment was and what the proper treatment should be, and the medical expert relied partly on prayer to help in the selection of a remedy. The gods did not give the same knowledge to all medical experts and some specialized in the various branches of medicine. There were those who concentrated on digestive disorders, while others specialized in dislocations and sprains. Surgery was not greatly emphasized, except that lancing was used in the treatment of boils and other infections. Some specialists used sorcery and magic in their treatment, while yet others were trained in methods of counteracting sorcery.

Amusements were primarily sports and games based on strength and skill. Great tournaments were held on large sports fields, especially during the *makahiki* season. Such games included boxing, various types of wrestling, and foot racing in which champions represented their districts against the skilled athletes of neighboring districts or islands. Water sports were popular with adults and children of both sexes and included surfboard riding, body surfing, and canoe racing, as well as various kinds of diving. Games of skill used implements that were thrown, thrust, or rolled, including javelins and darts which were slid along a course, disks rolled for accuracy or distance, and bows and arrows that were used in a game of shooting rats. *Kōnane*, a game similar to checkers, used pebbles on a prepared surface or on a specially carved wooden board. Finally, there were gambling games of guessing and forfeits in which players guessed where a pebble was hidden. Some sports and games had aristocratic forms that required special houses and chants, or prepared courses, such as the spectacular and extremely dangerous land sledding called *hōlua*.

Wars were usually waged over land disputes or for revenge. A ruling chief and his people might mount a war against other chiefs of his island, or a chief of a whole island might mount a large-scale expedition to conquer another island. Although there was no standing army, in reality all adult males constituted a reserve army and there was training in group fighting. Professional warriors often engaged in single combat, while both sides watched. Much of the training for war took the form of sport or amusement and there were sham battles on festive occasions. Javelins were used as weapons when armies marched upon each other, and warriors were trained to catch and return javelins as well as to dodge and to ward them off. But Hawaiian warfare was characterized primarily by hand-to-hand combat and the aim was to come directly to blows. Short clubs were used in close fighting and clubs tied with a long cord were thrown around an enemy's legs to trip him. Other weapons included daggers, shark-tooth weapons, slings, and strangling cords.

Music in Hawai'i was a complex integrated system of poetry, rhythm, melody, and movement, which served many functions, from prayer to entertainment.[3] The most basic element in Hawaiian music was poetry. The poetry was composed with a time pattern, but the melodic succession of pitches to which the poetry was sung was secondary and often interchangeable. A piece of poetry might be sung with one melody by one individual or school and quite a differ-

ent melody by another individual or school, but it was still considered to be the same song. Some songs were accompanied by percussion instruments, such as drums and rattles, which served to set the beat and keep it steady. *Hula* was a final extension of this poetry in the form of stylized visual accompaniment, and the movements alluded to selected words of the texts. Hawaiian music honored the gods, praised the chiefs and their ancestors, and reflected the everyday events of Hawaiian life—birth, love, war, and death.

The 19th century coat of arms of Hawai'i, which incorporates the motto of Hawai'i *Ua mau ke ea o ka aina i ka pono*, "The life of the land is perpetuated in righteousness," is symbolic of the Hawaiian world view of the time. Consisting of a European style crown with taro leaf decoration, Hawaiian chiefs wearing feather cloaks and helmets, *pūlo'ulo'u* standards with bark cloth padded terminals which designate *kapu* areas, *kāhili* feather standards, and a spear, the combination illustrates elements of importance for a 19th century ruling chief. It is instructive to compare this earlier coat of arms with the symbolism of the great seal adopted by the state of Hawai'i on its admission to the Union in 1959. A Western image, in the form of the goddess of wisdom, replaces one of the Hawaiian chiefs, and a phoenix rising from the flames has been added; the rising sun, an adaptation of the rising sun of the Orient, replaces the European crown, and the *pūlo'ulo'u* have been given a black dot at the center, perhaps to neutralize their sacred quality. But most important, the Hawaiian symbolism is now centered on Kamehameha I. Although a genealogical usurper, Kamehameha was instrumental in forming what became the Hawaiian Kingdom and, in recent times, has become a symbol of the great chiefs of the past— diversity has become standardized.

This stylistic change in coats of arms is indicative of the many changes that occurred during the 19th and 20th centuries. The relationship of many Hawaiians to the land has changed, but although many Hawaiians live an urban existence, they have ties to land in more rural areas. These ties are activated regularly during family reunions, modern holidays, "baby *lūau*" honoring a child's first birthday, funerals, and other important rites of passage. During these celebrations and family gatherings, traditions that bespeak one's Hawaiianness are most evident. Widespread persistence of tradition can be found in the sharing of food, the performance of music and dance, and the clothing worn. Knowledge of the traditions associated with these aspects of one's Hawaiian background, or at least the modern interpretation of these traditions, gives people status within the *'ohana*. It is a status one gains by sharing—not the competitive status as-

---

[3]Examples of the various styles of traditional Hawaiian music will be included in the Bishop Museum recording *Na Leo Hawai'i Kahiko, The Voices of Old Hawai'i*, Volume 1.

sociated with chiefs. This attitude of sharing and caring, derived from relationships within the 'ohana carried over into modern life, is the essence of the persistence of tradition.

Strict *kapu* were associated with clothing and bedcoverings (Handy and Pukui, 1958, pp. 181-182). Bark cloth skirts could not be worn over the shoulders. A daughter could not wear the clothes of her mother, but a mother could wear the clothes of a daughter. A man could wear his brother's clothes, but never his sister's clothes. Sleeping mats or bark cloths were only for sleeping (not sitting) and were kept separate, depending on whether they were to lie upon or to be used as a cover. Most important, clothing meant to be worn around the waist and hips could not be worn above the waist. Old clothing was not given away, but burned or buried, and even *lei* were not carelessly discarded. Clothing in the hands of a sorcerer could be dangerous.

All of these *kapu* were transferred to European clothes and bed coverings, and even today one never sits on a Hawaiian quilt. Even the same towel could not be used above and below the waist. Each item had its own place; clothes were never put on the floor or sat upon, and it was forbidden to sit on a trunk that held these things. Specific clothes were worn at home, others worn elsewhere, and when outgrown, they were not given away, except among brothers or sisters.

Although these *kapu* were strong in all families, they were especially important for chiefs, and this may account for the rarity of clothing associated with specific chiefs in museum collections. Traditionally, the clothing of the high-ranking chiefs required the prostrating or sitting *kapu* even when carried by an attendant—personal items carried one's personal *kapu*. Formerly, families who did not adhere to clothing *kapu* were considered careless, and were thus made vulnerable to sorcery. Even today, although it is not always expedient to abide by the *kapu*, they are usually not needlessly broken. One might give clothes away to persons unknown, but it is necessary to willfully retain the *kapu* so that neither the giver nor the recipient will be harmed.

Clothing evolved along with the changing world views of the Hawaiians. The so-called Mother Hubbard dress was introduced by missionaries in an effort to cover the unclad. These loose gowns, which often hung free from the shoulders without a yoke, were made of imported cotton or bark cloth and became a prototype for the *mu'umu'u*, still a popular style of dress among Hawaiians. More elegance was added with the addition of a yoke and train, which developed into a style called *holokū*, often worn today for formal Hawaiian occasions. Clothing of the chiefs during the 19th century, however, was based on European high fashion, with elaborate silk dresses for the women and military style dress for men. The two cultural styles so evident throughout Hawaiian culture during the 19th century are well presented in two illustrations made in London in 1824. The illustration of the Royal Party at Drury Lane Theatre by John Gear illustrates the European style of dress, while the romantic painting of Boki and Liliha by John Hayter illustrates Hawaiian ceremonial dress. (See No. 217.)

For her portrait,[4] the high female chief Liliha wore a *lei niho palaoa* neck ornament and a feather *lei* in her hair, which, along with her bark cloth skirt, must have symbolized to her the distinctive property of a female Hawaiian of high rank. Her husband, Boki, wears a feather cloak and helmet, the distinctive property of male Hawaiians of high rank. This painting, combining as it does traditional Hawaiian objects with the European attitudes suggested by their pose, marks the critical interface period of the 1820's, which overthrew the *kapu*, but retained traditional objects as symbolic showpieces of Hawaiian culture. The distinctive traditions that the *ali'i* wished to perpetuate were retained and, over the years, have been accepted as symbolic of Hawaiian culture in the search for identity by Hawaiians of all backgrounds.

Food was an important element of the interaction between man, his gods, and the environment. Certain foods were given as offerings to the gods. Planting, growing, harvesting, food preparation, and eating were all carried out under the auspices of the gods and were surrounded by *kapu*.

I'a (fish, pig, dog, fowl, or the meat of other birds) was considered a relish to be eaten with *'ai*, the staple vegetable foods—primarily *poi* and sweet potato. *Poi*, the steamed, pounded, and slightly fermented corm of the *kalo* plant, was considered the staff of life and was eaten in large amounts each day. One took care not to offend Hāloa, the god of *kalo*, who insisted, for example, that no discussions regarding business be conducted while eating. Mealtime was a time for pleasant conversation and joviality. Traditionally men and women did not eat together, but today feasting and hospitality of which eating is a large part are important times for the displaying and the passing on of tradition. The traditions that deal with food, eating, and utensils for food are among those that have changed the most from pre-European practices. Yet the legacies deriving from these traditions are among the most

---

[4]No. 165 in this exhibition, Color Plate XXIV.

conspicuous of the customs that persist from their evolved 19th century forms.

Traditionally in Hawai'i the making and serving of food was not a high-ranking occupation. Chiefs, however, required trusted servants to insure that leftovers did not come into the possession of sorcerers who could use food touched by an individual, as well as fingernail clippings or hair, as material to pray over to induce sickness or death. Scrap or refuse bowls, often inset with human teeth or pieces of ivory, were used to receive such leftovers, which were then buried or destroyed.

Two traditions dealing with food developed and co-existed during the 19th century. Formal dining in the European manner required magnificent china, crystal, and silver imported from Europe. This tableware acquired a kind of sacredness because of the individuals who owned or used it. Feasting in the Hawaiian manner used wooden, coconut, and gourd implements on a grand scale. Many of these containers have been preserved and passed on as Hawaiian heirlooms within Hawaiian families. The Hawaiian feast, 'aha'aina, continues in an evolved form under the name of lū'au, which refers to kalo leaves used for laulau and other dishes. Modern wooden bowls and plates augment the festive Hawaiian atmosphere of lū'au.

Wooden and gourd bowls are referred to as "calabashes" and are symbolic of extended family relationships—one refers to those with whom one can share humble food, all dipping fingers in the same poi bowl, as "calabash cousins." Ipu, gourd calabashes, however, are nearly a thing of the past. Traditionally ipu were used as containers for water, food, and other objects, and were often carried in nets balanced at the ends of carrying poles. Although ipu lent themselves to decorative elaboration, they were fragile and difficult to repair. Like the family relationships they symbolized, once broken they could never be perfectly mended. The demise of the gourd container has been offset by the elaboration of the wooden container— perhaps an appropriate metaphor here for traditions that have been selectively retained as guideposts for life in the modern world. Containers, too, are visual representations of social relationships that have changed over time and are objectifications of the metaphors and concepts that are the essential elements of the persistence of tradition.

2. The Death of Cook February 14, 1779, by John Cleveley

3. Tereoboo, King of Owhyee, 1779, by John Webber

4. An Inland View in Atooi (Kaua'i), 1778, unknown artist after Webber

Village of MACACOUPAH, OWHYEE.

5. "Village of Macacoupah, Owhyee," 1794, by Thomas Heddington

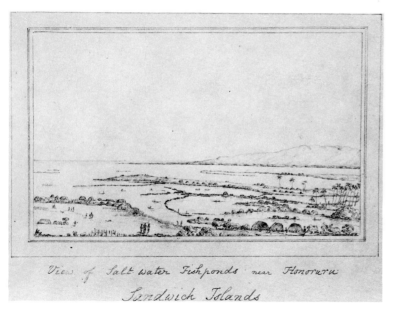

View of Salt water Fishponds near Honoruru
Sandwich Islands

6. "View of Salt Water Fishponds," 1825, by Robert Dampier

7a. "Town of Honolulu," 1834, unknown artist

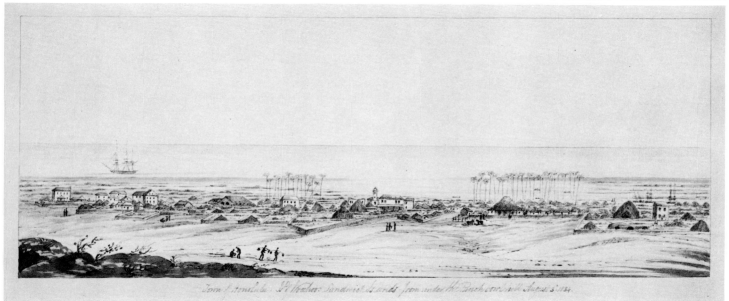

7b. "Honolulu from the Anchorage," 1834, unknown artist

8a. ''Panorama de l'ile d'Oahou . . .,''
1837, by Romuald-Georges Mesnard

9. View of Honolulu Harbor,
1849, by Robert Elwes

10. ''Port of Honolulu,''
by George H. Burgess, 1857

8b. ''Panorama de l'ile d'Oahou . . .,'' 1837, by Romuald-Georges Mesnard

11. ''Diamond Head . . .,'' by George H. Burgess, 1857

12. "Ewa from Honolulu,"
by George H. Burgess, 1857

14. Country Scene, unknown photographer, c. 1855

15b. Honolulu Looking Toward Punchbowl, by C. L. Weed, 1865

23. Canoe of the Sandwich Islands, 1779, by John Webber

Engraved from a Drawing made on the spot by Robt Dampier.

MORAI NEAR KARAKAKOOA.

31. "Morai near Karakakooa," 1825, by Robert Dampier

33. Wooden Image called Waiānuenue, or "Water-Rainbow"

32. Wooden Image from Hale-o-keawe

28. Wooden Image, Kālaipāhoa, the Poison God

35. Wooden Support Figure

72

36. Stone Owl God

38. Stone Image

73

40. Stone Image called Lononui-a-ehu

Necker Island Stone Image

41. Stone Image

42. Stone Fishing God

43. Urchin Spine Image from Kahoʻolawe

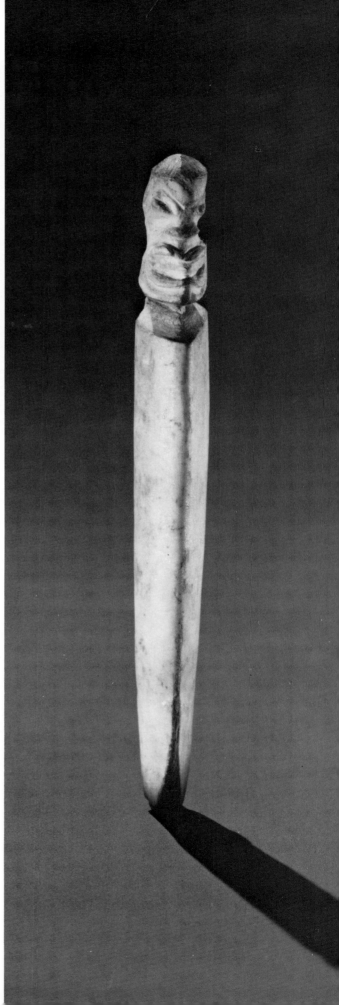

46. "Manière de punir
de mort un coupable aux îles
Sandwich," 1819, by
Jacques Etienne Victor Arago

47. "Manière d'étrangler un
coupable aux îles Sandwich," 1819,
by Jacques Etienne Victor Arago

77

54. Hawaiian Hymnal with Turtle Shell Covers, 1823

50. Four Hawaiian Christian Youths, by Samuel Finley Breese Morse, 1822

52. Levi Tenney Family, unknown photographer, 1851

53. "Grove of Tutui Trees Kauai," 1840, by Alfred T. Agate

56. "Diamond Hill as Seen from Honolulu," engraved by Momona, c. 1839

57. "Lahainaluna,"
engraved by Kepohoni, c. 1840

62. Father Damien, by E. D. Hale, 1889

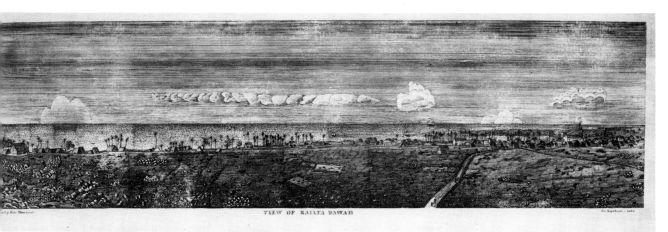

"View of Kailua Hawaii," engraved by Kepohoni, c. 1840

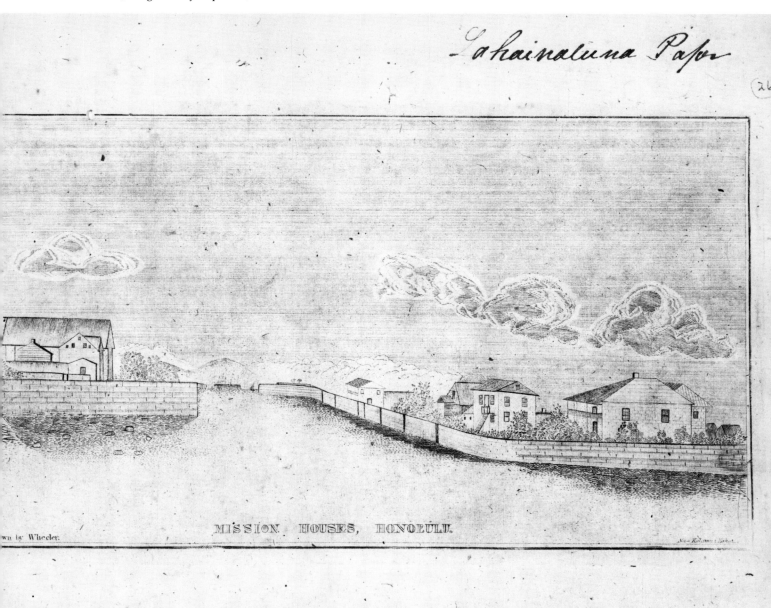

58. "Mission Houses, Honolulu," engraved by Kalama, 1837

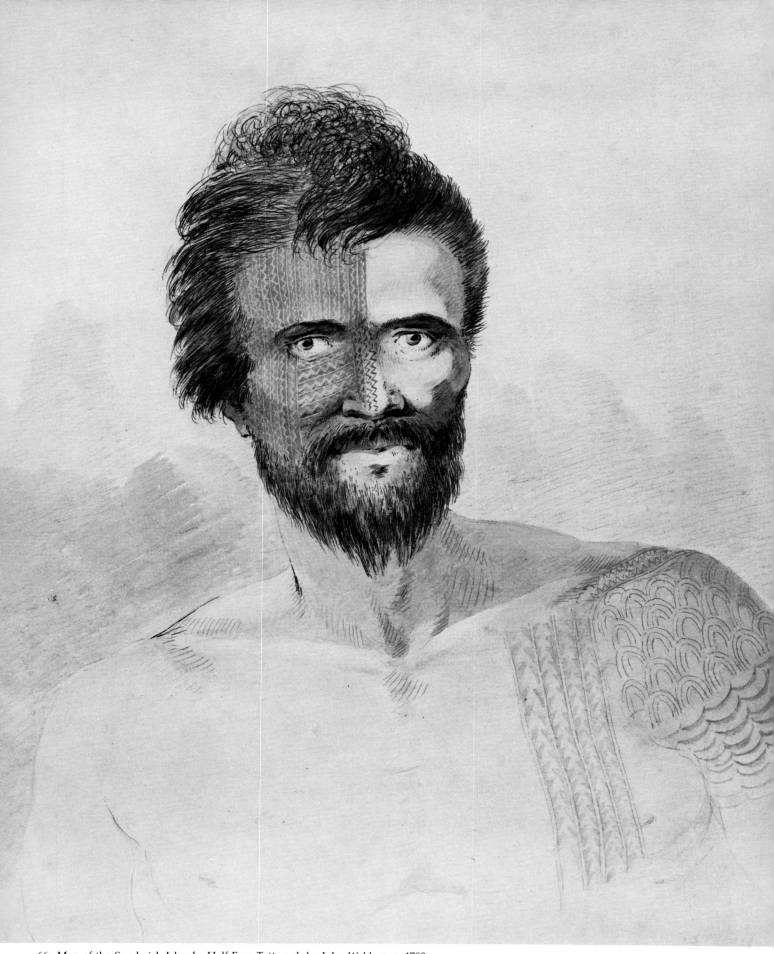

66. Man of the Sandwich Islands, Half Face Tattooed, by John Webber, c. 1780

67. "Ile Wahu Nomahanna," by L. Massard, c. 1830

68. "Vue d'une rue d'Honoloulou . . .," 1837, by Louis-Jules Masselot

69a. "Governor Hoapili,"
by Clarissa Chapman Armstrong, c. 1837

69b."Kaniu the Wife of Gov. Hoapili,"
by Clarissa Chapman Armstrong, c. 1837

73. "Princess Kaiulani in Japanese Costume,"
by Walter M. Giffard, 1889

74. Hawaiian Men Fishing, by Alonzo Gartley, c. 1905

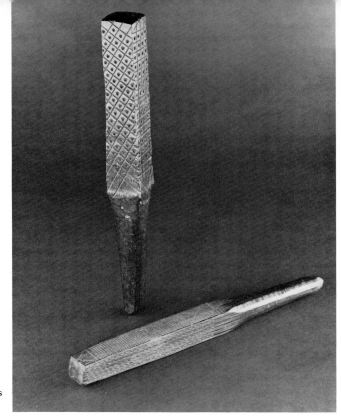

76. Two Bark Cloth Mallets

75. "Îles Sandwich: Maisons de Kraïmokou . . .," 1819, by J. Alphonse Pellion

A. Pellion delin.   Villeroy sculp.

ÎLES SANDWICH: MAISONS DE KRAÏMOKOU, Premier Ministre du Roi; FABRICATION DES ÉTOFFES.

77. Bark Cloth Loincloth

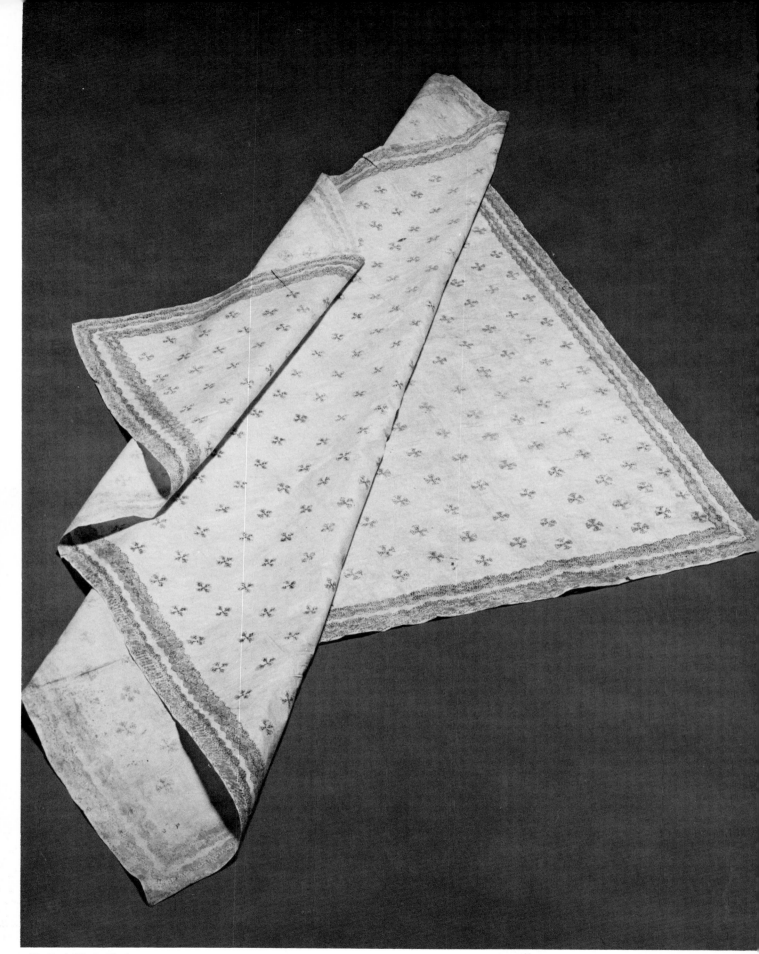

79. Bark Cloth Cloak

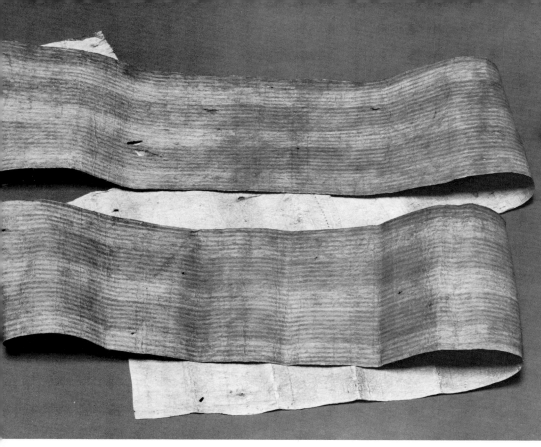

78. Bark Cloth Loincloth

80. Cloak or Blanket
used by Kamehameha III

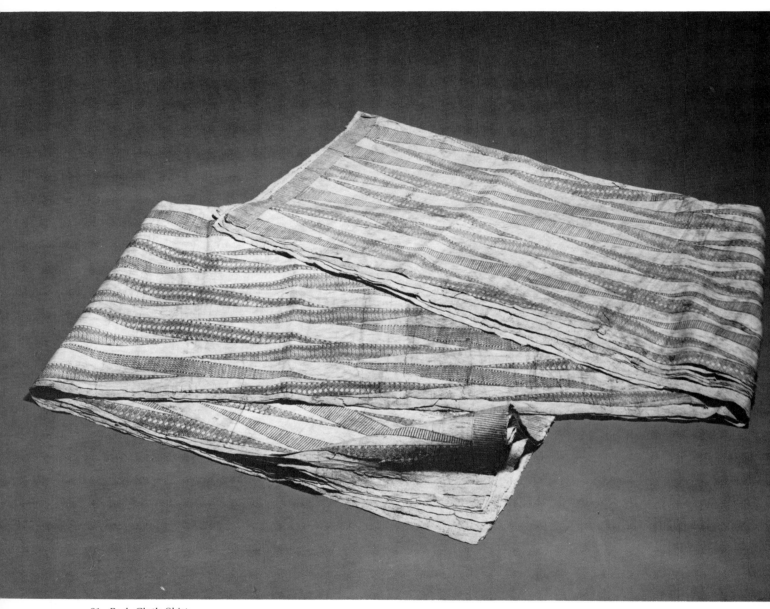

81. Bark Cloth Skirt

82. Bark Cloth Skirt

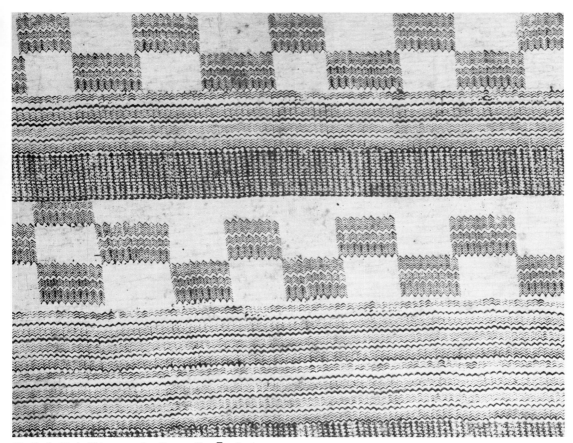

83. Bark Cloth Skirt worn by Queen Kamāmalu

84. Cotton Skirt

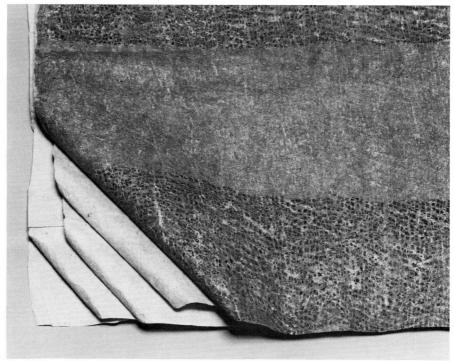

87. Bark Cloth Bed Cover

92

88. Bark Cloth Bed Cover

85. Bark Cloth Dress

86. Cotton Dress and Petticoat

90. 92, 93, 94. Hawaiian Hats

89. Hawaiian Quilt, Pineapple Design

95. Carved Meat Platter, owned by Princess Ke'elikōlani

95. Detail

97a-c. Poi Pounders

138. *Lū'au* at Moanalua Gardens, unknown photographer, c. 1885

98. Meat Bowl

100. Poi Bowl used by
Queen Emma when a child

99. Poi Bowl used by
Kamehameha I

103. Poi Bowl on Pedestal

104. Poi Bowl with Lid

105. Keōpūolani's Calabash Mounted on Stand

107. Double Finger Bowl

106. Finger Bowl

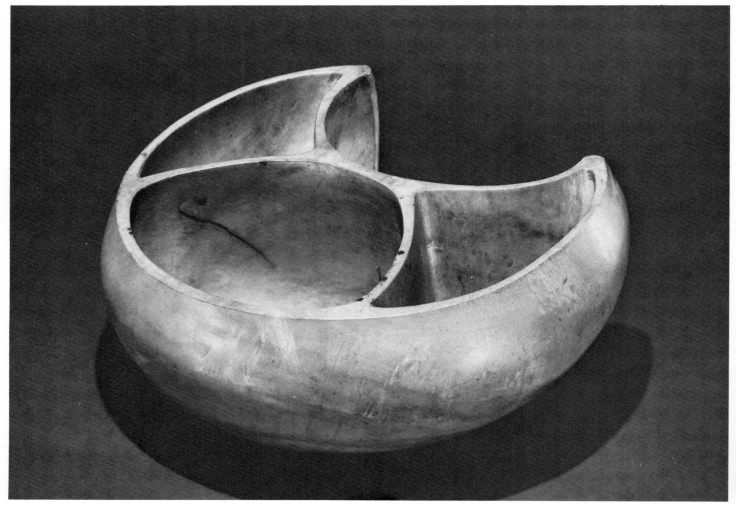

108. Finger Bowl with Three Compartments

109. Finger Bowl

110. Hand Basin

104

112. Refuse Bowl Inset with Human Teeth

111. Refuse Bowl

114. Spittoon used by Kamehameha I and Ka'ahumanu

113. Refuse Bowl

115. Spittoon

118. Storage Container

117. Refuse Bowl

120. Queen Kapi'olani's Covered Wooden Container

121. Medicine Pounding Bowl

128. Coconut Cup and Stand,
given by Queen Pomare
of Tahiti to Queen Emma

125. Coconut Shell Spoon

129. Carved Coconut Goblet,
detail, Queen Kapi'olani

129. Carved Coconut Goblet, with Views of King Kalākaua and Diamond Head

132. Decorated Water Bottle

130. Decorated Gourd Bowl

131. Decorated Gourd Bowl

113

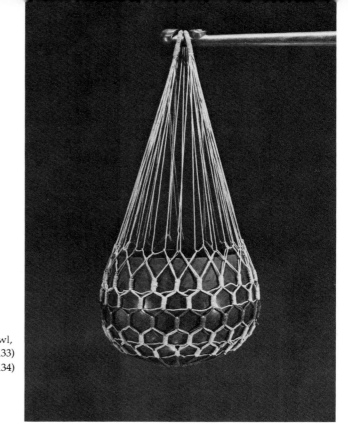

102. Poi Bowl,
with Carrying Sling (133)
and Pole (134)

136. "Pali, Oahu," 1840-1841, by A. T. Agate

114

135. Basketry Covered Gourd Container
and Burden Pole (134)

137. "A Calabash Carrier in Ancient
Hawaiian Dress in the Fern Forest,"
by Henry W. Henshaw, c. 1895

141. Men of the Sandwich Islands Dancing, by John Webber, c. 1780

143. "Scène de Danse, aux Îles Sandwich," 1836, by Barthélemy Lauvergne

144. Hawaiian Dancers, unknown photographer, c. 1858

146. "Hula Girls," unknown photographer, c. 1890

147. Hula Drum, preserved by the Kamehameha Family

148. Coconut Knee Drum

149. Carved Drum Support

119

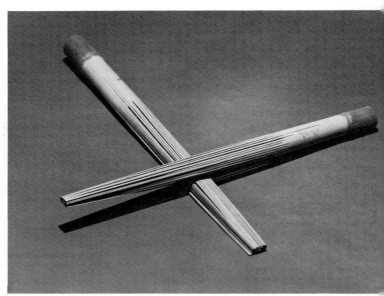

152. Pair of Bamboo *Hula* Rattles

156. Treadle Board and Pair of Wooden Hula Sticks, No. 155

151. Bamboo Stamping Tube,
and Conch Shell Trumpet, No. 160

157. Musical Bow, Gourd Whistle (No. 159),
Nose Flute (No. 158), Pair of Castanets (No. 154)

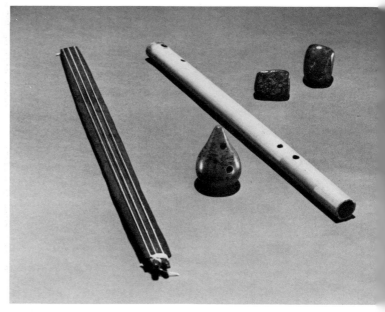

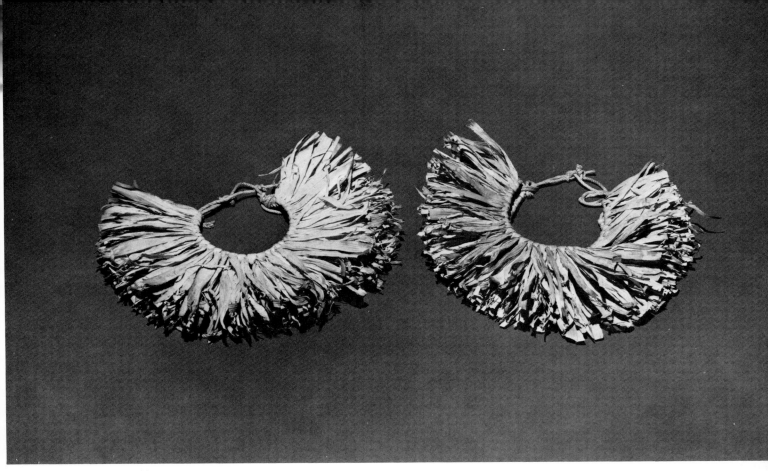

162. Pair of Corn Husk Anklets

163. Grass Skirt

169. Kiwala'ō Cloak

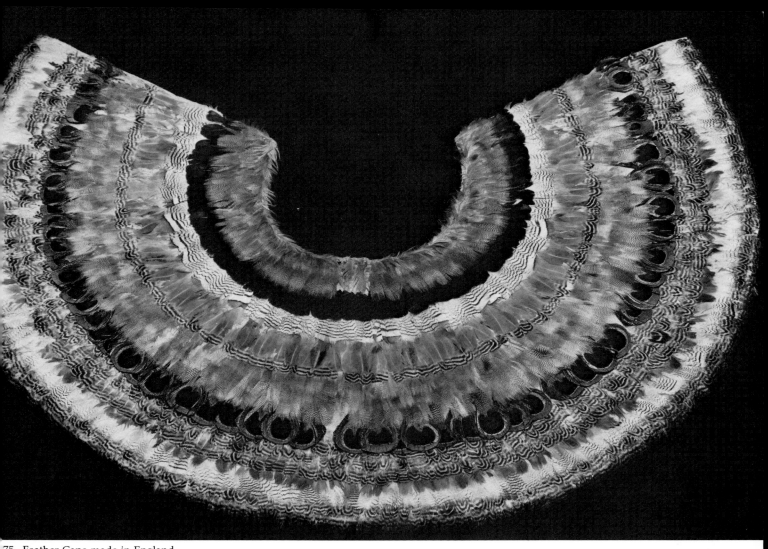

75. Feather Cape made in England

76. Transitional Period Feather Cape

123

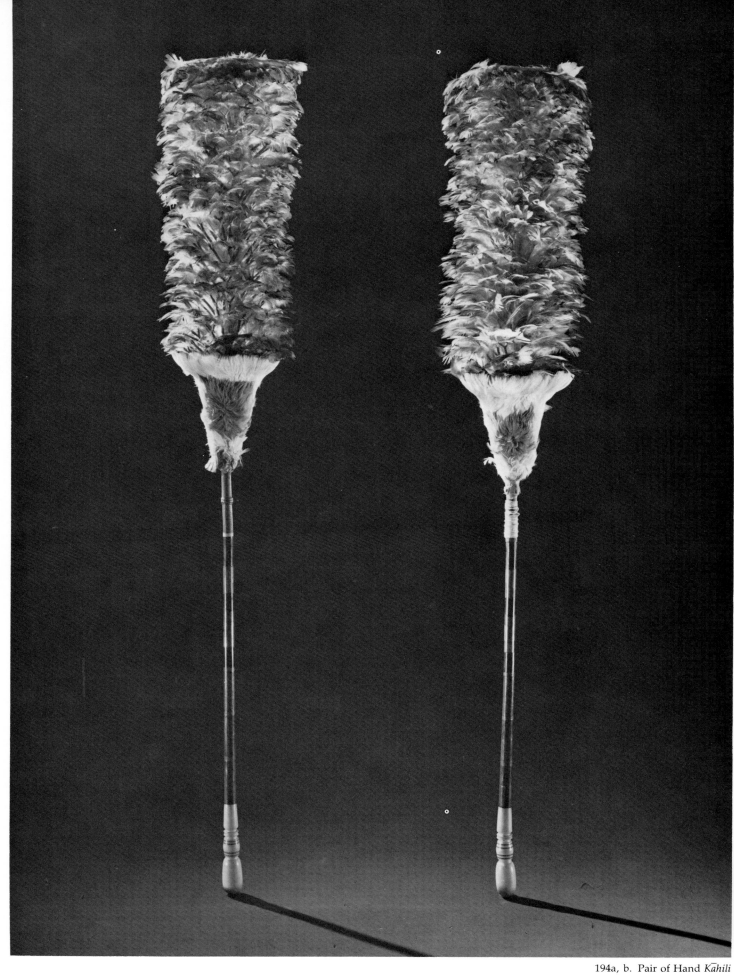

194a, b. Pair of Hand *Kāhili*

196. Hand *Kāhili* used by Queen Lili'uokalani

198. Hook Pendant Excavated from Bellows Beach, O'ahu, A.D. 800-1000

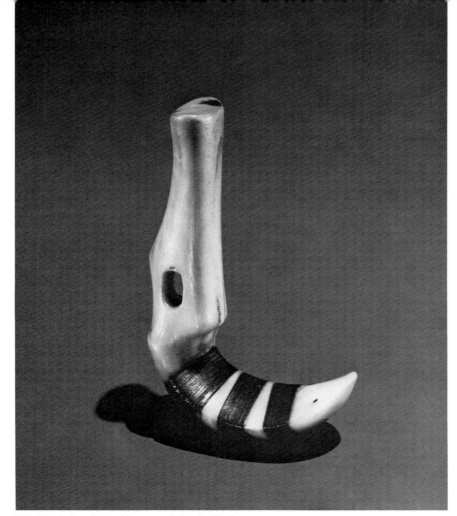

201. Hook Pendant of Ivory and Turtle Shell

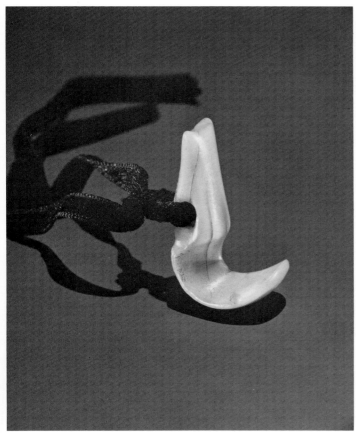

200. Hook Pendant on Velvet Ribbon Tie

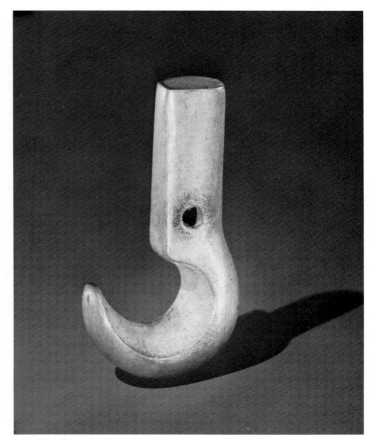

202. Wooden Hook Pendant

205. Ivory Necklace

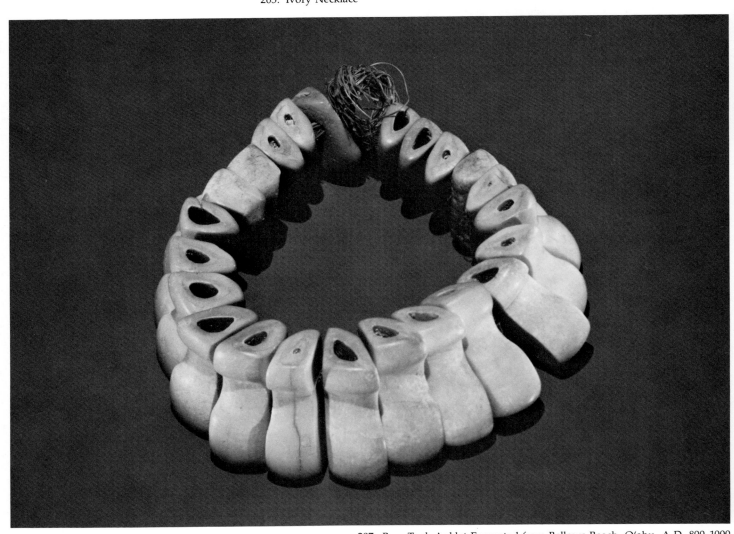

207. Boar Tusk Anklet Excavated from Bellows Beach, O'ahu, A.D. 800-1000

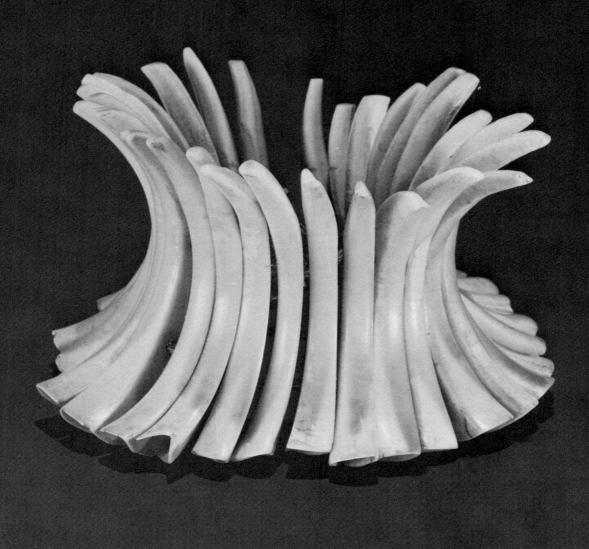

206. Boar Tusk Bracelet from Forbes Cave

209. Ivory Wristlet

211. Basalt Mirror Said to Have Belonged to Keawe, Paramount Chief of Hawai'i

212. Mirror used by Keōpūolani, wife of Kamehameha I

213. Ivory Comb

217. "Their Majesties King Rheo Rhio . . . and Suite . . . at the Theatre Royal . . . June 4th, 1824," by John William Gear

216. "Tamehamalu Queen of the Sandwich Islands . . .," 1824, unknown artist

222. "Assemblée des Chefs des Îles Sandwich . . .," 1837, by Louis-Jules Masselot

224. Clock of Kamehameha III, c. 1840

225a. ''Kamehameha III'' by August Plum, 1846

225b. ''H. Kalama,'' by August Plum, 1846

230. ''Iles Sandwich.—Funérailles du roi de l'Archipel . . .,'' attributed to Mesnard, c. 1870

237. King Kamehameha IV,
    unknown photographer, c. 1860

229. Prince Lot Kamehameha, Dr. Judd,
    and Prince Alexander Liholiho
    in Boston, May 23, 1850

238. Queen Emma, by Joseph W. King, c. 1860

239. Queen Emma's Silver Bracelet

242. Princess Ke'elikōlani with Featherwork, by Menzies Dickson, c. 1880

243. Keōua Hale, Home of Princess Ke'elikōlani, unknown photographer, c. 1883

244. Princess Ke'elikōlani's Grass House in Kailua, Hawai'i, unknown photographer, c. 1883

246. Mr. and Mrs. Charles Reed Bishop, unknown photographer, c. 1857

250. Lunalilo as a Young Boy, attributed to A. T. Agate, c. 1840

249. Bust of King Lunalilo, by Allen Hutchinson, 1890

259. Royal Order of Kapi'olani, Grand Cross, Commander and Cordon

258. Royal Order of Kalākaua I, Knights Grand Cross

260. Royal Order of the Crown of Hawai'i, Grand Cross

261. Royal Order of the Star of Oceania, Grand Officer

264. Kalākaua and Kapiʻolani Anniversary Medal (left) and King Kalākaua Jubilee Medal (No. 265)

266. Coat of Arms Medal (left) and Hail! Kalākaua Medal (No. 267)

268. King Kalākaua's World Tour Medal (left) and Kalākaua Election Medal (No. 263)

274. David Kalākaua in Youth, unknown photographer, c. 1850

276. King Kalākaua Lying in State, 'Iolani Palace Throne Room, by J. J. Williams, 1891

272. Queen Kapi'olani and Princess Lili'uokalani at Rackheath Hall, unknown photographer, 1887

270. 'Iolani Palace, unknown photographer, c. 1885

277. Queen Lili'uokalani, unknown photographer, 1892

281. "Aloha" Bracelet, given by Princess Bernice Pauahi Bishop to Liliʻuokalani

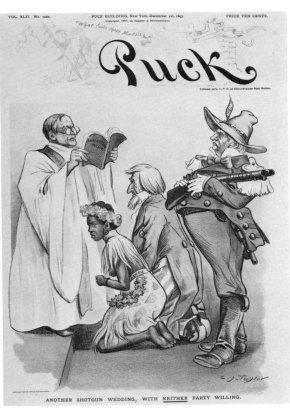

285. Great Seal of the Republic of Hawaiʻi, 1894

286. "Another Shotgun Wedding with *Neither* Party Willing," by
      Charles Jay Taylor, 1897

288. Hawaiian Flag Quilt

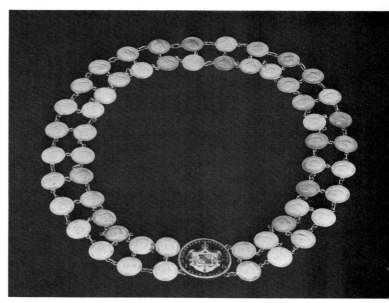

289. Hawaiian Coin Belt

292. Memorial Bust of King Kalākaua, by Allen Hutchinson, c. 1896

294. "Meeting Place of an Ancient Secret Society,"
by Robert C. Barnfield, 1886

295. "Hawaiian Godess [sic]—
Kiha Wahine or Lailai,"
by Robert C. Barnfield, c. 1885

298. Covered Container of the Hale Nauā Society

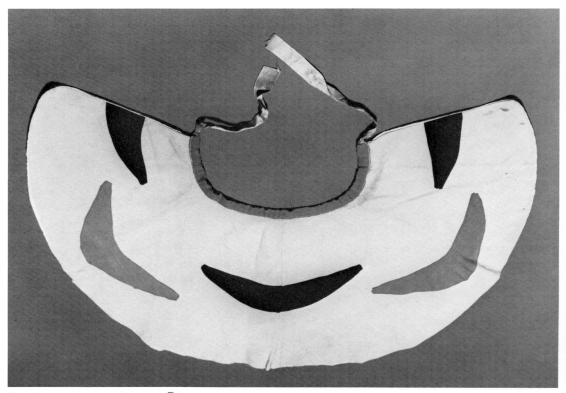

299. Cloth Cape of the Hale Nauā Society

300. Crepe Paper Cloak

302. Coconut Dance Rattle, by Kukui'ola

303. "Hula Ku'i," by A. C. Kahekiliuila Lagunero, 1979

305. "Wailua A'u (My Two Souls)," by Rocky K. Jensen, 1979

The Exhibition*
Roger G. Rose

Visions of Hawai'i

Through the eyes of Captain James Cook and his contemporaries were the first visions of Hawai'i given to the world. In words and engravings, the published journals of Cook and others depict the sights and events he and other explorers encountered in the late 18th and early 19th centuries, and which the pictorial artists of the day portrayed more or less imaginatively according to their purpose or ability. On these works, and on the accounts of whalers, merchants, and missionaries who later plied the Pacific, are the European and American visions of Hawai'i and her people based.

Literally hundreds of pictorial representations were left by these roving artists and early draftsmen.

The examples assembled here depict many of the same scenes and events and people that astonished or delighted earlier audiences, providing them with their first and sometimes only impression of this distant and provocative land. Many of the works afford fleeting glimpses into their creators' minds nearly as much as into the realities of the scenic wonders or events portrayed, yet the totality represents an unparalleled legacy depicting Hawai'i as perceived by the outside world.

Unfortunately, the view is one-sided, for the Hawaiians' vision of this strange new outside world that imposed itself upon them has remained largely unexplored.

---

1. The Death of Cook, by George Carter (1737-1794)

Oil on fabric, c. 1783
76 × 91 cm.
Gov. G. R. Carter Collection, 1959
Color Plate I

The death of Captain James Cook at Kealakekua Bay on February 14, 1779, thrust the Hawaiian Islands into the forefront of European thought. Numerous illustrations were made to commemorate the event, but few stirred the popular imagination more than the famous painting (several versions exist) by George Carter, a noted British painter of historical events.

Sailing north from the island of Tahiti into uncharted seas the year before, Cook sighted O'ahu, the first of the Hawaiian Islands, on January 18, 1778. Two days later his ships, the *Resolution* and *Discovery*, reached Kaua'i, and after a brief stay at the village of Waimea, and the nearby island of Ni'ihau, they headed toward the northwest coast of America for further discoveries.

Returning in November to winter, Cook anchored at Kealakekua Bay on the west side of the island of Hawai'i

on January 16, 1779, after seven frustrating weeks seeking a safe harbor. His ships generously provisioned and the men rested, Cook sailed away three weeks later, only to be driven back for repairs after a heavy gale. The wearied hosts, nearly exhausted of food as well as patience, found it increasingly difficult to avoid provocations with the English. When the *Discovery's* cutter was stolen during the night of February 13, an exasperated Cook went ashore next morning to take as hostage high chief Kalani'ōpu'u, ruler of the island. A skirmish erupted, and in its wake four marines, several Hawaiians, and the renowned navigator lay dead.

2. The Death of Cook February 14, 1779, by John Cleveley (1747-1786)

Aquatint with watercolor
Published 1790
49 × 65.3 cm. (plate mk.)
Gift of Mrs. A.W.F. Fuller, 1964

Cleveley's version of the death of Cook is the only one having a reasonable claim to "authenticity." A marine painter, Cleveley is thought to have based his work on an original sketch by his brother James, a carpenter aboard

*All items in this exhibition are from Bishop Museum unless otherwise indicated.

the *Resolution* and the only illustrator of the event who may have been present. This representation is from a set of four believed to be "proof states" of the four Pacific views aquatinted by F. Jukes and published in 1790. Perhaps handcolored by John Cleveley himself, it differs in minor details from the well-known published version, which is entitled simply, "View of Owhyee, one of the Sandwich Islands in the South Seas."

3. Tereoboo [Kalani'opu'u], King of Owhyee, Bringing Presents to Capt. Cook, by John Webber (1751-1793)

Pen and wash
40.2 × 63 cm.
Published in atlas to Cook's third voyage (B.T. Pouncy, engraver), 1784
Purchase from Spencer Bickerton, 1922.

Ten days after anchoring at Kealakekua Bay, Cook was formally received on January 26, 1779, by high chief Kalani'opu'u, who had come down to the Bay the day before to meet the explorer. The ceremony, captured in this impressive view by shipboard artist John Webber, was witnessed by Captain James King:

The next day, about noon, the king, in a large canoe, attended by two others, set out from the village, and paddled towards the ships in great state. Their appearance was grand and magnificent. In the first canoe was Terreeeboo and his chiefs, dressed in their rich feathered clokes [sic] and helmets, and armed with long spears and daggers; in the second, came the venerable Kaoo, the chief of the priests, and his brethren, with their idols displayed on red cloth. These idols were busts of a gigantic size, made of wicker-work, and curiously covered with small feathers of various colours, wrought in the same manner with their cloaks. Their eyes were made of large pearl oysters, with a black nut fixed in the centre; their mouths were set with a double row of the fangs of dogs, and, together with the rest of their features, were strangely distorted. The third canoe was filled with hogs and various sorts of vegetables. As they went along, the priests in the centre canoe sung their hymns with great solemnity; and after paddling around the ships, instead of going on board, as was expected, they made toward the shore at the beach where we were stationed.
As soon as I saw them approaching, I ordered out our little guard to receive the king; and Captain Cook, perceiving that he was going on shore, followed him, and arrived nearly at the same time. We conducted them into the tent, where they had scarcely been seated, when the king rose up, and in a very graceful manner threw over the Captain's shoulders the cloak he himself wore, put a feathered helmet upon his head, and a curious fan into his hand. He also spread at his feet five or six other cloaks, all exceedingly beautiful, and of the greatest value. His attendants then brought four very large hogs, with sugar-canes, cocoa-nuts, and bread-fruit; and this part of the ceremony was concluded by the king's exchanging names with Captain Cook, which, amongst all the islanders of the Pacific Ocean, is esteemed the strongest pledge of friendship . . . (Cook and King, 1784, Vol. 3, pp. 16-18).

4. An Inland View in Atooi (Kaua'i), unknown artist, after Webber.

Pencil, ink, and watercolor wash
44.2 × 99 cm.
From a set of 19 drawings (many on paper watermarked 1890) copied from Webber sketches in the British Museum.

Soon after Cook's first landing at Waimea, Kaua'i, on January 20, 1778, "a trade was set on foot for hogs and potatoes, which the people of the island gave us in exchange for nails and pieces of iron, formed into something like chissels." With amicable relations established, Cook's men, as this drawing after Webber suggests, "met with no obstruction in watering; on the contrary, the natives assisted our men in rolling the casks to and from the pool; and readily performed whatever we requested" (Cook and King 1784, Vol. 2, p. 199).
The village at Waimea consisted of about 60 houses near the beach and another 40 or so a bit inland:

Though they seem to have adopted the mode of living in villages, there is no appearance of defense, or fortification, near any of them; and the houses are scattered about, without any order, either with respect to their distances from each other, or their position in any particular direction. Neither is there any proportion as to their size; some being large and commodious, from forty to fifty feet long, and twenty or thirty broad, while others of them are mere hovels. Their figure is not unlike oblong corn, or hay-stacks . . . with two very low sides, hardly discernible at a distance. The gable, at each end, corresponding to the sides, makes these habitations perfectly close all around; and they are well thatched with long grass, which is laid on slender poles, disposed with some regularity. The entrance is made indifferently in the end or side, and is an oblong hole, so low, that one must rather creep than walk in . . . (Cook and King 1784, Vol. 2, pp. 233-234).

5. "Village of Macacoupah [Makakupu], Owhyee," by Thomas Heddington

Aquatint, with color added
Published 1814
41 × 55 cm. (plate mk.) 42.2 × 57.3 cm. (sheet)
Gift of Gwendolyn McGolrick, 1961

Some 30 vessels, mostly traders, visited Hawai'i in the interim between George Vancouver's first appearance with Cook and his own voyage in command of the *Discovery* and *Chatham* in 1792-1794. Counseling peace, and distributing seeds and livestock wherever he went, Vancouver was warmly regarded by many later Hawaiians as "the father of the nation." The apparent tranquility captured by midshipman and artist Thomas Heddington at Makakupu (near Pāhala, Hawai'i) on February 12, 1794, however, belies the changes beginning to take place as a result of contact with the Western world.
Just before sailing a few days later, Vancouver accepted Kamehameha's plea for protection from Britain's King George, and within a year the warrior king was well on his way to unifying the islands by conquest.

6. "View of Salt Water Fishponds near Honoruru Sandwich Islands," by Robert Dampier (1800-1874)

Pencil
18.4 × 23.5 cm. (sheet)
Later engraved and published in Voyage of H.M.S. Blonde *to the Sandwich Islands in the Years 1824-1825 (London: J. Murray, 1826)*
Gov. G. R. Carter Collection, 1959

Robert Dampier was the artist and draftsman aboard H.M.S. *Blonde,* which brought the bodies of King Kamehameha II and Queen Kamāmalu back from London in 1825 (see No. 31). Rich in visual detail, his numerous sketches and oil paintings are valuable supplements to the published records of the voyage. The description of fishponds near Pearl Harbor, situated just west of the growing port of Honolulu, is a case in point:

> Behind the town the plain extends nearly a mile to the foot of the hills. Here the taro fields, with their little water-courses, give a rich verdant appearance to the country: and beyond the town, along the shore, are the great saltwater tanks, which the natives have constructed by rolling large blocks of lava into the water so as to form great dikes, in order to secure a constant supply of fish (*Blonde*, 1826, p. 120).

This is No. 4 in a set of 26 original drawings later published in *Voyage of H.M.S.* Blonde . . . Some items are watermarked "J. Whatman 1824."

7a. "Town of Honolulu: Is.¹ᵈ of Woahoo. Sandwich Islands from under the Punchbowl Hill August 3: 1834," unknown artist

Pencil, pen, and ink wash
14.8 × 32.3 cm. (sheet)
Watermark J. Whatman 1832

7b. "Honolulu from the Anchorage outside the Reef. Is.¹ of Woahoo Sandwich Is.¹ᵈ August 4 1834," unknown artist

Pencil, pen, and ink wash
14.9 × 32.2 cm. (sheet)
Purchase 1962

This pair of pencil drawings presages the rapid growth of Honolulu from a sleepy village to a bustling port, destined in a few short years to become the crossroads of the Pacific. By 1823 the town boasted four general stores, abundantly, if expensively, stocked by New England merchant companies, and could attribute its early success to the safe harbor—Honolulu means "protected bay"—frequented by sandalwood and fur traders supplying the Canton markets. When the Hawaiian sandalwood trade expired in the 1830's, New England whalers quickly filled the void, virtually guaranteeing commercial prosperity. During the peak of whaling days, some 490 ships anchored off either Honolulu or Lahaina in 1844 alone, loosening their thirsty and pent-up crews onto the streets and waiting grog shops. While horrified missionaries preached doom and damnation, the struggling government did its best to maintain a semblance of order.

8a. "Panorama de l'ile d'Oahou pris du mouillage d'Honoloulou (Iles Sandwich) 1.ᵉʳᵉ. Feuille," by Romuald-Georges Mesnard

Lithograph, tinted
35.7 × 54.4 cm. (sheet)

8b. "Panorama de l'ile d'Oahou pris du mouillage d'Honoloulou (Iles Sandwich). 2.ᵐᵉ. Feuille," by Romuald-Georges Mesnard

Lithograph, tinted
32.9 × 54.3 cm. (sheet)
Published in Atlas Pittoresque *accompanying Du Petit-Thouars'* Voyage autour du monde . . . pendant les annés 1836-1839 . . . *(Paris: Gide, 1840-1864)*
Gov. G.R. Carter Collection, 1959

The French frigate *La Vénus*, under command of Abel Aubert Du Petit-Thouars, sailed into Honolulu on July 9, 1837. Although impressed at first by the harsh landscape, which on closer inspection seemed promisingly fertile, the French soon conceded that O'ahu merited the sobriquet bestowed upon it by former visitors—"garden of the Sandwich Islands."

> Approaching the eastern point of Oahou, we were struck by the dry and desolate appearance which was presented to us; from the seashore to the crest of the mountains, we saw nothing, not even the slightest trace of vegetation; everything is bare and dry. The mountains are wrought by grooves like furrows formed from lava flows, and, in several places the stones are black, as if, just recently, they had undergone the action of fire.
> After having turned the first point, formed by an ancient volcanic crater, we saw in the N.W., above the lowlands which join Diamond Head to the island, the flag of the Sandwich Islands; it waved over the fort constructed at the summit of the mountain called Punchbowl, which dominates the town of Honoloulou . . . After having passed around Diamond Head point, we discovered the bay of Wäi-titi [Waikiki], to which it serves as a shelter in the east. Alerted, too favorably, no doubt, to the beauties of the village of Wäi-titi, the sight of it caused in me only a painful sensation, like that that a sad and miserable place causes one to feel . . .
> (Translated from Du Petit-Thouars 1840-1843, Vol. 1, pp 322-323).

9. View of Honolulu Harbor, by Robert Elwes

Watercolor
33.4 × 47.6 cm.
Published as colored lithograph in Robert Elwes, A Sketcher's Tour round the World. *(London: Hurst and Blackett, 1854)*
Purchased with funds donated by Dr. and Mrs. Alfred D. Morris, 1978

Arriving for a brief sojourn aboard the frigate H.M.S. *Amphitrite* in May, 1849, Robert Elwes was also struck by the "sterile and barren" appearance of O'ahu when seen from a distance:

> As we approached, everything looked burnt up and desolate, and it was not till we were close to the shore that we saw little valleys running up into the mountains, dotted with some straggling cocoanut trees, and from the midst of which peered a few huts. But Honolulu itself looks quite a town, and boasts of stone houses, churches

and stores, while a fort, surmounted by cannon, guards the entrance of the harbour.

We anchored outside the harbour, as there was some doubt whether the 'Amphitrite' would be able to go in, no ship of her size having ever been in before. The next day, however, before the wind sprung up she was safely warped in. Numbers of boats came off to see us when she anchored, to get the ship's washing, the rowers wearing clean, well-ironed shirts, as specimens of what could be done, and calling out, 'Lookee here, Sir, my wife washee this' (Elwes, 1854, pp. 180-181).

10. "Port of Honolulu," by George H. Burgess (1831-1900)

Lithograph, 1857
27.5 × 38 cm. (sheet)

While the city prospered, life for its Hawaiian residents took on a colorful, if not always compatible, mixture of the old and the new. The vignettes of life in Hawai'i by George H. Burgess are among the numerous works the London-born artist completed during 20 some years of travel between California and Hawai'i, where his brother Edward was a Honolulu merchant and coffee shop owner. Burgess was one of the first artists to exhibit Hawaiian views commercially (at the San Francisco First Mechanics Institute Industrial Exhibit in 1857), and his idyllic yet animated scenes have been justly admired through the years.

11. "Diamond Head from Hon.[lu] Beach," by George H. Burgess (1831-1900)

Lithograph, 1857
27.6 × 38.3 cm. (sheet)

By the time this view was prepared, the population of the Kingdom's capital had reached nearly 14,000, of which the vast majority was Hawaiian or part-Hawaiian.

12. "Ewa. From Honolulu," by George H. Burgess (1831-1900)

Lithograph, 1857
27.6 × 38.3 cm. (sheet)

'Ewa, meaning "crooked," refers to an area of O'ahu west of Pearl Harbor. This view is not of 'Ewa itself, but of Moanalua, looking toward Pearl Harbor and beyond to 'Ewa (compare No. 6).

13. Honolulu Harbor, unknown photographer

Ambrotype, c. 1856
16.4 × 21.5 cm.
Photo Collection, 1976.192.10
Color Plate II

Not long after Elwes published his view (No. 9), an unknown photographer captured a strikingly similar image of a modern warship lying at anchor in Honolulu Harbor. These "splendid and permanent plates on glass, well known as the improved ambrotypes," were first introduced to Honolulu in 1856 by local photographer

Hugo Stangenwald. As the October 11, 1856, issue of the *Polynesian* noted, he had just returned from San Francisco prepared to execute the new "Photographic pictures on Glass and Paper!"

Although a local engineer named Theophilus Metcalf had experimented briefly with daguerrean portrait photography as early as 1845, scenic views did not become generally available until Hugo Stangenwald established his Honolulu Daguerrean Gallery about ten years later.

14. Country Scene, unknown photographer

Daguerreotype, c. 1855
9.7 × 13 cm.
Photo Collection, 1976.179.10.

Apart from a few city views, daguerreotypes of Hawaiian scenes are unusual. The difficulties involved in gaining access to rural areas and packing cumbersome photographic equipment did not make the effort worth most artists' time. Although the significance of the event and the location in this image have been lost, clearly it was a momentous occasion, bringing together a large group in an otherwise somnolent mid-19th-century setting.

15a,b,c. Honolulu (three views in sequence), by Charles Leander Weed (1824-1903)

Albumen print, 1865
a: Honolulu from Prison looking toward Nu'uanu Valley
41.8 × 53.5 cm.
b: Honolulu from Prison looking toward Punchbowl
43.3 × 53 cm.
c: Honolulu from Prison looking toward the harbor
41.9 × 53.3 cm.
Photo Collection, 1979.24.14-16.

By 1865, when Charles Leander Weed made these three "mammoth" prints, the town was beginning to resemble a Western frontier settlement. Although still dominated by stark hills rising abruptly from the dusty plain, Honolulu's tree-lined streets were already reaching out tentatively into newly settled residential areas flanking the harbor and the Kingdom's most important commercial center.

Weed, a well-known California landscape photographer, famous for his large scenic views of Yosemite Valley, opened a short-lived studio in Honolulu in 1865. Anticipating that he should be "equally successful in Honolulu and other parts of the islands," *The Friend* for April of that year noted approvingly, on his arrival from San Francisco, "He is about to take a large photographic view of Honolulu." The result proved to be the first panoramic sequence of Honolulu in photography.

16. Kīlauea, Day Scene, by Titian Ramsay Peale (1799-1885)

Oil on fabric, 1842
51.5 × 76.5 cm.
Gift of Albert Rosenthal, 1924
Color Plate III

Among the spectacular scenes that never failed to impress visitors was the live volcano of Kīlauea on the island of Hawai'i, captured in two dramatic views by Titian Ramsay Peale. The youngest son of Charles Willson Peale, and one of a growing number of pioneer American natural history illustrators, Peale visited Hawai'i in 1840-1841 as naturalist with the United States South Seas Surveying and Exploring Expedition. Commanded by Lieutenant Charles Wilkes, U.S.N., it was the government's only major expedition into the Pacific under sail.

Peale spent a day in the volcano area late in 1840 making several sketches that he incorporated into finished views when the expedition returned home in 1842. Evidently painted purely for his own pleasure (no record is known of their public exhibition), these views convey a freshness and quality not always evident in Peale's few other contemporary volcano paintings, or in much of his subsequent work.

17. Kīlauea, Night Scene, by Titian Ramsay Peale (1799-1885)

Oil on fabric, 1842
51.5 × 76.5 cm.
Gift of Albert Rosenthal, 1924
Not illustrated

When Wilkes visited the volcano, he wrote, "The most brilliant pyrotechnics would have faded before what we now saw . . . The [lava] streams were of a glowing cherry-red colour, illuminating the whole crater around . . . The sight was magnificent, and worth a voyage round the world to witness" (Wilkes, 1844, Vol. 4, p. 187).

Sacred to Hawaiians, Kīlauea was feared and avoided as the abode of the fire goddess Pele. Here in 1824, the chiefess Kapi'olani approached the flaming pit and, eating 'ohelo berries sacred to Pele, defied the goddess by crying for all to hear, "Jehovah is my God. He kindled these fires. I fear not Pele" (Feher, 1969, p. 178). Her act of extreme courage broke the hold of Pele and helped clear the way for the acceptance of Christianity.

18. Eruption of Mauna Loa Seen from Kawaihae, by Charles Furneaux (c. 1835-1913)

Oil on fabric, c. 1880-1881
84 × 143 cm.
Not illustrated

Charles Furneaux came to Hawai'i in 1880 with his friend William T. Brigham, a geologist, who was returning to study an eruption of Mauna Loa. When activity ceased, Brigham went back to Boston, but Furneaux stayed on. Later, the major eruption anticipated by Brigham took place, and Furneaux painted many scenes of the fiery spectacle. When Brigham moved to Hawai'i in 1888 to take charge of Bishop Museum, he commissioned Furneaux to paint additional volcanic scenes, some of which Brigham published in *Volcanoes of Kilauea and Mauna Loa* in 1909.

Furneaux served as American Counsular Agent and U. S. Shipping Commissioner at Hilo from 1888 until annexation in 1898, retiring afterward to 'Ōla'a to raise coffee and bananas.

19. "Mokuaweoweo Crater, Eruption of 1896," by David Howard Hitchcock (1861-1943)

Oil on fabric, 1896
51 × 153 cm.
Gift of David Howard Hitchcock, 1897
Not illustrated

Many artists and visitors from around the world made the pilgrimage to the volcanoes of Hawai'i, but it was a native son who created a lasting public demand for romantic views of the ominous fire pits. Born in 1861 of missionary parentage, David Howard Hitchcock had worked patiently at his easel until the late 1880's, when Charles Reed Bishop, a local philanthropist, spotted his developing talent and provided the means for study in America and Europe. In acknowledgment, Hitchcock presented four of his best works to Bishop Museum in 1897, expressing hopes that they "will be a satisfactory addition to the historical value of the Museum" (Kent, 1965, p. 301).

20. Diamond Head from Waikīkī, by Enoch Wood Perry (1831-1915)

Oil on fabric, c. 1865
66.3 × 97 cm.
Not illustrated

Among the professional artists who visited Hawai'i in the 19th century, few succeeded in depicting scenic views so pleasingly as Enoch Wood Perry. An inveterate traveler, Perry visited Hawai'i from New Orleans for a short time during the mid-1860's, before settling in New York to become a prominent international portrait painter. His genre paintings, however, are only recently being recognized for both their artistic and historical merit. Note in his view of Diamond Head, Honolulu's most imposing landmark, the figure of a standing woman, an earlier version of which is revealed through the partly translucent paint.

Diamond Head, a tuff crater formed by violent steam explosions some 100,000 years ago, was so named because of the calcite crystals early visitors found in the surrounding rocks. The highest point, 760 feet, is Lē'ahi Peak. Flanking Waikīkī on the east, the extinct cone was the site of a religious structure used for human sacrifices and important to Pele's younger sister Hi'iaka, who likened its profile to the brow of the 'ahi fish; hence its Hawaiian name.

21. Mānoa Valley, by Enoch Wood Perry (1831-1915)

Oil on fabric, 1865
66 × 94 cm.
Not illustrated

Perry was impressed with cool and lush Mānoa Valley, the epitome to many of how a tropical paradise should appear. Located directly behind Waikīkī, Mānoa (meaning "vast") for years remained primarily agricultural, until metropolitan Honolulu began to invade later in the 19th century. Today, the University of Hawai'i and East-West Center occupy part of the lower section and the remainder is a prime residential district. In legendary days, Mānoa was famed as the home of Kahaukani (a wind) and Kauahuahine (the rain), a brother and sister born of the mountains, whose marriage "brought to the valley as an inheritance the rainbows and showers for which it has since been distinguished" (Kalākaua, 1888, p. 512).

The Gods Were Many
Images of Deity

Generally regarded as invisible spirits, the gods of ancient Hawai'i could also be "symbolized" by material objects. Natural stones, wood, or carved and fabricated representations in human form, called *ki'i*, served as receptacles for divine essences during periods of ritual invocation. Supernatural intervention in human affairs was sought by reciting appropriate prayers and supplications, usually accompanied by offerings presented to such god figures.

Chiefs and commoners, men and women, craftsmen and warriors—in short, all ranks and classes of society—had their own special gods active in daily affairs. Lesser gods, generally of a personal nature, or associated with family, crafts, sorcery, or other endeavors, were known as *'aumākua;* their visual manifestations were termed *ki'i 'aumakua.*

The major gods, *akua*, were state deities activated in the interest of the nation. The four major ones, shared with the rest of Polynesia, were Kū, Kāne, Lono, and Kanaloa, and all four existed in multiple manifestations with individualized attributes and corresponding names. They were usually worshiped in religious structures called *heiau*, where their *ki'i akua* images were cared for by an officiating priesthood.

Besides these more formal aspects of religion, there were in the heavens, the oceans, the forests, and every other place, "countless multitudes of elves, sprites, gnomes and fairies . . . full of mischief . . . their hands in every pie" (Malo, 1951, p. 85). Colorfully referred to as the "40,000 and 400,000 and 4,000," the gods con-

trolled the destiny of every Hawaiian from birth to death—and beyond.

Of the 160 or so wooden images that survived the burning spree of 1819, when the official state religion was abrogated by chiefly decree, only a mere handful can be associated by name or function with the workings of the ancient religious system—and then often mainly by conjecture. Nevertheless, the examples selected here attest to the great diversity of Hawaiian religious iconography as much as to the individual craftsman's mastery of the body of socio-artistic conventions represented by these sculptural manifestations of the gods.

22. An Offering before Captain Cook in the Sandwich Islands, by John Webber (1751-1793)

Pen and wash
44 × 63 cm.
Published in atlas to Cook's third voyage (Middiman and Hall, engravers), 1784
Purchase from Spencer Bickerton, 1922
Color Plate IV

Perhaps because of the resemblance of his ships' masts and sails to the emblem of Lono, Captain Cook was initially believed by the Hawaiians to be a reincarnation of Lono, god of peace and agriculture. Reinforced in their beliefs by Cook's fortuitous arrival at Kealakekua Bay during the annual *makahiki* celebrations honoring their god, the priests of Lono-i-ka-makahiki were quick to accord Cook all the honors of his presumed divinity.

The eye-witness drawing by John Webber depicts a ceremony honoring Cook held on or about January 21, 1779, at Hikiau *heiau*, an important shrine of Lono at Nāpo'opo'o. With Cook were three ship's officers, including Captain James King, who wrote:

On his [Cook's] atrival [sic] at the beach, he was conducted to a sacred building called Harre-no-Orono [Hale-o-Lono], or the house of Orono, and seated before the entrance, at the foot of a wooden idol, of the same kind with those on the Morai. I was here again made to support one of his arms, and after wrapping him in red cloth, Kaireekeea [Keli'ikea], accompanied by twelve priests, made an offering of a pig with the usual solemnities. The pig was then strangled, and a fire being kindled, it was thrown into the embers, and after the hair was singed off, it was again presented, with a repetition of the chanting, in the manner before described. The dead pig was then held for a short time under the Captain's nose; after which it was laid, with a cocoa-nut, at his feet, and the performers sat down. The ava was then brewed, and handed round; a fat hog, ready dressed, was brought in; and we were fed as before (Cook and King, 1784, Vol. 3, pp. 13-14).

Three weeks later Cook was killed a short distance away, victim of a tragic misunderstanding brought about in part by shifts in the delicate balance of power between political and religious factions in Hawaiian society (Daws, 1968, p. 27).

23. Canoe of the Sandwich Islands, the Rowers Masked,
by John Webber (1751-1793)

Pencil, pen, and wash
30.5 × 45.5 cm.
Published in atlas to Cook's third voyage (C. Grignion,
engraver), 1784
Purchase from Spencer Bickerton, 1922

The double-hulled canoe is probably delivering gifts to
Captain Cook (see No. 3), a few days after the offering
previously described took place at Hale-o-Lono. The
helmeted rowers, wearing gourds decorated with plants
and bark-cloth streamers, are thought (on no very certain
evidence) to be priests of Lono. Two of the occupants
carry feather-covered basketry images, while a wrapped
bundle is lashed to the platform between the hulls.

24. Feather-covered Basketry Image
'Ie'ie aerial rootlets, human hair, mother-of-pearl shell,
wood, dog tooth incisors, olonā netting, red 'i'iwi and
yellow 'o'o feathers
H. 52.2 cm. W. 20.8 cm. Th. 31 cm.
Gift of Trustees of Oahu College (Punahou School), before
1892 (3900)
Color Plate V

Unique to the Hawaiian Islands, such feather gods
epitomize the high technical achievements of the featherworking and basketry arts. Constructed of split aerial
rootlets of a mountain vine arranged into warps and
wefts, the twined foundation is covered with a closely
woven *nae* netting of tough and durable *olonā* fibers, to
which are tied tiny clusters of red and yellow feathers,
now mostly disappeared. The image is finished with
disks of mother-of-pearl shell and wooden pegs to
represent the eyes, while some 74 dog incisors outline the
gaping mouth. On this and about half of the two dozen
surviving feather images, the head is adorned with tufts
of human hair, instead of the crests found on feather
helmets.

Traditionally, these images have been linked with Kū-
ka'ili-moku, the famous war god of Kamehameha I, but
the attribution is based mainly on incomplete historical
records of one particularly well-preserved specimen in
Bishop Museum, believed to have belonged to the great
warrior chief. Conceivably these images represent other
gods as well, but evidence is simply too tenuous to
assign to them any more definite role in the traditional
religious system.

25. Wooden Image
Kauila *wood*
H. 57 cm. W. 51.3 cm. Th. 9.5 cm.
Hawaiian National Museum Collection, 1891 (1363)
Color Plate VI

Purchased on May 7, 1877, for the Hawaiian National
Museum at the estate auction of Charles Kana'ina, father
of King Lunalilo, this image was at the time believed to
be Kū-ka'ili-moku (Kū-Snatcher-of-Islands), war god of
Kamehameha I. It is illustrated in King Kalākaua's book,

The Legends and Myths of Hawaii, and described in the
introduction by R. M. Daggett:

Among the celebrated war-gods of the kings of the
group was that of Kamehameha I. It was called *Kaili,* or
Ku-kaili-moku, and accompanied the great chief in all of
his important battles. It had been the war-god of the
Hawaiian kings for many generations, and was given in
charge of Kamehameha by his royal uncle, Kalauiopuu
[Kalani'opu'u]. It was a small wooden image, roughly
carved, and adorned with a head-dress of yellow feathers
[now lost]. It is said that at times, in the heat of battle, it
uttered cries which were heard above the clash of arms
(Kalākaua, 1888, p. 44).

While this attribution may be conjectural, the image is
a superb example of Hawaiian sculpture. J. Halley Cox
and William H. Davenport (1974, p. 165, Fig. 14) call
attention to the abstract form of the jaw line and head
crest, which is said to resemble the *lei niho palaoa,* a
whale tooth ornament worn by chiefs. Other authorities
liken the face to that of Kamapua'a, the pig demigod and
symbol of lechery, whose rootings created valleys and
springs throughout the islands.

26. Wooden Image
H. 36.5 cm. W. 7.7 cm. Th. 4.6 cm.
Gift of Helen Goo Carter in memory of Paul Leonard
Carter, 1971 (1972.44)
Color Plate VII

Possibly an *akua kā'ai,* or portable image with pointed
prop (to use the terminology of Cox and Davenport,
1974), this god figure is typically Hawaiian in sculptural
form, despite an old handwritten label inscribed, "Tahiti,
Gesellschafts-Inseln, vor 1775, Götzenbild" (Tahiti,
Society Islands, before 1775, God-figure). Purchased at
Sotheby's of London on December 7, 1971, nothing more
is known of its history except for an unexplained
collector's number written on the back in old script, "A.
K. 176." Probably carved in the mid- to late 18th century,
the image once held mother-of-pearl insets in the vacant
eye sockets, like those found on many other Hawaiian
images.

27. Wooden Image
Wood, mother-of-pearl, human hair, bark cloth, bone, black
pigment
H. 53.8 cm. W. 19.3 cm. Th. 10 cm.
Purchase, before 1892 (4044)
Color Plate VIII

Possibly a sorcery image because of the cuplike
appendage arising from the back (from which one
miniature companion is missing), the object is described
in early catalog records as "Kealoewa, a goddess of rain."
It is in fact a male image, confusion having arisen from
the conventionalized overdevelopment of the pectoral
region. The designation may be a misrendering of
Kū-ke-olo'ewa, a war god of Maui chiefs, or of
Kū-ke-ao-lewa, Kū-of-the-Hanging-Cloud, one of the Kū
god-forms with jurisdiction over the rains (Kamakau,
1976, pp. 30, 51).

163

In the possession of Mrs. Mercy P. Whitney of Kaua'i at least by 1865, it may have been one of the cast-off gods given to the Whitney missionary family by King Kaumuali'i (1780-1824). Probably one of two "idols" sold at the Whitney estate auction in February and March, 1873, it was acquired by an unidentified person in Boston, where it remained for 15 years before being returned to Hawai'i.

28. Wooden Image

Wood, human hair, paper, black pigment
H. 89.5 cm. W. 31 cm. Th. 24.5 cm.
J. S. Emerson Collection, 1889 (132)

Found about 1852 at the foot of a cliff near Waimea, O'ahu, having apparently fallen from a cave, this image is said to represent Kālaipāhoa, the poison god. The narrow cavity cut into the back would have been used to hold materials connected with sorcery. The lizards with four legs and long tail painted over each eye and on the cheeks and chin are unusual features of Hawaiian religious iconography.

29. Wooden Image

? Koa wood, human hair, mother-of-pearl shell
H. 74 cm. W. 34.5 cm. Th. 18.5 cm.
Purchase from William Wagner, 1907 (9072)
Color Plate IX

This is one of two similar female figures discovered in a lava-tube burial cave near Honokoa Gulch, Kawaihae, Hawai'i, in 1905 by David Forbes, William Wagner, and F. A. Haenisch. A particularly rich site, the cave contained two other wooden figures (see No. 30), a carved refuse bowl and game board, gourd bowls, bark cloth, remnants of a feather cape and helmet, glass trade beads, and several other objects—presumably deposited as part of the burial accouterments of a chief or priest.

In describing the "Forbes Cave" find, Bishop Museum Director William T. Brigham (1906, p. 7) considered this pair of female figures to be "the finest specimens known of Hawaiian portrait work." As Cox and Davenport (1974, p. 110) point out, "They exhibit the remarkable feeling for sculptural form, fine craftsmanship, and control achieved by the Hawaiian sculptors." Associated trade beads, a shard of Chinese porcelain, an Oriental fan, and other foreign items, suggest a late 18th- or early 19th-century date.

30. Wooden Image

H. 108 cm. W. 13.5 cm. Th. 11.3 cm.
Exchange from F. A. Haenisch, 1907 (9067)
Color Plate X

From the same Forbes Cave burial chamber, this and a nearly identical companion in Bishop Museum (9068) are the largest and best examples of a class of portable images sometimes called *akua kā'ai*. The elaborate headdress may represent abstractions of symbols associated with the gods—such as the rainbow or the "eight foreheads of Lono"—or perhaps proliferations developed simply for dramatic effect. The notched vertical extensions of the head, possibly conventionalized representations of hair braids, appear on other life-sized images thought to be characteristic of the Kona coast of Hawai'i. The facial expressions, suggesting contempt, ferocity, haughtiness, or power, are also typical of the so-called Kona style, which developed in the late 18th century after introduced steel tools facilitated an efflorescence and elaboration of the woodcarver's art.

31. "Morai near Karakakooa," by Robert Dampier (1800-1874)

Aquatint on India paper
22.8 × 27.8 cm. (plate mk.)
Published in Voyage of H.M.S. *Blonde to the Sandwich Islands in the Years 1824-1825. (London: J. Murray, 1826)*

In May, 1825, Lord Byron, commander of H.M.S. *Blonde*, returned to Hawai'i the bodies of King Kamehameha II and his favorite wife, Kamāmalu. Both had died of the measles in London the previous year while awaiting an audience with King George IV. Lord Byron's sad mission accomplished, the *Blonde* visited the nearby royal mausoleum of Hale-o-Keawe while paying tribute to Cook's memory at Kealakekua Bay.

Ship's artist Robert Dampier produced a pencil sketch of the sanctuary a day or two before the *Blonde's* departure for Tahiti, on July 18, 1825.

Built to house the bones of high chief Keawe and his relatives, the sacred enclosure at Hōnaunau (the present-day City of Refuge National Historic Park) had miraculously escaped the rash of burnings that swept the islands on abrogation of the *kapu* system in 1819. An astonished Dampier wrote in his journal:

[This] . . . pagan sanctuary . . . very prettily situated on the banks of a winding stream . . . [was] . . . in all directions . . . planted [with] rude looking carved wooden images, of all shapes & dimensions . . . [and contained within] . . . a great number of feathered Idols, protruding their misshapen heads thro' numberless folds of decayed Tapa . . . [also] . . . the bones of mighty kings and potent warriors, Sandwich heroes of other days . . . An old Priest, the Guardian of these relics, still looked upon each of these grim looking Deities with the utmost veneration . . . (Dampier, 1971, p. 67).

32. Wooden Image

H. 135 cm. W. 20.7 cm. Th. 38.3 cm.
Gift of H. R. Bloxam, 1924 (B. 7883)

Having been granted permission by Kalanimoku, Governor of O'ahu, to enter the royal mausoleum at Hōnaunau, "and take out any curiosities he chose" (Bloxam, 1925, p. 74), Lord Byron and a small party availed themselves of the opportunity with "rapacious inclination" (Dampier 1971, p. 67). Entering the sanctuary, expedition naturalist Andrew Bloxam (1925, p. 74) observed: "Before us were placed two large and curious carved wooden idols, four or five feet high, between which was the altar where the fires were made for consuming the flesh of the victims." Among the several articles believed to have been removed from Hale-o-Keawe that day is this image, preserved in the Bloxam family for nearly a century.

Unusual because of the extended arms and stylized representation of a beard, the figure provides another glimpse of the stylistic exuberance and innovation made possible through metal tools and fresh ideas introduced after Cook in 1778. A companion piece evidently made by the same artist, and also believed to have been removed from Hale-o-Keawe on that same voyage, is now in the Field Museum, Chicago.

33. Wooden Image

H. 160 cm. W. 49 cm. Th. 23.5 cm.
Gift of George N. Wilcox, 1896 (8049)

Recovered from a swamp in 1896 at Kealia, Kaua'i, this slab-type image with unusually large circular eyes was identified by local Hawaiians as the water deity Waianuenue, literally "Water-Rainbow." Captain Cook's men saw similar images on a *heiau*, or temple, near Waimea, Kaua'i, decorated with bark-cloth streamers. Notches at the base of the crest of this carving may also have carried bark-cloth streamers.

34. Wooden Image

H. 299 cm. D. 39 cm.
Gift of Evelyn Breckons, 1913 (11,096)
Not illustrated

The tallest of all Hawaiian carved images known was found deeply buried in the mud of a stream near Kapa'a, Kaua'i in 1909. A post image, its sculptural qualities are closely related to the natural shape of the tree trunk from which it is carved. Post images were sometimes placed around the outer edges of *heiau* compounds.

35. Wooden Support Figure

H. 39.5 cm. W. 16 cm. Th. 14 cm.
Gift of Mrs. S. W. Wilcox, 1912 (C. 8816)

Some carvings of the human figure had little if any religious significance, but were used decoratively as support devices—for example on wooden bowls, drums, carrying poles, spear racks, and the like. Carved in acrobatic or strange and twisted poses, many have a playful quality not apparent in the more formalized religious sculptures. With hands lashed to a horizontal bar, this figure may have supported poles or spears in the U-shaped notches (now partly broken) extending from the upraised feet.

36. Stone Owl God, *pohaku 'aumakua*

H. 19.5 cm. W. 16.5 cm. Th. 16.6 cm.
Hawaiian National Museum Collection, 1891 (4053)

Although its shape is unaltered by man, this waterworn stone of dense basaltic lava has been polished to a shiny black, probably by rubbing with coconut or other oils. It is a typical example of a class of natural products, such as stone, which, because of peculiarities of shape or some other mystical feature, become linked with the spirit world. According to records from the old Hawaiian National Museum, this is said to be an owl god, sometimes called Pueo.

The short-eared owl, also called *pueo*, was formerly widespread throughout the Hawaiian Islands, occupying wide climatic conditions from open grasslands to wet forests, and from sea level to 8,000 feet and above. "The *pueo*," noted 19th-century historian David Malo (1951, p. 38), "is regarded as a deity and is worshiped by many."

37. Stone Image, *pohaku 'aumakua*

H. 15 cm. W. 10.6 cm. Th. 6 cm.
Anonymous purchase before 1893 (7537)
Color Plate XI

Probably a personal *'aumakua*, this natural formation in soft basaltic stone can be scraped like clay. Suggestive of the human form, it is covered with a thin wash of reddish iron oxide or ocherous earth, called *'alaea*. Commonly used for coloring sea salt, for dyes, and medicines, *'alaea* also figured formerly in the *hi'uwai* purification ceremony, in which "people bathed and frolicked in the sea or stream after midnight, then put on their finest tapa and ornaments for feasting and games" (Pukui and Elbert, 1971, p. 67).

Scrapings from other soft stone images are credited with warding off evil influences (*'aumakua 'ino*). Shavings from unworked wood embodying the poison god Kalaipahoa were used in black magic, often with lethal effects.

38. Stone Image, *ki'i pohaku*

Vesicular basalt
H. 15.6 cm. W. 7.5 cm. Th. 6.5 cm.
Gift of Mrs. M. Yamashita, 1950 (D.27)

Discovered about 1930 by Tsuriuichi Yamashita at Hau'ula, O'ahu, this rough but engaging carving is typical of the numerous smaller stone images generally thought to represent family or craft *'aumakua*. No matter what the size, fineness of finish, or medium, it was not the workmanship that gave material representations of the gods their *mana*, or power, but a complicated series of prayers and offerings performed to activate and capture the divinity.

39. Necker Island Stone Image

Vesicular basalt, guano
H. 37 cm. W. 21.8 cm. Th. 10 cm.
Gift of George N. Wilcox, 1894 (7447)

Situated some 450 miles beyond Kaua'i, the northwesternmost island of the main Hawaiian chain, tiny Necker Island was uninhabited and apparently unknown to living Hawaiians at the time of its discovery by Compte de La Pérouse in November, 1786. Since exploration of the rocky pinnacle began in earnest in 1894, fewer than 20 of these mysterious and rigidly conventionalized male images have been recovered, mostly from a *heiau* or religious structure known as "marae 12" near the summit of Flagpole Hill (Emory, 1928). This specimen—one of the finest—was discovered there on May 27, 1894, by Captain William K. Freeman and engineer Benjamin K. Norton while accompanying Minister of the Interior James A. King on an expedition to annex the island to Hawai'i.

Differing substantially from stone carvings elsewhere in the archipelago in the full treatment of face and limbs, Necker images seem to represent an early phase of Hawaiian culture rooted deeply in Southeast Polynesia. These images have not been securely dated, so it is uncertain whether they stem from the proto-Eastern Polynesian influences that prevailed before the 13th century A.D., subsequent archaic Tahitian contacts, or other sources yet to be explained.

40. Stone Image, *ki'i pōhaku*

Vesicular basalt
H. 30.5 cm. W. 18 cm. Th. 10.3 cm.
Gift of Rev. Sam Kapu, 1895 (7662)

Although said to be modern, this image exhibits a degree of fine craftsmanship and imaginative sense of proportion not often found in Hawaiian stonework of any period. Discovered June 10, 1895, by the Reverend Sam Kapu in a special room in the house of a recently deceased uncle, Joe Oku, it had been part of the elderly man's ritual paraphernalia used in the Hale Naua Society. Possibly prehistoric, it might simply have been "touched-up" and rededicated for use in this semi-secret organization, founded by King Kalākaua in 1886 to revitalize and preserve ancient teachings. By 1895 the image was known as Lononui-a-ehu, perhaps a variant of Lono-ka-'eho (Lono-the-Stone), an eight-headed chief from distant Kahiki said by tradition to have been killed by Kamapua'a, the pig god.

41. Stone Image, *ki'i pōhaku*

H. 112 cm. W. 33 cm. Th. 15.5 cm.
Acquired before 1892 (4898)

Many images were either hidden or destroyed when the formal religious system was abandoned by official decree in 1819. This slab-type basalt image, discovered accidentally in a small cave during blasting operations for a road near Kailua, Hawai'i, is more realistic in facial details than most stone figures of comparable size.

42. Stone Fishing God, *kū'ula*

Vesicular basalt
L. 24.7 cm. W. 13 cm. Th. 7 cm.
J. S. Emerson Collection, 1889 (316)

Long after the overthrow of the official religion in 1819, stone images continued to be made and used, particularly by fishmen whose *kū'ula* served as good-luck talismans for increasing the supply of fish. This example, worked with steel tools, was purchased by J. S. Emerson on October 8, 1886, from Mary P. Ailau, a part-Hawaiian dealer who had obtained it from Governor Kanoa's caretaker at Kōloa, Kaua'i. It had been found on an elliptical stone basin (Bishop Museum No. 317) on which "offerings of ia ula (kumu) [*i'a 'ula, kumu*; introduced gold fish, or goatfish], awa and 5 leaves of the grass called Puaa lau [*pua'a lau*] were placed, to bring in the fish toward the shore. The grass Puaa lau is the same as kukai puaa [*kūkae pua'a*] & takes the place of a live pig" (Emerson, n.d., No. 1177).

According to tradition, Kū'ula-kai (Red-Kū-of-the-Sea), the god of fishermen, built the first fishpond and instructed his son 'Ai'ai to establish fishing stations *(ko'a)* and shrines *(kū'ula)* throughout the islands. All fishermen's stone images and shrines were named *kū'ula* in Kū'ula-kai's honor and were taboo. Fishing gods have continued to be propitiated well into the present century, but most examples survive as natural or minimally worked pieces of stone or coral.

43. Urchin Spine Image

"Slate pencil" sea urchin
H. 9 cm. W. 0.9 cm. Th. 1 cm.
Collected by John F. G. Stokes, 1913 (C.3526)

Altogether, nearly a dozen of these unusual images have been recovered, all but one from the presently uninhabited island of Kaho'olawe. This and several others (see also No. 44) were found on a fishing shrine at Kamōhio Bay during an early survey of the island's numerous archaeological sites by Bishop Museum Curator of Polynesian Ethnology J.F.G. Stokes.

While never a center of population, Kaho'olawe once supported a highly developed fishing culture, linked apparently to nearby settlements on Maui and perhaps elsewhere. Reminiscent in style of certain full-scale carvings in wood, sea-urchin spine images undoubtedly had some religious connection with fishing, but whether they were *'aumākua* or some special form of offering is unknown.

44. Urchin Spine Image

"Slate pencil" sea urchin
H. 6 cm. W. 1 cm. Th. 0.5 cm.
Collected by John F. G. Stokes, 1913 (C. 3527)
Not illustrated

45a & b. Pair of Kapu Staves, *pūlo'ulo'u*

Wood, bark cloth
L. 155 cm. D. (of head) 20 cm.
Exchange from Martha Brown Richards, 1938
(C.8941a/b)
Not illustrated

Balls of white or black bark cloth affixed to the upper ends of short poles were carried before sacred chiefs (*ali'i kapu*) as insignia of taboo. Their appearance served as a warning to the people to remove all coverings, to bow, squat, or, depending upon the rank of the *kapu* chief, prostrate themselves as a sign of humility. *Kapu* sticks were also placed at temple entrances, at the four corners of chiefly residences, or beside springs, groves, paths, or bathing places as a standing notice against trespass. Commonplace elsewhere in Polynesia, the *kapu* in Hawai'i developed to excessive limits and was oppressive, irksome, and dangerous to the masses. "Obey or die," it commanded, and even for thoughtless violations, death was the usual penalty.

46. "Manière de punir de mort un coupable aux îles Sandwich," by Jacques Etienne Victor Arago (1790-1855)

Lithograph
24.7 × 35 cm. (sheet)
Published in atlas accompanying Arago's Promenade autour du monde pendant les années 1817, 1818, 1819, et 1820 . . . *(Paris: LeBlanc, 1822)*
J. C. Earle Collection, 1969

In August, 1819, only three months before the *kapu* system was toppled, Jacques Arago visited the islands and was vividly impressed by the manner in which criminals and *kapu* breakers might be dealt with. "The punishment of death is inflicted here in various ways," he observed, "and as if suffering was regarded as nothing, they begin by subjecting the criminal to a forty-eight hours' fast . . ."

Here, as soon as the two days' fast is terminated, they conduct the criminal, bound, to a morai, at the door of which the high-priest is in waiting for him, and pronounces a certain formula, the meaning of which I have not been able to ascertain. Two or three persons then lay the criminal down on a piece of wood, placing his head on a stone; whilst the executioner, who is chosen indiscriminately from among the most athletic of the spectators, dispatches him by a violent blow on the forehead, with a club. His body is either interred immediately or left to the birds of prey, according to the will of the priest, or the nature of the crime (Translated from Arago 1823, Vol. 2, p. 137).

47. "Manière d'étrangler un coupable aux îles Sandwich," by Jacques Etienne Victor Arago (1790-1855)

Lithograph
24.4 × 35.1 cm. (sheet)
Published in atlas accompanying Arago's Promenade autour du monde pendant les années 1817, 1818, 1819, et 1820 . . . *(Paris: LeBlanc, 1822)*
J. C. Earle Collection, 1969

Arago (1823, Vol. 2, p. 137) also described and illustrated another mode of execution in which "the criminal is fixed with his back to a cocoa-nut tree, and strangled by two men, who pass a cord round his neck, and draw it with great force, supporting themselves by another tree at a short distance from the first."

48. Strangling Cord, *ka'ane*

Walrus ivory, olonā *cordage*
L. (of doubled cord) 93 cm. L. (handle) 5.5 cm.
Acquired before 1892 (4868)
Not illustrated

Hawai'i differed from the rest of Polynesia in having public executioners, termed *mū*, who were charged with procuring victims for sacrifice and executing *kapu* breakers. Strangling was a common form of execution, and a special cord of square, eight-ply plait attached to a carved grip was often employed. Delicate but deadly, the exquisitely crafted grip resembles necklace beads, except that perforations are drilled laterally rather than longitudinally. Unruly children were sometimes frightened by being told the dreaded *mū* would get them.

Arrival of the First Missionaries

Fed up with burdensome taboos (which foreigners violated flagrantly and fearlessly), and aware that Tahiti had abandoned its old ways in favor of Christianity four or five years earlier, many influential chiefs and priests were ready to urge abolition of the *kapu* system when steadfastly traditionalist Kamehameha I died on May 8, 1819. The symbolic event triggering the overthrow occurred at a feast held in Kailua in early November, 1819, about six months after Liholiho had succeeded his father as Kamehameha II. Urged by the two most powerful female chiefs, Queen Regent Ka'ahumanu and his mother, Keōpūolani, the 19-year-old king was persuaded to eat publicly at a table prepared for females in open violation of one of the most fundamental taboos. Thus, in this one dramatic gesture of "free eating," or *'ai noa,* the entire overt structure of the ancient religious system collapsed.

Although the inexorable move toward abolition had been building up for more than a quarter of a century, as one historian prophetically noted, Hawai'i presented to the world "the singular spectacle of a nation without a religion" (Jarves, 1843, p. 198).

Unaware of these happenings, 14 Congregationalist missionaries from New England arrived on the brig *Thaddeus* six months later, fired with piety and Calvinist fervor. They were also armed with instructions from Boston's American Board of Commissioners for Foreign Missions "to aim at nothing short of covering these islands with fruitful fields and pleasant dwellings, and schools and churches; of raising up the whole people to an elevated state of Christian civilization; of bringing them to the mansions of eternal blessedness" (Feher, 1969, p. 173).

During the next 28 years, twelve companies totaling 140 men and women followed, many with their families. Short of Western discovery of the islands in 1778, the landing of the first missionary company at Kailua on April 4, 1820, was one of the single most important events to affect the history of Hawai'i.

49. "Îles Sandwich: Baptême du Premier Ministre du Roi, à bord de L'Uranie," by Crépin after various sketches of Arago

Engraving, handcolored
22.9 × 32.9 cm. (plate mk.) 34.5 × 50.4 cm. (sheet)
Published in Atlas Historique *accompanying de Freycinet's* Voyage autour du monde . . . pendant les années 1817, 1818, 1819, et 1820 . . . *(Paris: Chez Pillet Aîné. Imprimeur-Libraire, 1824-1842)*
Gov. G.R. Carter Collection, 1959
Color Plate XII

Arriving at the critical juncture between the death of Kamehameha I and the November feast signaling the overthrow of the *kapu* system, the French expedition under Louis de Freycinet met with an unexpected request for baptism from high chief Kalanimoku, prime minister under Kamehameha I. After a council of state in which de Freycinet proffered France's eternal friendship, the Abbé de Quélen administered the colorful ceremony aboard *L'Uranie* on (or slightly after) August 13, 1819. The curious onlookers included members of the court of Liholiho, his five queens, Kauikeaouli (the future Kamehameha III), and numerous retainers dressed in appropriate splendor. Afterward, carped de Freycinet, "these royal guests drank and carried away, during a period of two hours, enough [brandy and wine] to take care of a mess of ten persons over a period of three months" (Wiswell, 1978, p. 28).

Two weeks later an envious Boki, Governor of O'ahu, was granted a similar request for baptism, but "political considerations" prevented Liholiho himself from accomplishing this desire—"for the moment" (Wiswell, 1978, p. 28). Doubtlessly aware that Kalanimoku had objected initially to the overthrow, yet relented when it appeared inevitable, the young king was unready to declare himself publicly a convert to the new religion.

In later years, Catholic missionaries suffered persecution, and an edict by staunchly Congregationalist Ka'ahumanu in 1829 prohibited Hawaiians from attending Mass. When priests were actually banished on Christmas Eve, 1831, the French government's demands for reinstatement were swift and predictable: even so, trouble persisted until a French gunboat finally enforced freedom of worship for Catholics in 1839.

50. Four Hawaiian Christian Youths, by Samuel Finley Breese Morse (1791-1872)

Engraving
Published, 1822
33 × 25 cm. (plate mk.) 31 × 46.5 cm. (sheet)
Gov. G.R. Carter Collection, 1959

The four youths depicted are Thomas Hopu (Hoopoo), George Kaumuali'i (Tamoree), William Kenui (Tenooe), and John Honoli'i (Honoree), each of whom had made his way independently to New England between about 1809 and 1815. Having worked variously as sailors or servants in Boston households, the young men gradually drifted to the Foreign Mission School established in 1817 at Cornwall, Connecticut. There, hopes for evangelizing the Hawaiian Islands were pinned on Henry Opukahaia of Kealakekua, a devout convert and exemplary scholar who had accompanied Hopu to New Haven in 1809. His affecting death in Cornwall in 1818 spurred the American Board of Commissioners for Foreign Missions to organize the first missionary company, which left Boston Harbor amidst rejoicing on October 23, 1819. Aboard the *Thaddeus* were the four "Owhyean Youths," who taught the missionaries the rudiments of the Hawaiian language during the long voyage out.

Once in Hawai'i, Hopu and Kenui joined Rev. Asa Thurston at the Kailua mission station, while Honoli'i proceeded to Honolulu with Hiram Bingham. George Kaumuali'i, favorite son of King Kaumuali'i of Kaua'i, soon tired of the mission on Kaua'i and, following his father's death in May, 1824, led an insurrection against Liholiho. Kenui turned into a drunkard and was excommunicated, but Hopu, having become a favorite of the king, gave many years of dedicated service. His marriage on August 11, 1822, to Delia, a young Hawaiian convert, was the first Christian marriage celebrated in Hawai'i.

The artist is more widely known as Samuel B. Morse, the inventor of the telegraph.

51. Elizabeth, Helen, and Laura Judd, unknown photographer

Daguerreotype; tinted, gold highlights, c. 1855
7.5 × 10 cm.
Gift of A. F. Judd, II, 1938 (1938.65.02)
Not illustrated

Prosperous and contented, these three daughters are among the nine children of Gerrit Parmele Judd, who arrived with the third missionary company on March 30,

1828. A physician, Dr. Judd made frequent visits to the 17 scattered mission stations before entering public life as a trustee of the Chiefs' Children's School to help care for the royal offspring. Although few missionaries bothered to follow literally their instructions "to abstain from all interference with local and political interests of the people," Judd resigned under pressure from the mission in 1842 to become government translator and recorder—and a member of the Treasury Board. Occupying in quick succession the posts of Secretary of State for Foreign Affairs, Minister of the Interior, and Commissioner to France, Great Britain, and the United States (see No. 229), Judd was instrumental in stabilizing and directing the infant Hawaiian government on its long path to maturity.

52. Levi Tenney Family, unknown photographer

New York (?), 1851
Daguerreotype
10.7 × 13.9 cm.
Gift of Philip Spaulding, III, 1979 (1979.262)

Despite Hiram Bingham's misgivings expressed aboard the *Thaddeus*—"Can we throw ourselves upon these rude shores, and take up our abode, for life . . .?" (Daws, 1968, p. 64)—material riches were not elusive to the missionaries. One of the latest services offered in the *Polynesian* for April 9, 1853, to the growing number of foreign families in thriving Honolulu was the sending of daguerreotypes taken by Messrs. Stangenwald and Goodfellow to destinations abroad. "The postage varies according to the weight of the picture, from $1 to $2," noted the tabloid, "which includes the Hawaiian and U.S. postage."

In the Levi Tenney family portrait are: (back row, left to right) Levi Tenney, Jr., Abigail Jackson, Lusina, Harriet. (Front row, left to right) Gertrude Tenney, Mary Kingsbury Tenney, Levi Tenney, Abigail Matteson, and her mother Nancy Tenney Matteson. It was sent in July, 1851, to the Tenneys' Honolulu daughter, Mary Tenney Castle, the second wife of Samuel Northrup Castle of the eighth missionary company of 1837. Assistant Superintendent of Secular Affairs for the mission, Castle had married his first wife's sister on a trip to Boston in 1842.

53. "Grove of Tutui Trees Kauai," by Alfred T. Agate (1812-1846)

Steel engraving
12.4 × 18.5 cm. 16 × 27.4 cm. (sheet)
Published in Charles Wilkes' Narrative of the United States Exploring Expedition, during the years 1838 . . . 1842
Purchase, 1977

Alfred T. Agate of the U.S. Exploring Expedition recorded this typical missionary scene about October 29, 1840, near Pīla'a, Kaua'i, while en route to Rev. William Patterson Alexander's mission station at Wai'oli. A description appeared in the published narrative of the voyage:

On their way they passed through a beautiful grove of tutui-nut trees, in which the Rev. Mr. Alexander is in the habit of preaching to the natives. These trees are large, and form a delightful shade. There are few places in the open air so well calculated to hold divine service in, and it is well fitted to create feelings of religion. The view, by Mr. Agate, will give a good idea of it (Wilkes, 1845, Vol. 4, p. 69).

54. Ellis, William (1794-1872), and Bingham, Hiram (1789-1869). *Na himeni Hawaii; he me ori ia Iehova, ke Akua mau* [Hawaiian hymns; being songs to Jehovah, the true God. O'ahu: printed at the Press of the Missionaries, 1823]

Duodecimo; brown patterned calf spine; turtle-shell boards; plain paper paste downs
Gov. G. R. Carter Collection, 1959

The missionaries' success was due in large part to their ability to reduce the previously unwritten Hawaiian language to a phonetic alphabet. A small printing press was introduced by the first missionary company in 1820, and the first imprint was a tentative alphabet and primer produced by mission printer Elisha Loomis on January 7, 1822. After prolonged discussion the alphabet was finally "solidified" by committee decision in 1826 to its present twelve letters: *a, e, i, o, u,* and *h, k, l, m, n, p, w.* The missionaries recognized but normally did not use the glottal stop (') and macron (ˉ).

Numerous books and translations followed, and by 1838 presses in Honolulu and Lahainaluna on Maui had printed about 100 million pages in Hawaiian and almost as many in English (Feher, 1969, p. 175). Notable achievements include *Ka Lama Hawaii*, the first Hawaiian newspaper begun at Lahainaluna on February 14, 1834, and the *Sandwich Island Gazette*, started in 1836 as the first English-language newspaper west of the Rocky Mountains. The Bible, translated from the original Greek and Hebrew by joint effort beginning in 1822, appeared in completed form in 1839. It remains to this day a masterpiece of classic Hawaiian literature.

The mission's fourth imprint and first bound book appeared in 1823, a 60-page Hawaiian language hymnal containing 46 "songs to Jehovah, the true god." Translated by Hiram Bingham and William Ellis, 40 selected passages of scripture introduced each hymn, many of which were original, or pointedly instructional translations such as Pope's "Taheite's Idols." At least nine copies were bound in local turtle shell by Moku, a Hawaiian, for use by the chiefs.

55. "Diamond Hill as Seen from Honolulu," engraved by Momona.

Copper plate, c. 1839
10.9 × 15.5 cm.
Seth Andrews Collection, 1959
Not illustrated

Crude wood-block illustrations by Hiram Bingham first appeared in local printing in 1831 but proved unwieldy and unsatisfactory. Two years later, Rev. Lorrin Andrews began experimenting with copper plate engravings when the original mission press was moved to Lahainaluna. Between 1834 and 1842, when Andrews left the mission to go into private business, about 150 "Lahainaluna engravings" were produced by Hawaiian students under Andrews' direction for textbooks and other instructional uses. Although only three plates are known to have survived, including this early view of Diamond Head, numerous prints provide a rich visual record of the period.

This plate of hammered and polished copper was probably engraved in 1839, when the artist, Rev. Edward Bailey, spent a year at Lahainaluna before transferring to Wailuku Female Seminary. Originally stationed at Kohala on arriving in 1837, Bailey resigned from the mission in 1850 to devote time to sugar plantation interests. After 45 years at Wailuku, Maui, where his house is now preserved as a museum, Bailey moved to California in 1885.

56. "Diamond Hill as Seen from Honolulu," engraved by Momona

Copper engraving, 1950
10.9 × 15.5 cm. (plate mk.) 16.2 × 21.2 cm. (sheet)
Seth Andrews Collection, 1959

Momona was one of Lahainaluna's lesser engravers, and his name appears on only four works. This print was struck from the original plate (see No. 55) at a later date.

57. "Lahainaluna," engraved by Kepohoni

Copper engraving, c. 1840
26.1 × 29.1 cm. (plate mk.) 30.5 × 24.3 cm. (sheet)
Gov. G. R. Carter Collection, 1959

Lahainaluna Seminary, today a public school, was established in 1831 by Rev. Lorrin Andrews to train Hawaiian men as teachers and assistant pastors for rural churches. Situated above Lahaina, an early whaling port and intermittent capital until the 1840's, the school was built and furnished by pupils working under the direction of Andrews, who was the sole teacher until 1834. Many graduates later rose to influential government positions, and among the better known early scholars are Hawaiian historians David Malo and Samuel Kamakau.

Although Kepohoni, the engraver of this view, was never a Lahainaluna student, he became the school's foremost engraver. Once a sailor, he took his name—Kepo Honi—to celebrate his having sailed around Cape Horn. The view is taken from one of the Reverend Mr. Bailey's many sketches immortalized by the Lahainaluna engravers.

58. "Mission Houses, Honolulu," engraved by Kalama

Copper engraving, 1837
26 × 15.7 cm. (plate mk.) 35 × 24.5 cm. (sheet)
American Board of Commissioners for Foreign Missions Collection, 1895

Today a museum in downtown Honolulu, the missionary compound's original frame house was brought around Cape Horn in 1820. A printing shop was added in 1823,

followed by the Levi Chamberlain home five years later. One of the most popular Lahainaluna prints, its English title suggests that it was intended primarily for sale to sailors and occasional visitors, or for missionaries to send home to their families. A ship captain named Daniel Wheeler did the original sketch, which was engraved by Kalama, one of the Rev. Andrews' students.

This is one of only two known impressions of Lahainaluna print on locally made paper—in this case, a variety of Hawaiian bark cloth, or *kapa*. Although it is a very fine impression, the experimentation with *kapa*, apparently during a temporary shortage of paper, proved unsuccessful—or unnecessary once supplies of imported stock became more dependable.

59. "View of Kailua, Hawaii," engraved by Kepohoni

Copper engraving, c. 1840
50.1 × 17.2 cm. (plate mk.) 58.9 × 23.9 cm. (sheet)
Seth Andrews Collection, 1959

Modern historians find this panoramic view so precise that individual buildings can be identified. In some cases, this picture is the only remaining record of the location and appearance of structures mentioned in written sources. Well known to tourists today, Kailua was still an important center of commerce and government when this print was produced in about 1840. Evidence favors Miss Persis Thurston, one of the two daughters of local resident missionary Rev. Asa Thurston, as the artist of the original sketch charmingly preserved in this fine engraving.

60. "Amerika Huipuia," engraved by Kepohoni

Copper engraving, c. 1839
27.5 × 44.5 cm. (plate mk.) 30.6 × 49.8 cm. (sheet)
American Board of Commissioners for Foreign Missions Collection, 1895
Not illustrated

Maps played a very important role in mission efforts to educate the Hawaiian people, and the first successful Lahainaluna engraving was a map produced in 1834. This map formed part of the complete world atlas engraved and published at Lahainaluna in 1840. Cartographers will be interested to note that the map is marked at the top with longitudinal lines based on a Washington, D.C., meridian, and at the bottom with London meridian lines. It represents a transition toward the present universal acceptance of the London scheme.

61. "Temperance Map by C. Wiltberger Jr."

Copper engraving, c. 1843
35.5 × 37.4 cm. (plate mk.) 49.2 × 59 cm. (sheet)
American Board of Commissioners for Foreign Missions Collection, 1895
Not illustrated

This map was a commercial endeavor by Lorrin Andrews after leaving the mission and directorship of Lahainaluna in 1842 to go into business for himself, with Kepohoni as a partner. Since the inscriptions are in English, the map was presumably intended for sale to errant sailors visiting the fleshpots of Lahaina and Honolulu. It was originally published with a 16-page booklet explaining the perils of intemperance and the benefits of abstinence. (One proof is known to be engraved with Hawaiian titles.) After Andrews' business failed a year or two later, he moved to Honolulu to become a judge. In later years, his old plates were pounded up and sold for scrap copper.

62. Father Damien, by E. D. Hale

Etching, 1889
20.3 × 15.5 cm.
John F. G. Stokes Collection, 1960

The first Catholic missionaries arrived in Hawai'i in 1827, but were expelled to Spanish California four years later (see No. 49). Reinstated in 1836—and expelled a second time the following year—the mission was finally allowed to remain after Captain Laplace of *L'Artemise* demanded that the chiefs pay $20,000 cash at gunpoint as guarantee of good behavior. The Constitution of 1840 provided for religious freedom (if not tolerance), and in this new climate Honolulu's great stone Cathedral of Our Lady of Peace was dedicated in August, 1843.

Perhaps the most famous of all Catholic missionaries was Father Damien (Joseph de Veuster), a Belgian priest who arrived on the island of Moloka'i in May, 1873, to work among the lepers at Kalaupapa. Long neglected by official apathy and lack of funds, the lepers had by the time of Damien's arrival become somewhat of an international embarrassment to the Hawaiian government. This likeness of Father Damien, possibly by Ellen Day Hale (1855-1940), may have been made from a photograph taken by William T. Brigham a few weeks before the holy man's death at Kalaupapa of nodular leprosy on April 15, 1889 (Daws, 1973).

63. Ka Buke o ka pule . . . [Translation of *The Book of Common Prayer* into Hawaiian by Kamehameha IV.] Honolulu Polynesian Book and Job Print, 1862

Octavo; bound in red small grain morocco; cover borders and cross on both boards are raised; gold and blind tooled borders; inner sunken panel has decorative line and corner pieces; cross is gilded, with terminating corner pieces; edge rolled boards; four raised bands on spine defined with blind and gilt lines; spine bands gilded with decorative fillet and panels decorated with gilt floral bud; all edges gilt.
Inscribed: "Miss Burdett Coutts, with the kindest regards of the translator Kamehameha Honolulu August 1863"
A.W.F. Fuller Collection, 1964
Not illustrated

Weary of Yankee puritans, intensely pro-British Kamehameha IV and his consort, Queen Emma, resolved to establish an Anglo-Catholic mission in Hawai'i. Correspondence initiated with the British Foreign Office finally bore fruit on October 11, 1862, when Dr. Thomas Nettleship Staley arrived in Honolulu as first Anglican Bishop.

While these proceedings were under way, Kamehameha IV had been busy translating into Hawaiian

The Book of Common Prayer, the first part of which was ready for use at the first native service held on November 9, 1862. An excellent and justly admired translation—as well as a fine example of local binding and printing—it appeared in completed form only weeks before the King's death at age 29 on Saint Andrew's Day, November 30, 1863. Saint Andrew's Cathedral, begun in 1867 and finished in 1960, was intended as a memorial in his honor.

The Life of the Land
"A Fine Handsome Sett of People"

In 1843, when a grateful Kamehameha III thanked Admiral Thomas for restoring the independence of his temporarily besieged Kingdom, he is said to have proclaimed to the nation: *Ua mau ke ea o ka aina i ka pono,* "The life of the land is perpetuated in righteousness." For Hawaiians, the message could never be forgotten, and the prophetic words were soon adopted as the national motto.

But the life of the land is and has always been its people—the chiefs and kings and unknown multitudes who have called this land home for more than a thousand years. Isolated by vast oceans from the rest of the world until two centuries ago, the people were characterized by one of the first outsiders in 1778-1779 as "strong and well made . . . a fine handsome sett of People" (Samwell in Beaglehole, 1967, Vol. 3, pt. 2, p. 1178). Ever since they, as well as their land, have proved ready and popular subjects for artists—and later photographers—who paused long enough to chronicle the passing scene.

Their fleeting visions, especially when supplemented with written accounts, reveal a great wealth of detail about the physical appearance, mode of dress, and manner of the inhabitants. Equally important are the subtle indications of change, as well as the persistence of traditional values, which are apparent in these vignettes of daily life in 19th century Hawai'i.

64. Hawaiian Woman with Dog, by John Mix Stanley (1814-1872)

Oil on fabric, 1849
Verso signed and dated
92 × 73.2 cm.
Gift of Frances Damon, 1963
Not illustrated

A native New Yorker, John Mix Stanley began as an itinerant portrait and landscape painter in the western and midwestern United States. Before visiting Honolulu in 1848-1849, he had already finished a large number of Indian paintings, which he eventually placed on free exhibition in Washington, D.C., hoping to convince Congress to purchase the collection and thereby establish a national gallery. Before the government could act, a fire in 1865 in a wing of the Smithsonian housing his Indian Gallery destroyed all but five of the paintings, a personal and national loss never to be regained.

Stanley's Hawaiian subject is unknown, but her dress and demeanor suggest that she is intended to portray a woman of the chiefly class. Although there is no evidence to confirm her identity as Queen Kalama (1817-1870), wife of Kamehameha III, she would have been a handsome addition to Stanley's proposed national portrait gallery, nevertheless.

65. "The Lei Maker," by Theodore Wores (1859-1939)

Oil on fabric, 1902
91.5 × 73.7 cm.
Frame designed by Jean Charlot and hand crafted by Alan Wilkinson of Hawaiian koa and mango wood
Loaned by Dr. A. Jess Shenson and Dr. Ben Shenson, San Francisco
Color Plate XIII

Wores's painting of another unknown Hawaiian woman was executed a half century after Stanley's work (No. 64) to "immortalize the vanishing spirit of old Hawaii." A San Francisco artist, Wores came to Hawai'i to work in 1901, after having made two previous trips to Japan in 1885 and 1892. Acclaimed for his Japanese works in the eastern United States and London, he soon gained praise in Honolulu, where his exhibitions were enthusiastically attended. His portrait of the young Hawaiian woman stringing a *lei*, or neck garland, of *'ilima* petals has become a symbol of the spirit of the old Hawai'i that Wores sought to immortalize.

66. Man of the Sandwich Islands, Half Face Tattooed,
by John Webber (1751-1793)

Pen and wash, c. 1780
39.5 × 31 cm.
Purchase from Spencer Bickerton, 1922

Tattooing (kākau), common throughout Polynesia, was practiced in Hawai'i as a form of body decoration, and sometimes as a mark of mourning. David Samwell (in Beaglehole, 1967, Vol. 3, Pt. 2, p. 1178), one of the surgeons on Cook's third voyage, wrote:

They are tattawed or marked in various parts; some have an arm entirely tattawed, others more frequently the Thighs and Legs, the Lines being continued from the upper part of the Thigh to the foot with various figures between them according to their fancy; their bodies are marked with figures of Men and other Animals; Some few among them had one side of their faces tattawed, & we saw 2 or 3 who had the whole of the face marked, differing something from the New Zealanders in being done in strait not in spiral lines.

This sketch by John Webber shows a variety of the half-facial tattoo in a pattern of zigzag lines similar to those carved onto wooden mallets for beating bark cloth.

Webber's drawing also illustrates a common mode of wearing the hair in late 18th-century Hawai'i, in which the hair on each side of the head is cut short, leaving a central ridge extending from front to back.

67. "Ile Wahu Nomahanna," by L. Massard (fl. 1830-1840)

Engraving, handcolored
20.1 × 12.3 cm. (plate mk.) 23.5 × 16.1 cm. (sheet)
Gift of Mrs. Gwendolyn McGolrick, 1961

Nāmāhana, the daughter of high chief Kekaulike of Maui, and one of the widows of Kamehameha I, was acting regent and co-ruler of O'ahu with high chiefess Kīna'u (see No. 68) when Otto von Kotzebue visited in December, 1824. Calling to pay his respects, Kotzebue found "Queen Nomahanna" to be "at the utmost not more than forty years old . . . exactly six feet two inches high, and rather more than two ells in circumference. She wore an old-fashioned European dress of blue silk . . ." (The ell varies from country to country, but in England was 45 inches.) "On seeing me," Kotzebue continued, "she laid down the psalm-book in which she had been reading, and having, with the help of her attendants, changed her lying for a sitting posture, she held out her hand to me in a very friendly manner, with many 'Arohas!'" (Kotzebue, 1830, Vol. 2, pp. 207-208).

Considered by many Hawaiian and foreign settlers to be "not only the cleverest and the most learned, but also the best woman" on O'ahu (Kotzebue, 1830, Vol. 2, p. 223), Nāmāhana also set the pace in local fashion, at least during the time of the Russians' visit. "Even among the lowest class of the people, some article of European clothing is universal," Kotzebue (1830, Vol. 2, p. 221) observed. "The females especially set their hearts upon the most fashionable mode of dress: whatever the Queen wears is their model, which they imitate to the utmost of their power . . ."

68. "Vue d'une rue d'Honoloulou, Capitale des Iles Sandwich. La Reine Kinau revient du Temple des Etrangers accompagnée de ses dames d'honneur," by Louis-Jules Masselot

Lithograph
33.4 × 54.1 cm. (sheet)
Published in Atlas Pittoresque *accompanying Du Petit-Thouars'* Voyage autour du monde . . . pendant les années 1836-1839 . . . (Paris: Gide, 1840-1864)
Gov. G. R. Carter Collection, 1959

Louis-Jules Masselot, one of the artists aboard La Vénus during Du Petit-Thouars' visit to Hawai'i in July and August, 1837, was particularly interested in costume, which he recorded with considerable fidelity. Here, Elisabeta Kīna'u, or Ka'ahumanu II (1805-1839), is depicted with two attendants returning from Kawaiaha'o Church, followed by a small crowd dressed in mixed local and European fashions of the day.

Kīna'u, a daughter of Kamehameha I and half-sister of Liholiho (Kamehameha II) and Kauikeaouli (Kamehameha III), was chosen by the chiefs to succeed Ka'ahumanu on her death in 1832 as regent and *kuhina nui* (prime minister) during the minority of King Kamehameha III. When the King terminated the regency on the eve of his 21st birthday in 1833, Kīna'u continued as *kuhina nui* until her death six years later. A woman of great power and influence, she had given up her earlier marriage to Liholiho to take as husband Mataio Kekūanao'a, to whom she bore several children, including the future kings Kamehameha IV and Kamehameha V.

During their visit in 1837, the French were highly critical of the American missionaries and the authority they wielded over the Hawaiian government through Kīna'u: "supreme power was exercised by two women, of which one, Kinau, sister of the king, made fanatical by Mr. [Hiram] Bingham, executed, and still executes only his orders; for, it is the head of the mission who was and is still, under the name of this woman, and more than ever, the true king of the Sandwich Isles" (translated from Du Petit-Thouars 1840-1843, Vol. 1, p. 371).

69. "Governor Hoapili," by Clarissa Chapman Armstrong (1805-1891)

Watercolor with pen, c. 1837
19.1 × 12.3 cm. (sheet)

"Kaniu the Wife of Gov. Hoapili," by Clarissa Chapman Armstrong (1805-1891)

Watercolor with pen, c. 1837
17.6 × 17 cm. (sheet)
American Board of Commissioners for Foreign Missions Collection, 1895

Regal and dignified in European dress, Governor Hoapili, of Maui, and Kaniu were among the first of the high chiefs to be married in a Christian ceremony on October 19, 1823, by the Reverend William Richards. An intimate companion of Kamehameha I, Hoapili had been entrusted with the sacred task of concealing the bones of the conquerer on his death in 1819. He lived on into the new era "to become a grand old man, a blameless Christian, fearless, and foremost among the chiefs in supressing vice and resisting foreign encroachments against law and order" (Alexander and Dodge, 1941, p. 41).

Following the death of an earlier wife, high chiefess Keōpūolani in 1823, Hoapili married Kaniu, sister of Ka'ahumanu and another former wife of Kamehameha I. After her marriage, she took the name of Hoapili-wahine and became a devout Christian, "furious if anyone repeated scandal, and her eyes would turn red if she heard of any wrongdoing" (Kamakau, 1961, p. 387). Extremely influential in the early years of the monarchy, Hoapili died in 1840, two years before his wife's death on January 16, 1842.

70. "Hawaiian Women at Rest," by Hjalmar Stolpe

Albumen print, 1884
17 × 22 cm.
Gift of Bengt Danielsson, 1969 (1969.228)
Not illustrated

Far different is the mood of this photograph, taken a half century after Madame Hoapili-wahine posed majestically for the wife of the Rev. Richard Armstrong (see No. 69).

In the interim of roughly two generations, when ethnologist and photographer Hjalmar Stolpe visited the islands with the Swedish scientific ship *Vanadis* during the summer of 1884, the Hawaiian and part-Hawaiian population had fallen from 130,000 in the 1830's to less than 45,000. Even so, the quiet dignity in repose remarked upon by several 18th-century voyagers is still to be seen in the bearing of these unknown women, notwithstanding dire predictions that the race was said to be dying as a result of introduced diseases and demoralization.

71. "Mrs. Dominis at her Little Mountain House," by Alfred Mitchell (1832-1911)

Cyanotype, 1886
20.2 × 15.3 cm.
Gift of Alfreda Mitchell Gregor, 1967 (1967.289)
Not illustrated

Photography in Honolulu by the 1880's had developed into a profitable business through exploitation of the islands' natural and cultural surroundings. But visions of Hawai'i by commercial photographers were often artificial or sterile; their typical studio portraits of native women or dancers relied upon painted backdrops of palm trees, of Diamond Head, or of grass houses to evoke a tropical setting.

Among the growing number of amateur photographers, however, one who visited in 1886 captured a more intimate and believable vision of island life. Alfred Mitchell's informal portrait of Lili'uokalani seated by her grass house shows the Princess (also known as Mrs. John O. Dominis) in a rare moment of intimacy that conveys, then as now, a compelling sense of nostalgia for bygone days.

72. Hawaiian Woman with 'Ukulele, by Alfred Mitchell (1832-1911)

Cyanotype, 1886
19.2 × 15.1 cm.
Gift of Alfreda Mitchell Gregor, 1967 (1967.289.06)
Not illustrated

Among the 400 or so photographs taken by Mitchell in 1886 is this portrait of an unknown Hawaiian woman dressed in a type of *holokū* and playing the *'ukulele*. Taken somewhere on the island of O'ahu, it evokes a feeling of reality far more convincing than the usual studio views distributed far and wide by commercial photographers attempting to satisfy demands for pleasant mementos of this "Paradise of the Pacific."

73. "Princess Kaiulani in Japanese Costume," by Walter M. Giffard (1856-1929)

Albumen print, 1889
18.9 × 11.8 cm.
Loaned by Hawaii State Archives

This photograph was one of Giffard's entries in the Hawaii Camera Club's first show for amateurs held in 1889. In reviewing the event, the *Hawaiian Gazette* for November 11 concluded: "the exhibition showed plainly that the amateur photographers of Honolulu, as represented by the Camera Club are capable of competing successfully with the professionals of the art of counterfeit presentment." The young Princess, niece of King Kalākaua, seems to have responded to the camera with appropriate charm, her costume inspired, no doubt, by the increasing number of Japanese arriving after 1886 to work as indentured laborers on the sugar plantations.

74. Hawaiian Men Fishing, by Alonzo Gartley (1869-1921)

Platinum print, c. 1905
15.5 × 20.4 cm.
Gift of Mrs. Alonzo Gartley, 1921 (1921.64)

Another amateur photographer, Alonzo Gartley, focused on the peaceful stability of Hawai'i at the turn of the century, suitably captured in this timeless image of men fishing at Nāpo'opo'o, Hawai'i. Gartley was manager of the Hawaiian Electric Company when "a gentleman" wrote this account for the May, 1906, issue of *Paradise of the Pacific* describing one of his photographic excursions:

I went into the country with Mr. Gartley one afternoon when he was taking pictures, and he is like your true artist—he won't hurry himself. When he finds a scene that is something beyond the ordinary he sets his camera aside and commences to study it in all its aspects. He will view it from as many points of the compass as possible and then scan the sky north, south, east and west. I have known him to contemplate a view two hours before he would point a camera at it.

75. "Îles Sandwich: Maisons de Kraïmokou, Premier Ministre du Roi; Fabrication des Etoffes," by J. Alphonse Pellion

Engraving
23.8 × 32.2 cm. (plate mk.)
Published in Atlas Historique *accompanying de Freycinet's* Voyage autour du monde . . . pendant les années 1817, 1818, 1819, et 1820 . . . *(Paris: Chez Pillet Aîné, Imprimeur-Libraire, 1824-1842)*
Gift of Gwendolyn McGolrick, 1961

The woman at work in front of the covered shelter is making *kapa* cloth using a wooden mallet and anvil. Two-inch-wide strips of the soft inner bark peeled from the *wauke* (paper mulberry) plant or three or four other less important plants, were beaten together into sheets of various size for a multitude of uses, ranging from clothing and bed covers to lamp wicks and burial wrappings. Hundreds of varieties were made, differing in texture, thickness, color, decoration, scent, watermark, and other characteristics. Once a chief occupation of women, *kapa* making gradually declined and disappeared altogether toward the end of the 19th century, as imported European and Chinese fabrics became plentiful.

This scene was recorded in August, 1819, in the house compound of high chief Kalanimoku at Kailua, Kona, by J. A. Pellion, an artist accompanying Louis de Freycinet on his voyage around the world. Even by 1819, de Freycinet noted (Wiswell, 1978, p. 61), "Some of the chiefs have adopted the European type of clothing either

completely or in part . . . The same is true of women living with whites on Wahou [O'ahu]. Cloth from India and China, as well as some manufactured in our factories—cotton, wool, and even silk—is also beginning to appear."

76. Two Bark Cloth Mallets, i'e kuku

Front: L. 34 cm. W. 3 cm. Th. 3 cm. (B.7020)
Rear: L. 37 cm. W. 4.2 cm. Th. 4 cm. (B.7019)
Kapi'olani-Kalaniana'ole Collection, 1923

Once the bark had been peeled from the tree and the rough outer layer discarded, the inner fibers were soaked in water for several days until pliable. In a complicated and time-consuming process, the narrow strips were first flattened into foot-wide segments with a heavy cylindrical mallet, then beaten together with square mallets carved in various designs. The beaters, skillfully wielded by women, imprinted into the slightly moist *kapa* continuous patterns similar to watermarks on paper. Visible through transmitted light, complex watermark designs became a hallmark of Hawaiian *kapa,* particularly in the late 18th and 19th centuries when introduced metal tools stimulated the carving of more intricate designs on the hard wood mallets.

77. Loincloth, malo

Wauke bark cloth
L. 264 cm. W. 35 cm.
Queen Emma Collection, 1886 (2451)

The loincloth, or *malo,* was the chief item of apparel for men. It was a long and narrow piece of *kapa* created from one strip of bark, beaten flat and joined or sewn end to end until the proper length of nearly 10 feet was obtained. Often coarse and thick, or sometimes ribbed like corduroy, *malo* for the chiefly classes were frequently decorated. This example is printed with vegetable dyes in crossing lines applied with a multipronged liner of wood or bamboo resembling a fork.

78. Loincloth, malo

Wauke bark cloth
L. 263 cm. W. 21 cm.
American Board of Commissioners for Foreign Missions Collection, 1895 (7772)

According to one authority, "The malo was put on by the wearer holding one end temporarily under the chin, passing the cloth back between the legs to cover the genitals, and then winding it around the waist after hooking it around the first turn at the back. The front end was then dropped to hang down in front" (Buck, 1957, p. 210).

79. Cloak, *kihei*

Wauke *bark cloth*
L. 153.6 cm. W. 153 cm.
Purchase from A. M. McBryde, 1911 (10,964)

The *kihei* was a mantle or cloak made from a square piece of bark cloth just long enough to reach to the knees or below when knotted over one shoulder. Worn by either men or women, it provided extra warmth and protection from the elements, as well as a covering for the upper body when needed. *Kihei* for the upper classes were often elaborately decorated, and fancy borders, such as on this glazed example probably from the island of Kaua'i, became popular in imitation of introduced foreign cloth. The overall four-lobed pattern and border in various shades of brown were applied mostly freehand. Glazing may have been done by rubbing with the smooth surface of a cowrie shell.

80. Cloak or Blanket, *kapa moe ipo*

Wauke *bark cloth*
L. 240 cm. W. 220 cm.
J. S. Emerson Collection, 1889 (2462)

Skilled *kapa* makers were capable of producing extremely fine, gauzelike material, which could be used for a variety of purposes. This famous *kapa moe ipo* once belonged to King Kamehameha III, who was in the habit of throwing it over the shoulders of the woman he chose to favor for the night. It was obtained through Kanoelehua, the coachman of Queen Kalama, his wife. *Moe ipo* means, literally, "To have an affair; to sleep with a lover . . ." (Pukui and Elbert, 1971, p. 230).

81. Skirt, *pā'ū*

Wauke *bark cloth*
L. 376 cm. W. 73 cm.
Seth Andrews Collection, 1959 (D. 2226)

"The ordinary costume of women," observed de Freycinet (Wiswell, 1978, p. 61) in 1819, "consists of very thin cloth, folded over several times . . . which they wrap around their bodies, either above or below the breasts, and is sometimes thrown over the shoulder . . ." Usually of one sheet, *pā'ū* for upper-class women could also be composite affairs consisting of up to ten sheets stitched together along the upper border, and ornamented on different surfaces for varying effect.

This boldly decorated *pā'ū* of ten rather thick sheets was collected by the missionary physician Dr. Seth Andrews, who was stationed at Kailua, Hawai'i, between 1837 and 1848. It combines stamped designs typical of the early 19th century with overall patterning in elongated triangles more characteristic of *kapa* collected in the late 18th century. It is an interesting transitional piece mixing traditional concepts of layout with motifs adapted in part from imported textiles.

82. Skirt, *pā'ū*

Wauke *bark cloth*
L. 252 cm. W. 89 cm.
Charles R. Bishop Collection, before 1894 (8826)

Consisting of four plain and one cover sheet, this *pā'ū* is decorated with red and black designs disposed in broad, widely spaced diagonal bands. The designs were applied by dipping carved bamboo stamps into a coconut or gourd cup of vegetable or mineral dyes, then carefully pressing the small stamp onto the bark cloth with patient repetition until the desired area was covered. "The tiny decorative designs used by the *loea* [skilled one] were as numerous as the patterns on the calico prints of today," boasted one 19th-century Hawaiian historian, "and so were their dye colors" (Kamakau, 1976, p. 110).

83. Skirt, *pā'ū*

Wauke *bark cloth*
L. 377 cm. W. 170 cm.
Gift of Evangeline Priscilla Starbuck, 1927 (C.209)

Queen Kamāmalu took this thin and intricately stamped *pā'ū* to London in 1823-1824. Before her death there she gave it to Captain Valentine Starbuck, who had carried the royal party to England (see No. 174). Originally the background is said to have been pale green, but the printing shows the skills that *kapa* makers had achieved with stamping techniques believed to have been by and large a post-European innovation.

84. Skirt, *pā'ū*

Cotton
L. 278 cm. W. 87 cm.
Queen Emma Collection, 1886 (2323)

Throughout the Pacific, wherever European fabrics replaced traditional bark cloth, the cotton sarong evolved as a common solution to practicality and Western notions of modesty. In Hawai'i, however, simple tailored garments introduced by body-conscious missionaries prevailed, and the traditional wrap-around *pā'ū* quickly fell into oblivion.

This unusual cotton *pā'ū*, stamped with motifs typically seen on 19th-century bark-cloth counterparts, seems to be an early attempt to synthesize extant Hawaiian dress codes and aesthetics with an imported technology. Had the experiment succeeded, it is quite possible that 20th-century Hawaiian dress would have evolved quite differently. But it failed, and with it vanished an early opportunity to amalgamate a highly developed component of classic Hawaiian material culture with Western technology. Instead, lamented Kamakau (1976, p. 116) in 1870, "All are dead who knew how to make coverings and loincloths and skirts and adornments and all that made the wearers look dignified and proud and distinguished."

85. Dress, *lole*

Wauke *bark cloth, cotton, thread*
L. 147 cm. W. (shoulders) 46.5 cm. Sleeves, 43 cm.
Purchase at Jeckel Auction, 1975 (1975.97.02)

In Hawai'i, as in much of Polynesia, where an ample, well-fed figure was a mark of the leisured upper classes, tailored garments such as those fashionable in Europe and America at the beginning of the 19th century proved unacceptable. In their efforts to clad the unclad, missionary wives taught sewing to Hawaiian women, and in the process introduced a simple gown with high yoke and loose waist perfectly adapted to the local figure.

In a very few instances, the cloth prototypes were translated back into indigenous bark cloth, such as in this mid-19th-century example complete with high ruffled neck, full length sleeves, and hem trimmed in pink. From these "Mother Hubbards," as the style was called, the formal *holokū* with train and the stately *mu'umu'u* developed, both popular items of apparel well into contemporary times.

86. Dress, *lole*

Cotton, mother-of-pearl buttons
L. 126.5 cm. W. (shoulders) 35 cm. Sleeves, 52 cm.
Loaned by Lyman House Memorial Museum
(LHM 79.66.1)

With petticoat
Cotton, modern silk
L. 101 cm.
Loaned by Lyman House Memorial Museum, Elvira Cravalho Rezents Collection (LHM 78.24.20)

When the missionary women arrived dressed in the fashion of the day—high-belted tight skirts, short waists, and long tight sleeves—the chiefly women brought out their stores of rich Chinese silks and brocades obtained from early traders. The day before anchoring at Kailua on April 4, 1820, it is recorded that missionary wives aboard the *Thaddeus* gave their first sewing lessons to Kalakua, Nāmāhana (see Nos. 67 and 68), and two wives of Kalanimoku, who had come to welcome the newcomers (Jones, 1973, p. 7).

The first garments introduced by the missionaries had full straight skirts attached to a yoke with long close sleeves, which Hawaiian women found more comfortable than the stylish but confining Empire gowns then in vogue. The new fashion proved so popular that it persisted well into the 20th century, with only minor elaborations in the trim being necessary from time to time to maintain fresh appearances. This Mother Hubbard of fine cotton lawn features a deep-ruffled yoke of white cotton lace, full length sleeves with cuff and lace ruffles, and gathered and tucked skirt with ruffled hem. Dresses of this type provided an understated but comfortable touch of elegance to informal social events of the later 19th century for Hawaiian and foreign women alike.

87. Bed Cover, *kapa moe*

Wauke *bark cloth*
L. 289 cm. W. 214 cm.
Princess Ka'iulani Collection, 1911 (10,333)

Bark cloth was used throughout Polynesia for sleeping covers, but in Hawai'i a special form evolved consisting of five or more sheets of uniform size stitched together along one edge. Called *kapa moe* (sleeping *kapa*) or *ku'ina* (from *ku'i*, meaning to join or sew), they were used as coverlets on bedsteads composed of layer upon layer of mats piled upon the floor.

Most *kapa moe* consist of four or five plain inner sheets called *iho*, and a colored or decorated cover called *kilohana*. Cover sheets after the widespread introduction of foreign cloth tended to be rather plain forms called *pa'i'ula*. These were made by overlaying shredded turkey-red cloth (sometimes mixed with red *kapa*) onto white *kapa* and beating the two together into one sheet. This example is further decorated with broad bands of charcoal-stained bark cloth beaten onto the cover sheet.

88. Bed Cover, *kapa moe*

Wauke *bark cloth*
L. 270 cm. W. 290 cm.
Gift of Kay Afong Kramer in memory of her father, Albert Fairweather Afong, 1950 (C. 10247)

The decoration of this unusual 19th-century *kapa moe* from Kaua'i seems to take its inspiration from the Hawaiian quilt, which gradually replaced bark-cloth coverlets during the last half of the last century. Here, cut-out fleur-de-lis and "snow flakes" in blue and salmon alternate with chains of interlocking hearts and other elements in pink and blue. Beaten or pasted onto the cover sheet, the applique designs resemble early quilts more than traditional *kapa moe*, suggesting an interesting cross-fertilization between the two arts.

89. Quilt, *kapa lau* or *kapa 'apana*

Cotton
L. 209 cm. W. 199 cm.
Gift of Mrs. Clayton J. Chamberlin, 1979 (1979.282.01)

Although it is not known when or where the first Hawaiian quilts appeared, the patchwork coverlets introduced from New England after 1820, and the traditional *kapa moe*, both provided ready prototypes for an exuberant folk art that is still pursued today with enthusiasm. Early Hawaiian quilts tended to be simple in design and were usually made of turkey-red cloth on white (such as this example), possibly a reflection of the *pa'i'ula* cover sheets found on many *kapa moe* (Jones, 1973, p. 11). The single color appliques cut freehand or from folded pieces of cloth were made more pleasing by follow-the-pattern quilting, which added to the beauty and complexity. Jealously guarded, designs belonged to their originators and were rarely copied without permission, for fear of embarrassment or shame should the "theft" be discovered.

This quilt, presented to Clayton J. Chamberlin when he was principal of Hilo Intermediate School in the 1930's, boasts a one-piece applique secured by overcast stitching, and follow-the-pattern quilting in finger-width rows averaging ten stitches per inch. Like many Hawaiian quilts, the pattern is derived from nature; it probably represents the pineapple, called *hala 'ai*. The rounded corners are considered unusual.

A noted authority observed years ago that balance in Hawaiian quilting is "maintained through exact repetition of motifs. Its primary motivation is expression rather than ornamentation. In its imagery and method of expression the Hawaiian quilt ranks as a distinct type of needlework" (Jones, 1973, p. 8).

90. Hat, *pāpale*

'Iwa (fern), cloth
H. 21 cm. D. 31 cm.
American Board of Commissioners for Foreign Missions Collection, 1895 (7793)

Although they normally went bareheaded, except for the feather helmets worn on ceremonial occasions in the past, Hawaiian men who associated with Europeans were beginning to acquire by 1820 a taste for straw and felt hats (Wiswell, 1978, p. 61). In time, foreign styles were copied in local materials by Hawaiian craftsmen expert in basketry and mat-plaiting techniques. The top hat of silk or beaver pelt is recreated here from a type of maidenhair fern, whose narrow, feather-shaped fronds on dark stems up to three feet long proved ideal for the purpose. The hat was collected by early missionaries for their museum in Boston sometime prior to 1895.

91. Hat, *pāpale*

'Iwa (fern), cloth
H. 14 cm. L. 23.5 cm. W. 16 cm.
Bernice Pauahi Bishop Collection, 1884 (5058)
Color Plate XIV

The close-fitting hat or cap recalls a type of "mushroom ornamented" helmet formerly worn by lesser chiefs and warriors, apparently in lieu of the more spectacular feather-covered examples. Said to be a riding hat, it was made before 1884 from narrow strips of braided *'iwa* fern stems coiled into the desired shape and stitched together with thread. The technique of overlapping strips of prepared braid differs from traditional methods of helmet construction, in which warps and wefts of split *'ie'ie* aerial rootlets were twined into the required form.

92. Hat, *pāpale*

Sugar cane flower stalks (pua kō)
H. 5.5 cm. D. 25.3 cm.
Bernice Pauahi Bishop Collection, 1884 (5067)

Another popular hat material was derived from dried flower stalks of the sugar cane, many varieties having been introduced in the 19th century by plantation owners seeking to improve the indigenous breed. The beauty and versatility of this novel material is readily evident in this mid-19th-century open work with low crown and narrow brim, which may have been intended for a woman.

93. Hat, *pāpale*

Coconut leaf
H. 13.5 cm D. 45 cm.
Bernice Pauahi Bishop Collection, 1884 (5050)

Coconut leaf was the most abundant of all hat-making materials, and Hawaiian women created many elaborate and distinctive patterns in the durable medium. Made before 1884, this hat is typical of a style that is plaited rather than built up from prepared braids. Still popular today, similar hats of coconut leaf or pandanus are frequently worn with a colorful hat band of feathers or shells encircling the base of the crown (see Nos. 184-189).

94. Cap, *pāpale*

Coconut leaf, pandanus, grosgrain ribbon
H. 9.5 cm. L. 20.5 cm. W. 9.5 cm.
Gift of Mrs. Donald Woodrum and Mary Elsie Krassas, 1979 (1979.241.15)

This boy's cap of coconut-leaf hat braid, typical of what might have been purchased by turn-of-the-century Waikīkī tourists, calls to mind an earlier concern for vanishing handiwork expressed by the Hawaiian newspaper *Ku'oko'a* for August 15, 1891:

The handcrafts produced by Hawaiian women who like to practice the arts of a generation ago are the plaiting of hat braids, fans, and mats. There are many types of hat-making and some hats made of Hawaiian braids are beautiful enough to rouse astonished thoughts. But there are few hats like that seen nowadays. Good prices can be received for such things, so why don't our women continue to make them?

Calabashes and Kings

Food dishes made of wood (and of gourd) formed part of the wealth of old Hawai'i (Malo, 1951, p. 79). From the durable, rich brown wood of such trees as the *kou*, the people of old made utensils and containers in a multitude of shapes and sizes to satisfy the needs of housekeeping. Boasted Samuel Kamakau (1976, p. 47) in 1869, "They were proud of the containers, *'umeke*, shallow bowls, *ipu kai*, and flat platters, *pa la'au*, they made . . ."

In the 19th century, calabashes often were prized for their link with traditional Hawaiian values as much as for their beauty and function. As a consequence, many fine examples were amassed as showpieces by 19th-century royalty, not least King David Kalākaua in the 1880's, whose family collection was deposited partly in Bishop Museum in 1923 by Princess Elizabeth Kalaniana'ole Woods in memory of her late husband, Prince Jonah Kūhiō Kalaniana'ole, and his aunt, Queen Kapi'olani. The collections of Dowager Queen Emma, Princess Ruta Ke'elikōlani, and other 19th-century royalty have also been preserved as important cultural treasures. Not surprisingly, calabashes from these collections exhibit wide variations in appearance, arising in part from the changing 18th- and 19th-century contexts in which they were made or used.

Historian David Malo (1951, p. 122), born in the closing years of the 18th century, gives his account of the manufacture and use of calabashes in the early days:

> Those who were skilled in the art carved bowls and dishes out of different woods; but the *kou* was the wood generally used for this purpose. After the log had been fashioned on the outside it was either deeply hollowed out as a calabash, *umeke*, or as a shallow dish or platter, *ipukai*, to hold fish or meat. A cover also was hollowed out to put over the *ipukai* and the work was done.
>
> The dish was then rubbed smooth within and without with a piece of coral, or with rough lava (*oahi*), then with pumice or a stone called *oio*. After this, charcoal was used, then bamboo-leaf, and lastly it was polished with bread-fruit leaf and *tapa*; the same was done to the cover, and there was your dish.

Malo goes on to say: "Sometimes a *koko*, or net, was added as a convenient means of holding and carrying, and the work was then complete. The *umeke* was used for holding *poi* and vegetable food (*ai*), the *ipukai* to hold meats and fish (*ia*)."

Although the technology changed, the manufacture of calabashes persisted throughout the 19th century. To be sure, exposure to new kinds of tableware and other items imported from Europe and Asia fostered the development of innovative shapes and styles; besides, flat bottoms and annular or pedestal bases were much more suited to table service than traditional round-bottomed calabashes, which had been intended primarily for use with mats on the ground. Changing tastes of the late 19th century also caused the traditional hand-rubbed finish of *kukui* nut oil to give way to shellac and French polish, to the extent that many older calabashes were refinished in the new style.

Mechanical lathes replaced the simple stone adzes and their metal substitutes more than a century ago, but even contemporary craftsmen sometimes disagree whether a given calabash was made by machine or by hand, so perfectly were they shaped and finished. So, too, do modern craftsmen sometimes find it difficult to identify the woods of older calabashes, for the traditional Hawaiian woodcarver was expert in selecting unusual grain or color in seemingly the most familiar of woods.

The manufacture of calabashes nearly vanished in the early decades of this century, but the tradition is slowly reviving as today's craftsmen respond to the persistent symbolism of the Hawaiian calabash.

95 a,b. Carved Meat Platter, *pā ki'i*

Kou *wood*
H. 30.5 cm. L. 115.5 cm. W. 27 cm.
Princess Ruta Ke'elikōlani Collection, 1883 (408)

Large enough to hold a small pig or dog, this meat platter was carved to commemorate the victory of Chief Kahekili of Maui over Chief Kahahana of O'ahu, about the year 1785. In servile position supporting the meat dish of the conqueror, one figure represents the slain Kahahana, and the other his wife Kekuapoi. Heads bent back, their large open mouths double as receptacles for salt, *kukui*-nut relish, or other condiments. It was not unusual to defile enemies in this manner, but only 14 or so magnificent carved vessels of this type have been preserved. This one, apparently handed down in the Kamehameha family, was in the possession of Princess Ke'elikōlani at her Hulihe'e Palace residence at least by 1875, as it is mentioned in a Honolulu literary magazine called *The Islander* for March of that year.

96. Circular Plate, *pā poepoe*

Koa *wood*
D. 35 cm. H. 5.2 cm.
Queen Emma Collection, 1886 (643)
Not illustrated

Besides elongated platters, circular dishes and plates were also made for serving solid foods, like fish, meats, and so forth. Wooden plates were probably used by individual chiefs, but persons of lesser rank had to be content with leaves or simple gourd plates and bowls.

97. Three Poi Pounders, *pōhaku ku'i poi*

Vesicular basalt

Left: Ring pounder
H. 14.2 cm. L. 15.5 cm W. 7 cm.
Kapi'olani-Kalaniana'ole Collection, 1923 (B.6914)

Center: Stirrup pounder
H. 11.2 cm. L. 12 cm. W. 8 cm.
Kapi'olani-Kalaniana'ole Collection, 1923 (B.7178)

Right: Conical pounder
H. 22.2 cm. D. 13.5 cm.
Princess Ka'iulani Collection, 1911 (10,417)

Poi was the Hawaiian vegetable staple pounded from baked taro, or *kalo*, tubers and mixed with water into a thick, nutritious paste eaten with the fingers. People of Kaua'i used two kinds of oval-based pounder for the task, while elsewhere the conical form common to the rest of Polynesia prevailed.

98. Meat Bowl, 'umeke ipu kai

Koa *wood*
H. 32.4 cm. D. 61 cm.
Queen Emma Collection, 1886 (411)

Low, wide bowls were the largest made, their diameter far exceeding their height. Although some may have been used for *poi*, this was probably intended for salting down or serving other foods, such as pork, dog, or large fish.

Because of their value, calabashes were often repaired, and this bowl exhibits four of the six general methods employed: the inset wooden patch (*poho*); wooden pegs (*huini* or *kui lā'au*); wedges (*kepa* or *kepakepa*), which are usually hammered in obliquely across cracks in a zigzag pattern (see No. 130); and small wedges fitted into slightly open cracks (*kiki*). Other methods of repair included sewing, usually on gourds, and butterfly patching with small hourglass-shaped pieces of wood (see Nos. 102 and 118).

99. Poi Bowl, 'umeke palapa'a

Kou *wood*
H. 24.5 cm. D. 28.8 cm.
Hawaiian National Museum Collection, 1891 (1355)

The thick-bottomed bowl is so named because it will not upset easily from the weight of *poi* clinging to the sides. The shape is sometimes also called *puahala* from its resemblance to the key from a pandanus fruit. This particularly well-finished example was probably purchased in 1877 for the former Hawaiian National Museum at the estate auction of Charles Kana'ina and his son, King Lunalilo. It is said to have descended in the family from Kamehameha I, who used it while on canoe trips.

100. Child's Poi Bowl, 'umeke māna 'ai

Kou *wood*
H. 9.2 cm. D. 12.6 cm.
Queen Emma Collection, 1886 (5028)

Small *poi* bowls called *'umeke māna 'ai* "were made for favorite children, such as the first born (*makahiapo*), after weaning from the breast. They were tapu to the child, and others were not allowed to use them. A *kahu*, or attendant, looked after them. Bowls of this kind were sometimes made from a *kou* tree which had been planted over the afterbirths (*'i'ewe*) of grandparents" (Buck, 1957, p. 43).

According to an old label, this was Queen Emma's "own little poi bowl of kou wood when a child."

101. Covered Poi Bowl, 'umeke kūmau, or 'umeke kumauna

?Koa *wood*
H. 35.3 cm. D. 41.3 cm.
Queen Emma Collection, 1886 (420)
Color Plate XV

Too heavy to carry about easily, large deep bowls were used to store taro or sweet potato *poi*. Sometimes the pounded but undiluted taro *poi*, called *pa'i'ai*, was mixed with water in bowls of this size before serving. Such bowls often had wooden or gourd lids (called *po'i*) to keep out flies and to prevent the *poi* from crusting within.

102. Poi Bowl, 'umeke 'ai

Kou *wood with* koa *wood patches*
H. 21 cm. D. 27 cm.
Princess Ka'iulani Collection, 1911 (10,286)

This medium-sized *poi* bowl has been refinished and the base repaired with a square inset and several butterfly or hourglass-shaped patches. An old example from the collection of Princess Ka'iulani, it was no doubt repaired for display in a 19th-century curio cabinet or on a parlor table. Bowls of this size were made for *poi* that was soon to be used.

103. Poi Bowl, 'umeke 'ōpaka

Kou *wood with* koa *wood plugs*
H. 13.9 cm. D. 18.9 cm.
Kapi'olani-Kalaniana'ole Collection, 1923 (B. 6996)

In the late 19th century machine-turned bowls mounted on pedestals were used for individual servings of *poi* at feasts and meals in the homes of upper-class Hawaiians, when dipping into the communal *poi* bowl was inappropriate. Often richly finished, certain varieties with vertical panels and ridges, called *'ōpaka*, were said to be associated with the island of Maui, where they were used when serving chiefs (Buck, 1957, pp. 42, 51).

104. Poi Bowl with Lid, 'umeke 'ai

Kou *wood*
H. 11.6 cm. D. 18.9 cm.
Acquired before 1892 (591)

Lathe-turned bowls with flat bottoms were made in great numbers by any one of several cabinetry shops in Honolulu and elsewhere during the late 19th century. They were intended principally for individual service at large feasts, such as the *lū'au*, and a few examples are known with lids. The distinctive shape was no doubt inspired by the Japanese soup bowl, which began to appear with the influx of Japanese laborers after 1886.

105. Mounted Calabash on Stand

Kou and koa *woods, brass, felt*
Crowned KIX branded on lid, bowl, and base
H. 55.5 cm. D. 41.6 cm.
Kapiʻolani-Kalanianaʻole Collection, 1923 (B. 6960)

The ordinary *poi* bowl reached its zenith in the late 19th century, when older examples were mended, refinished, and sometimes mounted on ornate stands. This one is fitted with a turned *koa* lid and engraved brass bands—one bearing miniature Hawaiian and foreign views. It was probably a Jubilee gift to King Kalākaua, who celebrated his 50th birthday on November 16, 1886, with appropriate pomp and circumstance. Said to have belonged to Keōpūolani (see No. 69), the heirloom was thus converted to an object of display in ʻIolani Palace.

106. Finger Bowl, *ipu holoi lima*

Koa wood
H. 7.7 cm. D. 28 cm.
Acquired before 1892 (620)

An article of convenience for Hawaiian upper classes, particularly in the 19th century, finger bowls were used to wash sticky or greasy hands after a meal eaten with the fingers. The small flanges found on many finger bowls were helpful in scraping away adhering *poi* while the exterior lugs perforated for suspension cords provided ready means for storage afterward.

107. Double Finger Bowl, *ipu holoi lima*

Koa wood
H. 9 cm. L. 34.5 cm. W. 18 cm.
Queen Emma Collection, 1886 (628)

Finger bowls vary considerably in shape, but this one dating to the mid-19th century is unusual. One of the compartments possibly held water, and the other may have been for fresh clean leaves, to serve as napkins (Brigham, 1908, p. 182). The hook-shaped handle, imitating the chiefly *niho palaoa* whale-tooth ornament, no doubt doubled as an external flange for cleaning the royal fingers. The bowl is neatly repaired in several places with wedges and inset patches (see No. 98).

108. Finger Bowl with Three Compartments, *ipu holoi lima*

Koa wood
H. 18.2 cm. L. 34.2 cm. W. 18.4 cm.
Princess Ruta Keʻelikōlani Collection, 1883 (611)

If indeed this is a finger bowl, the three compartments could have provided separate receptacles for water, fresh leaves for wiping the fingers, and a place to deposit soiled leaves or other debris (Brigham, 1908, p. 182). Carved from a single piece of wood, the bowl was perhaps converted into this unusual configuration when one wall of the vessel was damaged during manufacture. Considering the confined interior working space, it is superbly crafted.

109. Finger Bowl, *ipu holoi lima*

Koa wood
H. 13.2 cm. L. 46 cm. W. 27.4 cm.
Kapiʻolani-Kalanianaʻole Collection, 1923 (B. 6896)

The raised pedestal base, lustrous finish, and nontraditional shape, calling to mind Aladdin's lamp, mark this finger bowl as a product of the later 19th century. More commodious than elegant, it has an internal flange for scraping the fingers free of *poi*, and a hook-shaped handle recalling the *niho palaoa* ornament.

110. Hand Basin, *ipu holoi lima*

Koa wood
H. 12.8 cm. L. 33 cm. W. 33.5 cm.
Purchase from A. F. Judd II, 1921 (B. 3994)

Although some voyagers and missionaries characterized the common Hawaiians as "dirty in the extreme," many of the upper classes were fastidious and washed their hands before meals. This vessel may have served as a kind of 19th-century wash basin, since its unusual shape is more in keeping with the variability of finger bowls than of food dishes. Besides being refinished, it has passed through the hands of many owners, including one who used it to feed chickens. It is said to have belonged originally to Queen Emma or her grandfather.

111. Refuse Bowl, *ipu ʻaina*

Wood, bone, human teeth, olonā cordage, brass nail;
molten lead repair in interior
H. 11 cm. D. 22.3 cm.
Queen Emma Collection, 1886 (4144)

Fearful of sorcery under the *kapu* system, chiefs used scrap bowls during meals to deposit fish bones, banana peels, and similar refuse in order to prevent it from falling into the hands of enemies. Food that had been touched was an excellent medium (*maunu*) for *kahuna ʻanāʻanā* sorcerers; therefore, influential chiefs with jealous rivals found it prudent to retain special attendants or *kahu* to dispose of food remains, usually by secret burial or by dumping into the sea. Refuse containers ornamented with human teeth and bone served the double purpose of insulting the memory of enemies whose corpses had furnished the decorative insets.

112. Refuse Bowl, *ipu ʻaina*

Douglas fir, human teeth, olonā cordage
H. 14.5 cm. D. 28.1 cm.
Gift of the Provisional Government of Hawaiʻi, 1893
(6927)

Made from driftwood from the Northwest Coast of America, this unusual refuse container, inset with no less than 289 human molars and premolars, was handed down by the Kamehameha and Kalākaua dynasties until the end of the Monarchy. Unfortunately, its historic associations are now lost, but the object must have been considered important, for Kamehameha V sent it to the Paris *Exposition Universelle* of 1867. Later, King Kalākaua seems to have taken it from its place of honor in the old Hawaiian National Museum for occasional display by his Hale Naua Society.

113. Refuse Bowl, *ipu ʻaina*

Koa *wood*
H. 14.2 cm. D. 27.8 cm.
Princess Ruta Keʻelikōlani Collection, 1883 (634)

Refuse bowls were occasionally used by some 19th-century Hawaiians careful to maintain certain of the old traditions. Naturally, the form of the vessels changed somewhat, and instead of human teeth and bone, lugs, ring bases, and faceted surfaces appeared, sometimes in very harmonious proportions. This example was owned by Princess Keʻelikōlani, whose preference for Hawaiian over Victorian ways typified the ambivalence felt by many Hawaiians, as foreign life styles from the East and West slowly engulfed the islands.

114. Spittoon, *ipu kuha*

Koa *wood, human teeth*
H. 8 cm. D. 15.7 cm.
Hawaiian National Museum Collection, 1891 (4143)

"Among the Hawaiians there was a deep-rooted belief (and three generations of Christian civilization have not much weakened the belief) that the kahunas or priests had a power over the lives of men which was brought into action by the *pule anaana* [*pule ʻanaʻana*] or praying to death," wrote William T. Brigham in 1908. "The person desiring the death of an enemy secured a lock of his hair, the pairings of his nails, or his spittle: the last perhaps most easy to obtain under ordinary circumstances without exciting suspicion: hence the existence of ipu kuha" (Brigham, 1908, p. 185). Beautifully proportioned, this spittoon belonged to Kamehameha I and one of his royal wives, the powerful and prestigious Kaʻahumanu.

115. Spittoon, *ipu kuha*

?Koa *wood*
H. 15.5 cm. D. 19.3 cm.
Lucy K. Peabody, Kalani and Edgar Henriques Collection, 1932 (C. 6234)

Obviously inspired by the Victorian brass spittoon, this example no doubt saw considerable service before it was mended and refinished, probably in the late 19th century. Smaller spittoons, fitted with handles of various sorts carved from the same block of wood, were sometimes carried even into church as late as the end of the last century (Brigham 1908, p. 186).

116. Waste Basin, *ipu mimi*

Kou *wood*
H. 10.9 cm. D. 25 cm.
Queen Emma Collection, 1886 (678)
Not illustrated

Although some authorities do not believe the chamber pot "to have been an ancient implement, nor was it used by the common people, who were very careless about the natural excretions of the body" (Brigham, 1908, p. 187), its use is consistent with the chief's fear of sorcery under the *kapu* system. Shaped much like enlarged versions of certain hand-carried spittoons, *ipu mimi* were quickly replaced by cheap crockery successors, and wooden examples are uncommon in museum collections. This one has been neatly repaired with wooden pins, wedges, and a dab of red sealing wax.

117. Refuse Bowl, *ipu ʻaina*

Kou *wood*
H. 19 cm. D. 30.1 cm.
Kapiʻolani-Kalanianaʻole Collection, 1923 (B.6895)

Handmade and beautifully finished to reveal the grain of the wood, this refuse bowl from the Kalākaua family collection is typical of the variability seen in such containers. It has no specific function assigned to it, though a suspension cord would have been knotted through the square perforation.

118. Storage Container, *hōkeo lāʻau*

Koa *wood*
H. 61.5 cm. D. 37 cm.
Gift of Elizabeth Kahalelaumoa Booth and family, 1947 (C.9967)

Some very large calabashes were used for storage of important valuables, such as clothing, featherwork, or other objects. This example, machine turned from fiery grained *koa* wood, would have been an imposing furnishing in nearly any Hawaiian home of the Victorian period. *Koa* wood, not traditionally used for food bowls because of the bitter taste said to be imparted to *poi*, was much favored for canoes, surfboards, and other domestic implements. The most important native cabinet wood in the 19th century, it is still a favorite of local artisans and craftsmen. Note the skillful use of butterfly or hourglass patching.

119. "Calabash of the Winds," *Ipu makani o Laʻamaomao*

Koa *and* kou *woods, brass, felt*
Red sealing wax on base of container.
H. 105.3 cm. D. 28.3 cm.
Kapiʻolani-Kalanianaʻole Collection, 1923 (B.6958)
Color Plate XVI

According to legend, this container is the sacred home of Laʻamaomao, a goddess of winds and the mother of Pākaʻa, to whom she gave a calabash containing the bones of her mother (Pukui and Elbert, 1971, p. 391). It was obtained by King Kalākaua in 1883 and refitted for display in ʻIolani Palace at the time of his 50th-birthday Jubilee in 1886. A local cabinet maker named William Miller provided the ornate stand and turned lid of *koa* wood, and a jeweler from Wenner & Co. of Honolulu later executed the scenes on the decorative bands from engravings published in Cook's voyages and elsewhere.

Shaped like traditional wooden containers for valuables, it can almost be said to symbolize the uneasy amalgamation of Hawaiian and Victorian values evident toward the end of the 19th century. A brass plaque placed on the cover, probably by King Kalākaua, reads in translation:

> The wind container of La'amaomao that was in the keeping of Hauna, personal attendant of Lonoikamakahiki I. It passed on to Paka'a, a personal attendant of Keawenuia'umi. It was placed in the royal burial cave of Ho'aiku, on the sacred cliff of Keoua, at Ka'awaloa, island of Hawai'i. Received by King Kalākaua I on January 1, 1883, from Ka'apana, caretaker of Ho'aiku.

120. Covered Wooden Container

Kou wood
H. 24.5 cm. D. 21.5 cm.
Kapi'olani-Kalaniana'ole Collection, 1923 (B.6963)

Machine turned and provided with a domed lid to accentuate its globular form, this late 19th-century "calabash" once belonged to Queen Kapi'olani, consort of King Kalākaua. Never intended for food, it epitomizes the evolution of the traditional *poi* bowl into a work of Victorian decorative art.

121. Medicine Pounding Bowl, *ipu ku'i lā'au*

?Kou wood
H. 37 cm. D. 25.6 cm.
Hawaiian National Museum Collection, 1891 (1143)

Some wooden containers are difficult to classify by their shape, but this rare form may have been used for pounding medicine. The bottom is thick, and the scalloped lip, useful for pouring, would have prevented a pestle or stirrer from accidentally rolling off when laid across the top. It appears to have entered the Hawaiian National Museum in 1877 from the estate auctions of Charles Kana'ina and King Lunalilo, whose combined collections included many old and significant objects associated with late 18th- and 19th-century chiefs and royalty.

122. Medicine Bowl, *'umeke 'ea lapa'au*

Turtle shell, wood, brass pins, sealing wax, pitch
Bottom stamped Kameh . . . in red sealing wax
H. 18.5 cm. D. 19.7 cm.
Hawaiian National Museum Collection, 1891 (5010)
Color Plate XVII

Tradition holds this to have been the vessel used by Kamehameha I for a dose of medicine. It holds about three quarts, and typical medicines were pounded infusions of herbs mixed with coconut milk. Similar in shape to No. 121, it is made from two plates of molded turtle shell laced together and pegged to a thick wooden base with tiny brass pins. Red sealing wax and a dark gummy substance, perhaps breadfruit sap, make a watertight seal, while turtle-shell patches close gaps at the rim. It was purchased for the Hawaiian National Museum on May 7, 1877, for $5.50 from the estate auctions of Charles Kana'ina and King Lunalilo.

123. Ivory Medicine Pounder, *palaoa ku'i*

Elephant ivory
H. 15 cm. D. 9.8 cm.
Hawaiian National Museum Collection, 1891 (5007)
Color Plate XVIII

This ivory pounder is also claimed by tradition to have belonged to Kamehameha I. Shaped much like the ordinary basalt conical pounders used for mashing taro and other foods, it was apparently used for medicines, ivory being especially preferred for the task because of its supposed pharmaceutical qualities. The fact that it is made of elephant ivory, imported by some early trader, may have added to its efficacy. Along with several other objects, the pounder was purchased (for $3.50) from the Kana'ina and King Lunalilo estate auctions on May 7, 1877, for the former Hawaiian National Museum.

124. Wooden Mortar and Pestle

Various Hawaiian woods
Mortar: H. 9.2 cm. D. 12 cm.
Pestle: L. 6 cm. D. 4.5 cm.
Gift of A. Brodie Smith, 1971 (1971.288.02a/b)
Not illustrated

Side by side with Western concepts, traditional Hawaiian medical practices persisted well into the 20th century. Native medical practitioners called *kahuna lapa'au* enjoyed considerable respect, and King Kalākaua himself is known to have written prescriptions based on Western remedies. Probably more decorative than functional, this mortar and pestle turned from a block of laminated Hawaiian woods is representative of the imagination and skill achieved by artisans familiar with the Hawaiian woodworking tradition.

125. Coconut Shell Spoon, *ipu kī'o'e*

Coconut shell, elephant ivory, brass pins
L. 16.5 cm. W. 8.5 cm. H. 7.6 cm.
Gift of J. K. Hewett, 1979 (1979.53.02)

Western travelers in the South Pacific recognized immediately the utility of the native coconut, whose nuts provided, in addition to food, cups and bowls, water bottles, scoops, and other domestic utensils. Hawaiians used small spoons made from coconut-shell segments for mashed sweet potato, *pālau*, which did not stick to the fingers as well as taro *poi*, hence necessitating the use of a scoop. Cut longitudinally and polished, this hemispherical section of coconut shell has a carved ivory handle attached with tiny brass pins. Perhaps modeled after spoons or ladles seen aboard visiting ships, it might have been intended for European guests reluctant to eat with their fingers in the traditional Hawaiian manner.

126. Condiment Dish, *ipu 'inamona*

Coconut shell
L. 10 cm. W. 6.4 cm. H. 3 cm.
Kapi'olani-Kalaniana'ole Collection, 1923 (B.7077)
Not illustrated

At 19th-century *lū'au*—a term said to have been coined in the 1850's for the traditional *pā'ina* or *'aha'aina* feasts where young taro tops (*lū'au*) were often served baked with coconut cream and chicken or octopus—condiments might be served in small coconut dishes. Some, like this one from the Kalākaua family collection, were polished and provided with flat bottoms and scalloped rims. Usual condiments included sea salt mixed with red earth (*'alaea*), many varieties of seaweed or *limu*, and *'inamona* relish prepared from roasted and ground *kukui* nuts mixed with salt.

127. Coconut Bowl on Pedestal, *'umeke pūniu*

Coconut shell, kou wood, metal screw and washer
H. 20.5 cm. D. 15 cm.
Gift of John K. Mehrten, 1923 (B.6391)
Not illustrated

"As the coconut shell takes a beautiful polish, the manufacture of cups, bowls, and small dishes has been much modified under foreign influence," noted W. T. Brigham (1908, p. 149). "Among Hawaiians these polished nut cups, foreign even to the glue that unites the cup and base, the latter the work of the turner, are still popular for individual poi bowls at feasts." This example with turned base and cover comes from a set of about two dozen, which once belonged to Rosalia I. K. Tripp.

128. Coconut Cup and Stand

Coconut shell, silver, brass
H. 15 cm. D. 14.4 cm.
Gift of Bruce Cartwright, 1927 (C.318)

A touch of Polynesian sentiment is apparent in this royal token, believed to have been sent from Queen Pomare IV of Tahiti to Dowager Queen Emma. Ambitious and proud, both women faced political intrigues in their own countries, so the humble coconut perhaps helped reaffirm their kindred Polynesian ancestry. Since Queen Pomare died on September 17, 1877, the inscription may have been added at a later date; it comes from the family of Queen Emma's trusted business manager and executor, Alexander Joy Cartwright.

129. Carved Coconut Goblet, *'umeke pūniu ki'i*

Coconut shell, wood, metal, glue, nails
H. 25.3 cm. D. 14.6 cm.
Bequest of Helen Irwin Fagan, 1967 (HH 1801)

The coconut has in this ornately carved goblet reached a pinnacle in 19th-century Hawaiian decorative art. The carved likenesses of King Kalākaua and Queen Kapi'olani indicate manufacture in the 1880's, quite possibly for the King's Jubilee in 1886 when a number of similarly ornate

items were produced. The scenes of Diamond Head and the grass house at Hulihe'e Palace, where the King and Queen maintained a country retreat at Kailua, Hawai'i, are prophetic forerunners of the tourist souvenirs that later developed from prototypes such as this sentimental memento of the closing years of the Monarchy.

130. Decorated Gourd Bowl, *'umeke pāwehe*

Bottle gourd, olonā cordage
H. 24.5 cm. D. 39.7 cm.
Purchase from A. M. McBryde, 1911 (10,996)

Ordinary gourd utensils were utilized by the lower classes in lieu of the difficult-to-produce and therefore more costly wooden calabashes. Gourd utensils were also decorated for aristocratic tastes by means of a technique believed to have been restricted to the island of Ni'ihau and parts of neighboring Kaua'i. This involved, according to one report, cutting a pattern through the outer skin of the gourd, peeling away unwanted areas to isolate the design, then immersing the gourd in swamp mud after soaking in an infusion of bark (Buck, 1957, p. 36). (The art was forgotten in the early 20th century, when the Hawaiian gourd is thought to have become extinct.) This example, with typical geometric motifs, has been painstakingly mended by zigzag stitching through paired holes along the edges of the cracks. Since the resulting lozenges resemble the meshes (*maka*) of a net, the repair technique is sometimes called *'aha maka*.

131. Decorated Gourd Bowl, *'umeke pāwehe*

Bottle gourd
Crowned L . . . U branded on bottom
H. 21 cm. D. 28 cm.
Gift of Lili'uokalani Estate, 1920 (B.3729)

Leaf and floral patterns are uncharacteristic of old Hawai'i, so this gourd from the Queen Lili'uokalani collection is thought to be an acculturated product influenced by European design. It was probably a food bowl, although larger gourds, generally left undecorated, were provided with covers and used for storage and transport of valuables.

132. Gourd Water Bottle, *hue wai pueo pāwehe*

Bottle gourd
H. 30.5 cm. D. 16 cm.
Purchase from Hanna Cook, 1901 (10,059)

Hawaiian farmers were expert in selecting seeds and in training gourds to grow in a multitude of forms which they bred for special needs. The hourglass variety, *pueo*, with two globes separated by a constriction, was especially favored for water bottles by devotees of the owl god, Pueo. Some water gourds were enclosed in cord supports (*aha hāwele*) for carrying, and stoppered with small shells or wads of bark cloth. This example from Ni'ihau is said to date to the end of the 19th century, just before the art of decorative staining was lost.

133. Carrying Net, kōkō

Coconut sennit, olonā cordage
L. 73 cm.
Acquired before 1892 (4414)
Illustrated with No. 102

Net slings were made in a great variety of forms, plain and fancy, for carrying wooden and gourd bowls by means of the burden pole. More complicated nets, such as this one of mixed sennit and *olonā*, were usually favored by the upper classes. Despite their attractive and utilitarian qualities, they dropped out of fashion around the turn of the century and are no longer made today, except by students interested in reviving the old techniques.

134. Decorated Burden Pole, 'auamo ki'i

Wood
L. 124 cm. D. 4.2 cm.
Purchase from John Howells, 1964 (D.3357)
Illustrated with Nos. 102 and 135

Carrying poles were balanced over one shoulder, with wooden or gourd calabashes and baskets slung in nets from the notched ends. Poles belonging to households of chiefs of note sometimes had figures (*ki'i*) carved on the terminal knobs, and a few are known with multiple notches. Whatever their form, however, they were important for transporting goods on land, even after horseback riding was introduced. In former days, chiefs' stewards were called *'a'ipu'upu'u* because they often had calluses (*pu'upu'u*) on their shoulders from carrying heavy loads of food.

135. Basketry Covered Gourd Container, hīna'i poepoe

Bottle gourd, 'ie'ie rootlets, olonā cordage
H. 36.5 cm. D. 21.7 cm.
J. S. Emerson Collection, 1889 (1404)

Hawaiian women were expert at twining several kinds of baskets and other containers from *'ie'ie* aerial rootlets, and a type fashioned around gourd bases with fitted gourd covers was apparently unique in Polynesia. Used for storage and transport, a few, like this one, had carrying nets attached. Some were also decorated by dyeing selected weft plies black before incorporating them into banded patterns.

136. "Pali, Oahu," by A. T. Agate (1812-1846)

Steel engraving
18 × 11.7 cm. 27.3 × 16.4 cm. (sheet)
Published in Charles Wilkes' Narrative of the United States Exploring Expedition, during the years 1838 . . . 1842, *Vol. 3 (Philadelphia: Lea & Blanchard, 1845)*
Purchase, 1977

A. T. Agate depicted (against a still dramatic backdrop) a sight that U. S. Exploring Expedition personnel found common in 1840-1841:

One cannot but be struck with seeing the natives winding their way along the different thoroughfares, laden with all kinds of provisions, wood, charcoal, and milk, to supply the market and their regular customers. Indeed, there are quite as many thus employed as in any place of the same number of inhabitants in our own country.

Their usual mode of carrying burdens is to suspend them with cords from the ends of a stick; this is laid across the shoulders, and so accustomed are they to carry the load in this manner, that they will sometimes increase the weight by adding a heavy stone, in order to balance it. The stick on which they carry their load is made of the Hibiscus tiliaceus, which is very light and tough. Instead of baskets, they use a kind of gourd, which grows to a large size, and seems peculiar to these islands; these are thin and brittle, but with the care the natives take of them, are extremely serviceable: they are used for almost everything, such as dishes, for carrying water, &c. It takes two gourds to make one of the baskets used for transporting articles; and the smaller one being turned over the opening cut in the larger one, effectually protects the contents from rain. Some of these gourds will contain upwards of two bushels. For travelling on these islands, they are almost indispensable (Wilkes, 1845, Vol. 3, pp. 389-390).

137. "A Calabash Carrier in Ancient Hawaiian Dress in the Fern Forest," by Henry W. Henshaw (1850-1930)

Platinotype, c. 1895
16 × 20.9 cm.

Henry Wetherbee Henshaw's photograph of a calabash carrier taken near Hilo about 1895 documents a method of balancing gourd calabashes on a burden pole—at the same time recording a bit of vanishing Hawai'i. Henshaw, formerly with the Bureau of American Ethnology at the Smithsonian, had come to the islands for reasons of health in 1894, but managed to lead an active life as a bird collector and photographer. "Just before leaving California," Henshaw (1920, p. 95) reminisced, "I had learned to use platinotype paper which is unexcelled for permanency and for artistic effect, and I was the first, I believe, to introduce the use of the paper into the islands." Henshaw stayed on, became famous, "and was induced by my friends to place the results of my handiwork of the camera on sale both in Honolulu and Hilo, the result being the sale of some thousands of prints, which are now scattered all over the world."

138. Lū'au at Moanalua Gardens, unknown photographer

Albumen print, c. 1885
16.9 × 23.5 cm.

Princess Likelike, younger sister of King Kalākaua and mother of Princess Ka'iulani (see No. 73) is seated third from the left, enjoying a common pastime of mid-Victorian Hawai'i. Although the *lū'au* persisted as a social institution well into modern times, ordinary kitchen crockery (or mass-produced wooden utensils imported from the Philippines) replaced the traditional assortment of calabashes. Moanalua, a cool and pleasant valley where travelers bound for Honolulu from 'Ewa rested, belonged to members of the Kamehameha family in the 19th century, until it was bequeathed by Princess Bernice Pauahi Bishop to Samuel M. Damon in 1884. It is today threatened by freeway construction.

139. "Scène prise dans l'ile d'Oahou (Iles Sandwich)," by Louis-Jules Masselot

Lithograph
35.5 × 50.3 cm. (sheet)
Published in Atlas Pittoresque *accompanying Du Petit-Thouars'* Voyage autour du monde . . . pendant les années 1836-1839 . . . (Paris: Gide, 1840-1864)
Gov. G. R. Carter Collection, 1959
Not illustrated

Masselot's romanticized vignette showing life around the *poi* bowl in 1837 is relatively unchanged from former days, except for the introduction of clothing inspired by early missionary wives. Note the calabash carrier, a favorite subject of artists, in the background.

140. "Hawaiian Child and the Poi Bowl," by Theodore Wores (1859-1939)

Oil on fabric, 1901
76.2 × 61 cm.
Frame designed by Jean Charlot and handcrafted by Alan Wilkinson
Loaned by Dr. A. Jess Shenson and Dr. Ben Shenson, San Francisco
Color Plate XIX

Like Wores's painting of "The Lei Maker" (No. 65), the Hawaiian child with a *poi* bowl has come to symbolize a part of old Hawai'i no longer readily apparent beneath the overlay of Western values and a competitive monetary economy. What had been a common enough sight for artist Louis-Jules Masselot (see No. 139) some 60 years before was passing out of existence in turn-of-the-century Hawai'i. While utensils and costumes may have changed, however, the enduring social relationships of the *'ohana,* or family, symbolized by the *poi* bowl, are still fundamental to the Hawaiian life style of today.

The *Hula*

Soon after becoming entrenched in the 1820's, Calvinist missionaries from New England made persistent but ultimately unsuccessful attempts to eradicate *hula* from Hawaiian culture. As a consequence, according to a recent evaluation of the *hula* in historical perspective (Barrère, Pukui, and Kelly, 1980, pp. 1-2), public *hula* performances disappeared from locations near mission stations almost immediately, then vanished soon afterward from residences of Christianized chiefs. Embracing religion with devout fervor, Queen Regent Ka'ahumanu went so far as to ban public performances altogether in 1830, but to hardly anyone's surprise, tradition-minded chiefs and many commoners ignored the edict. King Kamehameha III openly flouted the regulations for a short time after her death

in 1832 but soon repented under pressure, and by 1835 the Kingdom returned to the rigid constraints of Calvinist morality.

Even so, the *hula* continued to be taught and practiced away from prying missionaries and pious chiefs. Laws passed in 1851, and later, attempted to regulate public performances through payment of fees and levying of fines and penalties for noncompliance, but with mixed success. Nor could private performances be easily controlled, and throughout the 1860's clandestine *hula* schools continued to operate. Many chiefs and rulers reverted to the old custom of maintaining trained performers of *po'e hula,* or *hula* people, who provided entertainment at home and during royal excursions about the islands.

Although moralistic Hawaiians and foreigners continued to protest, public *hula* performances became fully re-established during the reign of King Kalākaua (1874-1891). Having somehow managed to keep the tradition alive, the *po'e hula* reasserted their arts with enthusiasm at the Coronation of 1883, and Kalākaua's 50th-birthday Jubilee three years later. In the reformist atmosphere after the fall of the Monarchy in 1893, however, public *hula* performances declined once again, and sporadic attempts at revival in the early 20th century met with varying success. Nevertheless, popularity of the *hula* as public entertainment could not be denied, and by midcentury the *hula* flourished once more. Today, the *hula* is in the full bloom of a renaissance that shows no signs of abatement.

Over the span of 200 years since first contact with outsiders, the *hula* has ebbed and flowed with changes that have come to the islands. While many features of the dance seen today bear faint resemblance to *hula* of the late 18th century, or even the 1880's, the tradition has shown a remarkable ability to adapt to changing tastes and pressures.

A fusion of 20th-century aspirations and forces rooted in ancient traditions, Hawaiian dance persists today as living *hula.*

141. Men of the Sandwich Islands Dancing, by John Webber (1751-1793)

Pencil, pen and wash, c. 1780
30.6 × 47.6 cm.
A single figure in pencil and wash at the Dixson Library is probably the source for the published version engraved by C. Grignion in the Atlas to Cook's third voyage.
Purchase from Spencer Bickerton, 1922

Although Captain Cook and his men had little opportunity to observe formal *hula,* they witnessed a brief performance at Kealakekua Bay toward the beginning of February, 1779:

> We were this day much diverted, at the beach, by the buffooneries of one of the natives. He held in his hand an instrument . . . some bits of sea-weed were tied round his neck; and round each leg, a piece of strong netting, about nine inches deep, on which a great number of dogs' teeth were loosely fastened, in rows. His style of dancing was entirely burlesque, and accompanied with strange grimaces, and pantomimical distortions of the face; which though at times inexpressibly ridiculous, yet, on the hole [sic], was without much meaning, or expression. Mr. Webber thought it worth his while to make a drawing of this person, as exhibiting a tolerable specimen of the natives; the manner in which the maro [loincloth] is tied; the figure of the instrument before mentioned, and of the ornaments round the legs, which, at other times, we also saw used by their dancers (Cook and King, 1784, Vol. 3, p. 27).

Shipboard artist John Webber's drawing illustrates two of the more common accouterments of the *hula*—the feathered rattle called *'ulī'ulī*, and the dogtooth anklet, or *kūpe'e niho 'īlio* (see Nos. 153 and 161). Note that Webber shows the anklets loosely fastened to the upper calves with individual teeth pointed downward, rather than tightly secured to the ankles with teeth pointing upward, as recorded by later artists, such as Louis Choris in 1816.

142. "Îles Sandwich: Femme de l'île Mowi Dansant," by Jacques Etienne Victor Arago (1790-1855)

Engraving, handcolored
32.1 × 22.1 cm. (sheet; platemk. trimmed)
Published in Atlas Historique *accompanying de Freycinet's* Voyage autour du monde . . . pendant les années 1817 . . . 1820 . . . *(Paris: Chez Pillet Aîné, Imprimeur-Libraire, 1824-1842)*
Gift of Mrs. A. W. F. Fuller, 1964
Not illustrated

The female dancer from the island of Maui is performing a seated *hula,* or *hula noho,* which Jacques Arago depicted during the voyage of Louis de Freycinet in August, 1819. Richly tattooed in patterns typical of the day (including a line of introduced goats over each breast), the young woman has streaks of hair around her face "bleached white by using a mixture of clay and lime" (Wiswell, 1978, p. 62). She wears a necklace of ivory beads and a full billowy *pā'ū,* or *hula* skirt, donned in graceful folds for the occasion. Describing dancing and music, de Freycinet (Wiswell, 1978, pp. 81-82) commented:

> The Sandwich Islanders have various types of dances and participate in this amusement with great fervor. Women, it is said, usually perform the principal parts, but in general it is not a case of exhibiting the agility of leg movement or of jumping in cadence, for the arms are almost the only agents of their choreography. Whether the dancer is standing or squatting on his heels, he applies himself mostly to gesticulating.
> While performing his pantomime, the dancer sings, and musicians almost always join their voices to his, accompanying themselves on various instruments . . .
> The lyrics of their songs are adaptable, depending on the occasion, and either deal with historic and religious traditions or describe some particular and individual event.

143. "Scène de Danse, aux Îles Sandwich," by Barthélemy Lauvergne (1805-1875)

Lithograph, sepia-toned
29.7 × 45.2 cm (sheet)
Published in Album Historique *accompanying Vaillant's* Voyage autour du monde . . . pendant les années 1836 et 1837 . . . *(Paris: A. Bertrand, 1840-1852, 1866)*
Gov. G. R. Carter Collection, 1959

By the time marine painter Barthélemy Lauvergne visited the islands in 1836, the *hula* had already entered a period of decline. It was revived somewhat after the death of Ka'ahumanu in 1832, and members of the *Bonite* were invited to a formal entertainment "disencumbered of all etiquette" at King Kamehameha III's country place near the outskirts of Honolulu.

Lamenting how "Dancing has also fallen into great disfavor in consequence of missionary influence," Théodore-Adolphe Barrot, the French Consul for Manila then traveling with the *Bonite,* noted further that only one female dancer took part in the performance. She wore a calico shirt under her skirt, composed of "Pieces of cloth, suspended from the hips, and hanging in graceful folds, [which] imparted a sort of originality to their movements."

Arriving on the scene on a late afternoon in October, 1836, Barrot (1978, p. 50) noted:

> Everything had been previously arranged; mats were spread in front of the cottage, and chairs were placed in a circle, and first, five singers appeared and kneeled down. Each of them was armed with a large calabash, which was made thin towards the middle; this calabash, held in the left hand by a string, aided the expression of their gestures in a singular manner. They were naked to the waist; their arms and breast were tattooed, and loose folds of tapa of various colors covered the lower part of their bodies. Their songs were a sort of recitative, or of modulated conversation, animated or slow, as the subject required.
> The theme they had chosen, or which had been suggested to them, was an eulogy of the King . . .

144. Hawaiian Dancers, unknown photographer

Ambrotype, c. 1858
16.2 × 10.6 cm.
Photo Collection, 1976.192.16

The earliest known photographic image of Hawaiian *hula* dancers, this wet plate collodion positive on glass shows two women posed against a cloth backdrop and standing on a floor retouched to give the appearance of sand. Their dress is typical of *hula* costume during much of the 19th century: loose blouses, wide *kapa* or cloth skirts (sometimes brightly patterned) tied around the waist with a drawstring, a handkerchief tucked into the belt to wipe the face of perspiration, fiber anklets, and various *lei* or garlands for the neck and hair.

Although missionary influence never succeeded in wiping out the *hula,* laws regulating their performance were passed by the Legislature in 1851. A licensing act followed in 1859 permitting public *hula* displays, "not of an immoral character, to which admission is obtainable by the payment of money" (cited by Barrère, Pukui, and Kelly, 1980, p. 41). More liberal laws in 1864-1865 and in 1870 reduced fees and penalties and lifted restrictions on venues, opening the way for wide participation in *hula* performances throughout the islands.

145. Ioane Ukeke and Hula Troupe, by Menzies Dickson (d. 1891)

Albumen print, c. 1880
16.2 × 19 cm.
Not illustrated

These dancers are from the troupe of *hula* master Ioane Ukeke, the distinguished "Honolulu Dandy" of Coronation festivities staged for King Kalākaua and Queen Kapi'olani in February, 1883. They are, left to right: Sister of Ioane Ukeke's wife, Ioane Ukeke's wife, Ioane Ukeke, Ann Kapule, Mary Kapule. Although moralistic Hawaiian and foreign residents decried the "return to paganism," *hula* performers outdid themselves in chanting and dancing, many of their creations having descended as reflections of ancient *hula* (Barrère, Pukui, and Kelly, 1980, p 50). "Dandy Ioane was in his glory on this occasion," the *Pacific Commercial Advertiser* reported three days after the February 24th performance; "he was floor-manager, and the master of the situation. He marshalled the performing girls in their short skirts and hula buskins, and accompanied their gyrations with his tremulous-toned instrument" (see No. 157).

Menzies Dickson's view is posed against a painted backdrop of Diamond Head and Waikiki Beach. According to *The Friend* for February, 1876, his studio also offered a full range of "curiosities" for "one desirous of studying the history and ethnology of the Polynesian Islands."

146. "Hula Girls," unknown photographer

Albumen print, c. 1890
24.3 × 18 cm.

Provocative "hula girl pictures" were produced as early as 1870 by one Honolulu photographer, J. W. King, who was fined $400 and run out of town for his "disgusting traffic in obscenity." While virtuous Honolulu citizens congratulated themselves that salacious photographs were purchased mostly by passing tourists, the *hula* itself eventually responded to prurient interests in its own fashion. "Hula girls of the olden days did not dance with bared thighs as they do today, for they were taught that to leave their thighs uncovered was immodest. Even down to the days of our last rulers hula dancers wore knee-length skirts . . . Today's hula costumes," noted Mary Kawena Pukui in 1942, "consist of brassieres, abbreviated panties, leis and grass skirts, and almost all of both thighs is glimpsed. Grass skirts were not Hawaiian and were introduced to Hawaii by laborers from the Gilbert Islands" (Barrère, Pukui, and Kelly, 1980, p. 72).

147. Hula Drum, *pahu hula*

Wood, shark skin, coconut sennit, olonā cordage, black pigment
H. 37.8 cm. D. 31 cm.
Hawaiian National Museum Collection, 1891 (4849)

Wooden drums are associated with the very core of Hawaiian music. Historical legends relate that the instrument was brought to Hawai'i during the period of semi-mythological contact with the Society Islands between the 13th and 16th centuries by La'a-mai-Kahiki (La'a-from-Tahiti), who in later times assumed the role of Laka, the Hawaiian god/goddess of *hula*. Large drums were used for religious activities in the temples, or *heiau*, while smaller ones accompanied *hula* chants and dancing. They are played with the fingers and palms of both hands on various parts of the drumhead to produce sounds characterized by tonal and rhythmic diversity, and sometimes unpredictability (Tatar in Kanahele, 1979, p. 289).

This 19th century *pahu hula* is believed to be one of several preserved by the Kamehameha family in the first 'Iolani Palace, and transferred to the Hawaiian National Museum in 1874. It was included among the exhibits sent by the Hawaiian Government to the Paris *Exposition Universelle* of 1889, where, incidentally, the display of "ancient Hawaiian musical instruments" was awarded an honorable mention.

148. Coconut Knee Drum, *pūniu*, or *kilu*

Coconut shell, shark skin, bark cloth, coconut sennit, olonā cordage
H. 11.1 cm. D. 12 cm.
Purchase from A. M. McBryde, 1911 (11,005)

Apparently unique to Hawai'i among the islands of Polynesia, the coconut shell knee drum was tied to the thigh just above the knee, or sometimes cradled in the musician's leg while seated cross-legged. It was played with a stout cord of twisted and knotted fiber, or with a flexible stick. Not considered a solo instrument, it was ordinarily used in combination with the *pahu* drum and produces a high-pitched tone that contrasts to the basic low tones of the larger wooden drum. Musically, the rhythmic beats of the *pūniu* occur between the beats of the *pahu*, producing a contrasting yet complementary effect (Tatar in Kanahele, 1979, p. 317).

149. Carved Drum Support

Wood
H. 17 cm. D. 18.3 cm.
Gift of T. Clive Davies, 1952 (D. 309)

A few old Hawaiian drums have human support figures carved on their lower portions, rather than the more typical arch or zigzag fretwork still being used to decorate contemporary drums. This 19th-century example probably once held a coconut shell drum chamber covered with a shark or fish skin tympanium.

150. Double Gourd Drum, *ipu hula, pā ipu,* or *ipu heke*

Bottle gourd, ?breadfruit gum, cotton cloth, olonā cordage, European trade cordage
H. 71 cm. D. 35.7 cm.
Gift of Carrie J. Robinson and Frank L. Kaleimamahu, 1933 (C. 6373)
Color plate XX

The double gourd drum is still used extensively in traditional and some contemporary Hawaiian music. Made from two hollow gourds joined at the neck with adhesive pitch, the drum is held by the left hand through the bark cloth or fabric loop attached just below the neck. It is sounded by stamping the base on a pad of bark cloth or similar material and emits deep hollow tones from the circular opening in the top. Slapping the sides of the lower gourd with the fingers of the right hand produces sharp, higher sounds that present all kinds of subtle rhythmic possibilities. Single gourd drums called *ipu heke'ole* are also made, but the smaller and thicker-walled gourds now imported from Mexico and elsewhere have somewhat different sound characteristics from those found in old instruments of both types.

This instrument was used by U'a, the court drummer of Kamehameha III, Kamehameha IV, and Kamehameha V. U'a died a few months after Kamehameha V in 1872, leaving it to his daughter, Pilahi Kaleimamahu. She later gave the drum to Carrie J. Robinson, who said it was used in the *'ala'apapa* and *kuolo* dances.

151. Bamboo Stamping Tube, *'ohe kā'eke'eke,* or *pahupahū*

L. 49.3 cm. D. 4.8 cm.
Acquired before 1928 (10,099)

According to legend, bamboo stamping tubes were brought to Hawai'i by the same La'a-mai-Kahiki who introduced the *pahu* drum (see No. 147). Made of different lengths of bamboo, usually with one end open and the other end closed by the natural septum, they were held vertically one in each hand and played by stamping alternately or simultaneously on the ground or on mats. The length of the bamboo determined pitch, and several musicians performing a *hula kā'eke'eke* could produce varied and pleasing sounds. Stamping tubes have been recently re-established in the musical repertories of some contemporary Hawaiian groups, though their use is still limited (Tatar in Kanahele, 1979, p. 196).

152a, b. Pair of Bamboo Hula Rattles, *pū'ili*

a: L. 63 cm. D. 4.6 cm
b: L. 65 cm. D. 4.7 cm.
Princess Ruta Ke'elikōlani Collection, 1883 (884a/b)

Made by splitting one end of a segment of bamboo opposite the node into many narrow tines of equal width, bamboo rattles produce a murmurous, breezy rattling sound highly appreciated for certain kinds of *hula*. Charles Warren Stoddard described a *hula pū'ili* for *Paradise of the Pacific* in June, 1888:

Then began a singularly intricate exercise, called *pu'ili*. Taking a bamboo in one hand, they struck it in the palm of the other, on the shoulder, on the floor in front, to the left and right; thrust it out before them, and were parried by the partners opposite; crossed it over and back, and turned in a thousand ways to a thousand metres, varied with chants and pauses . . . for a half hour or more.

153. Pair of Coconut Dance Rattles, *'ulī'ulī*

Coconut shell, chicken feathers, cotton and silk, leaf stems, wire, trade cordage, thread, ?wild canna seeds (ali'ipoe)
Left: H. 28.5 cm. D. 21.8 cm. (870)
Right: H. 23.5 cm. D. 21.5 cm. (871)
Hawaiian National Museum Collection, 1891
Color Plate XXI

Also a Hawaiian specialty, small coconut or gourd rattles containing a few seeds or pebbles were used to accompany many different kinds of *hula*. Decorated with feathers, bark cloth, or imported fabrics, they add an interesting visual component to the rhythmic movements of the dancers, who shake and strike the rattle against their palms and other parts of the body. Traditionally only one *'ulī'ulī* was used, but new *hula* styles in the 20th century introduced two rattles, one in each hand (Tatar in Kanahele, 1979, p. 408). Second in importance only to the gourd drum as an accompanying instrument in the early 20th century, *'ulī'ulī* decorated with bright red or yellow dyed feathers are still one of the most popular accouterments of the modern *hula*. This pair was probably exhibited by the Hawaiian government at the Paris *Exposition Universelle* of 1889 (see No. 147).

154a, b. Pair of Castanets, *'ili'ili*

Hematite
a: L. 4.3 cm. W. 3.5 cm. Th. 1.8 cm.
b: L. 4.2 cm. W. 3.3 cm. Th. 1.4 cm.
George H. Dole Collection, 1889 (895a/b)

Pebbles held in each hand were used to accompany and accentuate movements of the *hula*, much as Spanish castanets are employed. Small, waterworn lava pebbles free of air pockets or other irregularities usually sufficed, but this pair (from a set of four probably from Kaua'i) is shaped from dense, reddish brown hematite, a rarely used material sometimes found among chiefly possessions. Still used today in performances of traditional *hula*, *'ili'ili* also contribute on occasion their distinctive sharp clicking sounds to contemporary Hawaiian music (Tatar in Kahanele, 1979, p. 164).

155a, b. Pair of Wooden Hula Sticks, *kāla'au*

a: L. 80.5 cm. D. 3.3 cm. (10,309)
b: L. 53 cm. D. 3.6 cm. (10,310)
Princess Ka'iulani Collection, 1911

When Cook first visited Hawai'i in 1778, the *hula kāla'au* was one of the most popular dances in the islands (Kamakau, 1961, p. 105). Despite attempts at suppression, *hula* of this type continued throughout the 19th century, and *hula* rhythm sticks are occasionally still used by contemporary Hawaiian music ensembles specializing in slack key guitar, bass, and *'ukulele*—often with the trademark *ipu* rhythmic pattern (Tatar in Kanahele, 1979, p. 200).

Shaped hardwood rhythm sticks, traditionally of unequal length but today sometimes not, were described by Edward Bell at a *hula* performance given for Captain George Vancouver (see No. 5) in February, 1794, when the court of Kamehameha was located at Kealakekua Bay:

> Six men first entered—these were musicians—they had no drums . . . but they had in their left hands long poles—or Blunt pointed Spears, being very small at one end becoming thicker gradually towards the other end, made of their mahogany—this they strike with a piece of the same kind of Wood, which they accompanied to a song in which they all joined, keeping the most exact time with their right foot beating against the ground (Bell, 1929, Vol. 2, Pt. 2, p. 125).

156. Treadle Board, *papa hehi*

Wood
L. 32.6 cm. W. 16.3 cm. Th. 5 cm.
Purchase from A. M. McBryde, 1911 (10,870)
Illustrated with No. 155

Papa hehi were timekeeping instruments played with the right foot as a treadle over wooden crosspieces to accompany the *hula kālaʻau* on Niʻihau and Kauaʻi. The first Hawaiian *hula* seen by Europeans included the treadle board and *kālaʻau*, which Cook described in January, 1778:

> We had no opportunity to see any of their amusements and the only musical instrument that was seen among them was a hollow vessel of wood like a platter and two sticks, on these one of our gentlemen saw a man play: one of the sticks he held as we do a fiddle and struck it with the other, which was smaller and something like a drum stick and at the same time beat with his foot upon the hollow Vessel and produced a tune that was by no means disagreeable. This Musick was accompanied with a song, sung by some women and had a pleasing and tender effect (Beaglehole, 1967, Vol. 3, Pt. 1, p. 284).

Interest in the treadle board was reawakened sometime in the 1930's when this and a companion instrument in Bishop Museum were copied in order to revive a Kauaʻi form of the *hula kālaʻau* (Barrère, Pukui, and Kelly, 1980, p. 83).

157. Musical Bow, *'ukeke*

Kauila wood, restrung with olonā cordage
L. 47 cm. W. 3.5 cm. Th. 1.7 cm.
Lucy K. Peabody, Kalani and Edgar Henriques Collection, 1932 (C.5572)
Illustrated with No. 154

The only "string" instrument in pre-European Hawaiʻi, the musical bow is thought to have been introduced before A.D. 1200 by settlers from the Marquesas, where a similar instrument called *'utete* is found. Helen Roberts (1926, pp. 24-25) recorded the following method of playing the *'ukeke* from old Hawaiian musicians during field work in the 1920's:

> They grasped the instrument in the left hand, with the palm next to the convex side, and the thumbs pressing the lower edge . . . The end containing the slits was held between [or against] the lips and the entire instrument extended horizontally to the left. The mouth cavity acted as a resonance chamber. With a small fiber, or more usually with a bit of cloth [or bark cloth] twisted into a point, the strings were picked with almost incredible rapidity . . . As the strings were picked, the shape of the mouth and lips changed, and the tongue was used exactly as it would be in speech, with the result that the sound issuing from the mouth almost resembled speech.

The soft sound was considered most appropriate for love songs rendered in private, although a standing *hula* of the *'ōlapa* type was formerly accompanied by the musical bow. Difficult to play, the instrument is used only occasionally today, and rarely by contemporary musical groups because of its delicate sound (Tatar in Kanahele, 1979, p. 393).

158. Bamboo Nose Flute, *'ohe hano ihu,* or *'ohe kani*

L. 39.9 cm. D. 2.4 cm.
Kapiʻolani-Kalanianaʻole Collection, 1923 (B. 6736)
Illustrated with No. 154

Made from a joint of bamboo with the septum left intact near the blowing end, nose flutes usually have two or three burned or drilled finger holes. Spacing, and thus pitch, are dependent upon individual preference. When played, the flute is normally extended horizontally forward from the right nostril, the left one being closed with the thumb or a finger of the left hand to increase the draft of air. Functionally similar to the *'ukeke* (see No. 157) in being a voice-extension instrument, the nose flute in skillful hands could reproduce the rhythmic subtleties and approximate pitches of a chanted text. An instrument for love songs (until condemned by the missionaries), it is said that lovers could convey messages to one another in the still of the night. Nose flutes are sometimes used today by popular music groups, but the melodies are much simpler versions of older styles (Tatar in Kanahele, 1979, pp. 270-272).

159. Gourd Whistle, *ipu hōkiokio,* or *ipu hoehoe*

Bottle gourd
H. 7.2 cm. D. 5 cm.
Queen Emma Collection, 1886 (4859)
Illustrated with No. 154

Similar to the nose flute in being an instrument for love making, gourd whistles produced two or three soft notes of approximate halftone intervals when blown through one nostril. Most are made from small, pear-shaped gourds (or occasionally small coconuts) and have two or three finger holes through which a skillful player could imitate the sounds and words of a *mele hoʻoipoipo*, or love song. Rarely played today, some older ones are decorated with burned designs, typically triangles and circles with radiating lines. This one once belonged to Princess Nāhiʻenaʻena, a tragic figure of the early 19th century whose love for her brother, Kamehameha III, could never be reconciled between approving Hawaiians and noncomprehending Westerners (Sinclair, 1976).

160. Shell Trumpet, *pū*

Conch shell
L. 30 cm. W. 17.5 cm. Th. 11.5 cm.
Kapi'olani-Kalaniana'ole Collection, 1923 (B.6910)
Illustrated with No. 151

Although not musical instruments, strictly speaking, shell trumpets were frequently employed in ancient Hawai'i as signaling devices, but only occasionally to accompany chants. In early Christian times they were used to call people to worship. Properly blown, shell trumpets were capable of emitting sounds audible two miles away. They were usually perforated at the apex, like the helmet shells used for similar purposes. A few contemporary groups have attempted to incorporate the shell trumpet into their music, but the instrument remains primarily a symbol of the past. As such, it has been used to announce special ceremonies, and even to convene the State Legislature (Kanahale, 1979, p. 307).

161. Dog Tooth Ankle Rattle, *kūpe'e niho 'īlio*

Dog incisors, olonā cordage
L. 22.5 cm. W. 35 cm. Th. 3 cm.
Purchase from A. M. McBryde, 1911 (10,958)
Color Plate XXII

Traditionally worn in pairs by male dancers, dog tooth rattles were another peculiarity of the Hawaiian Islands. Consisting of some 1,000 or so dog incisors per anklet (requiring about 250 dogs each), the teeth were perforated through the roots, strung onto *olonā* cord chains, then fastened together in parallel rows by various techniques. They were laced to the dancer's calf or ankle by means of sturdy loops attached to two sides of the surprisingly heavy trapezoidal pads.

Early pictorial sources differ in whether they were worn with the teeth pointing upward or downward. Whatever the case, the anklets produced sharp rattling sounds to accentuate the vigorous movements of feet and legs in certain kinds of *hula*. Similar anklets were also made from shells and seeds, but the dog tooth variety seems to have persisted into the first half of the 19th century. Recently a few dance groups have attempted to revive these anklets by using shells and imitation teeth.

162a, b. Pair of Corn Husk Anklets, *kūpe'e*

Corn husks, trade cordage
a: L. 35 cm. W. 9 cm. Th. 5 cm.
b: L. 33 cm. W. 9.5 cm. Th. 2.7 cm.
J. S. Emerson Collection, 1889 (980a/b)

When the eating of dog's flesh as a delicacy fell into disfavor in the 19th century, dancers' anklets could no longer be made from surplus canine incisors. Instead, substitutes were created in worsted yarn and other materials, such as in this pair made in June, 1887, from the introduced maize plant. Here, shredded strips of dried corn husk are knotted onto imported fishing cord ties and arranged in double bands meant to encircle the ankle. Photographs taken before and after the Kalākaua Coronation and Jubilee festivities of 1883 and 1886 show

fiber anklets of one type or another to have been in general use during the last half of the 19th century.

163. Grass Skirt

Coconut leaf, trade cordage
L. 103 cm. W. 58 cm. Th. 5 cm.
Gift of Princess Kawānanakoa, 1920 (B.2144)

Irrevocably linked in the popular imagination to the *hula* of ancient Hawai'i, the "grass skirt" is, as most persons are surprised to learn, an adaptation of the last century. Apparently introduced by Gilbertese contract laborers in the 1870's and 1880's, fiber skirts are, moreover, not made from grass but from shredded *ki* leaves or some other suitable material, including cellophane in the 20th century.

During the Kalākaua period, when traditional bark cloth was becoming obsolete, *hula* costumes were normally fashioned from foreign cloth and covered the performers in billowy skirts and blouses, not infrequently over long underwear. The so-called grass *hula* skirt did not come into general use until tourists, and later movie patrons, learned to expect and then demand the revealing attire in *hula* entertainments. Lorrin Tarr Gill pointed out in *Paradise of the Pacific* in May, 1923:

. . . the hula has been popularized and commercialized . . . it has suffered the addition of imported steps from the mainland, and the vulgarities introduced to pander to tourists; yet it has been called the national dance of Hawaii, and its grass skirt, unknown to early Hawaii, has been called the national costume.

This typical example made of shredded coconut leaves knotted over a tie cord of imported fishing line comes from the collection of Prince David Kawānanakoa Pi'ikoi (1868-1908), a nephew of King Kalākaua.

164. 'Ukulele

Koa wood, mother-of-pearl, brass, plastic, metal, wood, cat gut
L. 52.4 cm. W. 14.8 cm. Th. 6.2 cm.
Purchase from Gail Ann Maule, J. N. Wilcox Fund, 1976 (1976.129)
Color Plate XXIII

Music in Hawai'i entered a new era when Portuguese immigrants in 1878-1879 introduced a small four-stringed instrument called the *braguinha*. Immediately captivated, Hawaiians adopted a version they called *pila li'ili'i*, "little fiddle," which soon acquired the name 'ukulele, or "jumping flea." According to one popular account, this was the nickname of Edward Purvis, one of King Kalākaua's chamberlains—a small and nimble Englishman who enthralled the court nobles with his artistry on the *braguinha*.

Within ten years, the 'ukulele reached the west coast of the United States spreading onward via traveling musicians, the Buffalo Exposition of 1901, vaudeville, and returning tourists. By the time of the 1915 San Francisco Exposition, "The thing [that] makes a sweet jingle somewhat as fetching as the melody of mandolins . . ."

(cited in Kanahele, 1979, p. 400) had become a fad. Popularity waned in the 1920's, but entertainers such as Cliff "Ukulele Ike" Edwards in the 1930's and Arthur Godfrey in the 1950's created momentary bursts of enthusiasm for the musical idiom that had now encircled the world.

This unusual violin-shaped 'ukulele, richly decorated with pearl-shell inlay, was made in the 1930's by David Mahelona, one of the lesser known instrument makers of Hawai'i.

Symbols of Sovereignty
Featherwork

Feather cloaks, capes, and helmets were sacred insignia of the highest chiefs of Hawai'i. As battle uniforms and robes of state, their "beauty and magnificence," to use Captain James King's words in 1779, were "perhaps nearly equal to that of any nation in the world" (Cook and King, 1784, Vol 3, p. 136).

Early Polynesian immigrants probably introduced a reverence for red feathers as symbolic representations of their gods and chiefs, and later Hawaiians elaborated the concept by adding the precious yellow feathers of two endemic birds to their featherwork. Nineteenth-century Hawaiians referred literally to all full-length and shorter capes, regardless of color, as "red shoulder garments," or 'ahu'ula, doubtless a reflection of these ancient Polynesian connections.

In Cook's day, Hawaiians made cloaks and capes in a surprising variety of styles and shapes, using differing techniques of manufacture. While the district of origin or owner's rank and status seemingly influenced the appearance of pre-European capes and cloaks, such items became much more standardized by the early 19th century. Rectangular capes of sea bird and other coarse feathers seen by early visitors soon disappeared, replaced by circular ones with flat or shaped collars and made predominantly from red and yellow feathers.

Except for a few early or very late examples, most 'ahu'ula are made from the tiny feathers of four or five indigenous forest birds. Most important are the red 'i'iwi (see No. 190) and 'apapane, and two black birds called 'ō'ō (see No. 191) and mamo, which have tufts of yellow under the wings, tail, or thighs. With such raw materials to work with, it is no wonder that Cook compared the brilliant cloaks "to the thickest and richest velvet . . . both as to the feel, and the glossy appearance" (Cook and King, 1784, Vol. 2, p. 206).

Because of their restriction to male chiefs of high rank exclusively, feather garments were made by men working under rigid ceremonial restrictions. Professional bird hunters (po'e hahai manu) captured the birds using sticky bird lime, nets, and other devices—releasing the 'ō'ō and mamo after plucking the sparse yellow feathers, but killing and often eating the 'i'iwi and 'apapane, which had so many red feathers they would not have survived plucking. Once selected and cleaned, a dozen or so feathers were bound into a cluster with fine olonā bast thread, then the clusters were tied in overlapping rows to the meshes of a fine netted foundation made from twisted fibers of the same plant. A painstaking and time-consuming task, it is estimated that some half-million feathers representing 80,000 to 90,000 birds were required to complete the famous all-mamo cloak of Kamehameha the Great, since each mamo yields only six or seven suitable feathers. It is obvious that only great chiefs could have accumulated the wealth necesssary to commission or acquire major items of featherwork.

Besides capes, cloaks, and helmets, Hawaiians also produced feather-covered images (see No. 24), lei, kāhili, and more esoteric items. Brilliantly colored feather chaplets, or lei, were worn by aristocratic women as personal ornaments for the hair or neck, and heirlooms are still to be seen at appropriate social functions. Although traditional capes and cloaks ceased to be manufactured long ago, lei are still made in great numbers and variety, both in the old circular form and in the newer flat style used for hat decorations. Dyed feathers of domestic fowl and various exotic birds, such as pheasant or mallard duck, have replaced the indigenous species, however, many of which are either extinct or endangered.

Kāhili, sometimes likened to segments of a rainbow standing on a shaft, were important symbols of royalty used by both men and women. They were borne in processions of chiefs, such as at funerals, or set up at royal residences during ceremonies. Attaining heights in excess of 20 feet, large kāhili were dismantled when not in use, and the individual feather branches comprising the crown, or hulumanu, were carefully preserved in large storage calabashes until needed again. Throughout the 19th century, kāhili remained an important embellishment of royalty and many innovative features of construction and decoration were devised to reflect changing tastes of the Victorian era.

Before Hawaiian chiefly tradition had been greatly changed by missionary influence, the Reverend C. S. Steward (1828, pp. 117-118) witnessed an impressive state procession in May, 1823, commemorating the late Kamehameha I. "So far as the feather mantles, helmets, coronets [lei] and kahilis," he wrote, "I doubt whether there is a nation in Christendom which . . . could have presented a *court dress* and insignia of rank so magnificent as these . . . There is something approaching the *sublime* in the lofty noddings of the kahilis of state as they tower far above the heads of the groups whose distinction they proclaim: something conveying to the mind impressions of greater majesty than the gleamings of the most splendid banners I ever saw unfurled."

165. Boki and Liliha, by John Hayter (1800-1891)

Oil on fabric
56 × 71 cm.
Loaned by The Kamehameha Schools, courtesy of Mr. and Mrs. John Dominis Holt
Color Plate XXIV

High chief Boki, Governor of O'ahu, and his wife Liliha were among the royal suite that accompanied King Kamehameha II and Queen Kamāmalu to London in 1823-1824, where the handsome couple posed for one of the most important portrait painters of the day. Boki is attired in a feather helmet and cloak, while Liliha wears a feathered head *lei* and necklace of braided human hair with ivory pendant. Her skirt of intricately printed bark cloth is a reminder that women traditionally were not permitted to wear featherwork other than head or neck *lei*.

166. Man Wearing Hawaiian Featherwork, unknown artist.

Oil on fabric
76.2 × 63.2 cm.
Bequest of Helen Irwin Fagan, 1967
Not illustrated

The circumstances of this painting are unknown, but its romantic style and classical pose epitomize the 19th-century sentimental view of Hawai'i. The subject appears to be Caucasian and undoubtedly a live model was used, perhaps selected to represent the artist's own fanciful concept of the appearance of a Hawaiian chief. Details of the featherwork indicate that actual specimens were copied, but they have yet to be identified among surviving examples. The helmet resembles, but is not identical to, one in the Peabody Museum of Harvard collected before 1841, probably from Maui or Hawai'i.

167. Man from the Sandwich Islands with Feathered Helmet, Helmet Band, and Cape, by John Webber (1751-1793)

Watercolor, c. 1780
44 × 31.5 cm.
Gift of Mrs. A. W. F. Fuller in memory of her husband, 1963. Formerly in the Edge-Partington Collection
Color Plate XXV

Webber's bearded Hawaiian wears a feather helmet surmounted by a low and wide crest, similar to certain ones known from late 18th-century Kaua'i. The separate helmet band, rare today in museum collections, "gives the whole headdress the appearance of a rich and elegant Turband," as Surgeon Samwell (Beaglehole, 1967, Vol. 3, Pt. 2, p. 1231) remarked during Cook's voyage in 1778-1779. His cape of long black feathers bordered by narrow bands of red and yellow was common enough in the late 18th century, but the type soon gave way to ones made entirely of red and yellow feathers.

168. Feather Helmet, *mahiole*

'Ie'ie aerial rootlets, olonā cordage, red 'i'iwi, yellow 'ō'ō and black feathers.
L. 42.5 cm. H. 25.5 cm. W. 17.2 cm.
Hawaiian National Museum Collection, 1891 (959)
Color Plate XXVI

Kamehameha I is believed to have given this beautifully preserved helmet to King Kaumuali'i of Kaua'i in 1810, when Kamehameha subdued Kaua'i by peaceful conquest and united the Hawaiian Islands for the first time under one ruler. It is the only feather helmet whose former ownership is definitely known.

Following Kamehameha's death, Kaumuali'i was summoned to Honolulu in 1822 to marry Ka'ahumanu, one of the conqueror's widows. Held a virtual prisoner of state, he died there on May 26, 1824, his former island passing to the Kamehameha dynasty. His helmet was preserved in the home of the Reverend Samuel Whitney of Kaua'i and was acquired by the Hawaiian National Museum at the Whitney estate auction in 1873. It has not been seen outside Hawai'i since it was exhibited by the Hawaiian government at the Paris *Exposition Universelle* of 1889.

Hawaiian historian Samuel Kamakau (1961, p. 254) wrote about 1868:

Ka-umu-ali'i was a handsome man, light in complexion and with a nose and general features like a white man's. He was rather slight in build, but he had a good carriage and dressed well. He was gentle in temper, spoke English well, was kind and simple in his ways. It would be well for the nation if there were more chiefs like him.

169. Feather Cloak, *'ahu'ula*

Yellow 'ō'ō, yellow mamo, and red 'i'iwi feathers, olonā cordage and netting
L. 164 cm. W. 248 cm.
Gift of the Provisional Government of Hawai'i, 1893 (6829)

Many chiefs of high rank went into battle wearing feather cloaks and helmets, which became spoils for the victor in case of death. This cloak belonged to Kiwala'ō, son of Kalani'ōpu'u (see No. 3), the high chief of Hawai'i at the time of Cook's visit in 1779. Kiwala'ō, the rightful successor to the chieftainship, was killed by Kamehameha's ally, Ke'eaumoku, at the battle of Moku'ōhai in 1782, during struggles for supremacy then engulfing the island. His ambitious cousin Kamehameha took the cloak as a battle prize, then went on to usurp Kiwala'ō's place as paramount chief by military conquest.

170. Feather Cloak, 'ahu'ula

Red 'i'iwi, yellow 'o'o, yellow mamo feathers, olonā
cordage and netting
L. 1612 cm. W. 291 cm.
Purchase from Mrs. C. H. Joy, 1912 (11,094)
Color Plate XXVII

One of the largest known, this cloak must have belonged
to a chief of imposing stature, since Hawaiian
featherwork was never allowed to drag on the ground.
Collected in August, 1789, during the voyage of the
Columbia Rediviva, the first American ship to
circumnavigate the globe, it was taken to Boston and
worn by a young Hawaiian named Attoo—the so-called
"Prince of Kaua'i," who walked down the streets
"looking like a living flame." The cloak acquired its
present name after falling into the hands of the Joy
family, who at one time had lined it with green fabric for
a sleigh robe.

The Joy cloak is one of two known with yellow disks
on a red background. Most cloaks and capes have
triangular or crescent designs in various configurations,
which have no known or decipherable meanings.

171. Feather Cloak, 'ahu'ula

Red 'i'iwi, yellow 'o'o, and black feathers, olonā cordage
and netting
L. 143 cm. W. 244 cm.
Deposited by Walter F. Dillingham, 1927 (C.9558)
Color Plate XXVIII

King Kamehameha III gave this cloak to Commodore
Lawrence Kearny of the U.S. frigate *Constellation* in
1843—a token of appreciation for his help during Lord
George Paulet's temporary occupation of the islands.

Forced to cede his Kingdom to Britain earlier that
year, Kamehameha III was greatly relieved when Kearny
arrived in July to protest the act by diplomatic means,
and by hoisting the outlawed Hawaiian flag from his
foredeck. A few days later Admiral Thomas arrived to
revoke the provisional cession on behalf of the British
government, and Hawaiian independence was formally
restored on July 31, 1843. It was on this occasion that
Kamehameha III uttered his now-famous words, "The life
of the land is perpetuated in righteousness."

A replica of this cloak made by the King Kamehameha
Civic Club was dedicated by its president in 1975 as "a
living symbol of Hawaiian culture and arts that are not
dead" (*Honolulu Advertiser*, Nov. 3, 1975).

172. Feather Cape, 'ahu'ula

Red 'i'iwi, yellow 'o'o, and black feathers, olonā cordage
and netting, cotton, thread
L. 70 cm. W. 110 cm.
Kapi'olani-Kalaniana'ole Collection, 1923 (B.7236)
Not illustrated

This exceptionally large cape with split crescents darting
like lightning across a field of red is named for
Kekaulike-nui, a celebrated chief of Maui who died in the
early 18th century. Of probable 19th century manufacture,

it was given by Lot Kamehameha (later King
Kamehameha V) in 1857 to E. Faulkner, paymaster of
H.M.S. *Havannah*. Queen Kapi'olani purchased the cape
in London in 1887 for $600 while attending Queen
Victoria's Golden Jubilee, and apparently bestowed the
name herself in honor of her sister Kekaulike and of the
famed chief, whose distant relationship to her family she
sought to publicize. The name is perpetuated among
Kapi'olani's collateral descendants.

173. Feather Cape, 'ahu'ula

Yellow 'o'o and red 'i'iwi feathers, olonā cordage and
netting
L. 50 cm. W. 82 cm.
Kapi'olani-Kalaniana'ole Collection, 1923 (B.7234)
Color Plate XXIX

In exchange for a royal decoration, Honolulu resident
Henry Riemenschneider gave this cape to King Kalākaua
after having acquired it at Mercy P. Whitney's estate
auction in 1873. With the feather helmet (No. 168), it is
said to have been a gift from Kamehameha I in 1810 to
Kaumuali'i, the maternal grandfather of Queen
Kapi'olani. This is sometimes called the second
Kaumuali'i cape, one other of similar history having
survived.

174. Feather Cape, 'ahu'ula

Yellow 'o'o, red 'i'iwi and black feathers, olonā cordage
and netting
L. 64 cm. W. 108 cm.
Gift of Evangeline Priscilla Starbuck, 1927 (C.208)
Color Plate XXX

Kamehameha II took this cape to London in 1823, intent
on an audience with George IV regarding a possible
British protectorate over his Kingdom. The visiting King
died before the audience could be arranged, and the cape
was given to Captain Valentine Starbuck, who had
carried the royal suite to England aboard *L'Aigle*. Of
unique checkerboard design, the cape had belonged to
the dead King's father, Kamehameha I.

175. Feather Cape

Peacock, mallard duck, parrot, chicken, and other feathers,
linen, thread
L. 57 cm. W. 71 cm.
Gift of Mrs. A. W. F. Fuller, 1964 (1964.19.01)

The royal visit to London in 1824 rekindled an interest in
Hawaiian featherwork first stirred in 1780 when some 50
or more capes, cloaks, helmets, *lei*, and other objects
were taken to England on Cook's third Pacific voyage.
When Kamehameha II's entourage suddenly appeared 45
years later dressed conspicuously in their own feather
regalia, fashionable ladies emulated the style by wearing
capes such as this one to soirées and other social affairs.
It is an interesting example of the colorful, but brief,
influence the Hawaiian visitors exerted on English
fashion of the day.

176. Feather Cape, *'ahu'ula*

Red 'apapane, black, and dyed yellow feathers, cotton netting, olonā, thread, rayon
L. 44 cm. W. 70 cm.
Lucy K. Peabody, Kalani and Edgar Henriques Collection, 1932 (D. 4579)

Feather cloaks and capes ceased to be made by the middle of the 19th century, when bird-catching and featherworking skills largely disappeared. Since many of the older pieces had been given away, sold to outsiders, or lost, capes had to be manufactured anew using experimental techniques and materials when elements of Hawaiian culture were revived after King Kalākaua ascended the throne in 1874. The design and color of this cape are typical of earlier 19th-century styles, but the rarely used *'apapane* and dyed feathers are tied to imported cotton netting sewn to a fabriclike backing, a transitional step in the revival of cape-making.

177. Feather Cape, *'ahu'ula*

Dyed red and yellow duck feathers, black chicken feathers, mattress ticking, cotton, satin, thread, linen braid
L. 68 cm. W. 57 cm.
Purchase from Elizabeth Kalaniana'ole Woods Estate, 1935 (HH 741)
Color Plate XXXI

At least a dozen capes nearly identical to this one in pattern, color, and craftsmanship exist, apparently relics of King Kalākaua's attempt to revitalize ancient science and lore through the semisecret Hale Nauā Society he founded in 1886. Unfortunately, few details survive concerning their use, but capes made entirely of cloth figured prominently in pageants and parades during the early 20th century. It is apparent that skilled hands have carefully arranged the dyed feathers in familiar patterns and colors, even though materials and technique of manufacture differ radically from traditional capes.

178. Feather Lei, *lei hulu*

Yellow 'ō'ō, red 'i'iwi feathers, cordage, thread, grosgrain ribbon
L. 51 cm. D. 4.3 cm.
Kapi'olani-Kalaniana'ole Collection, 1923 (B.7432)
Color Plate XXXII

Single color *lei* of yellow feathers were considered the most valuable, such as this full and rich example made from *'ō'ō* rump feathers. It is accented with a tinge of red at each end and fitted with modern ties. Many older *lei* have been refurbished with newer materials so they could continue to be worn.

179. Feather Lei, *lei pani'o,* or *lei 'oni*

Red Vini kuhli, red 'i'iwi, yellow 'ō'ō, and dyed red and yellow feathers, cordage, thread, wool, yarn, velvet ribbon
L. 36.5 cm. D. 3.8 cm.
Purchase from the Ward Estate, 1962 (D.2620)
Color Plates XXXII and XXXIV

Spiral designs, called *pani'o* or *'oni*, were difficult to make, and therefore treasured for their artistry. Each color had to be carefully laid out as the feather clusters were tied, a few at a time, to the stiff inner core, working upward from one end. Dyed and natural feathers have been mixed in this late 19th-century *lei*, which also includes feathers from a red and green lorikeet (*Vini kuhli*) native to the Polynesian islands south of the Hawaiian chain.

180. Feather Lei, *lei paukū*

Yellow mamo, black 'ō'ō, and dyed yellow and black feathers, cordage, thread, wool yarn, satin ribbon
L. 51.9 cm. D. 3.5 cm.
Purchase from the Ward Estate, 1962 (D.2631)
Color Plate XXXII

Simpler to make, banded *lei* are about three times more common than spiral ones, and two-color patterns predominate. Here, five of the eleven yellow bands or "links" (*paukū*) are dyed, while the black feathers are a combination of natural and dyed.

181. Feather Lei, *lei paukū*

Yellow and green Vini kuhli feathers, cordage, thread, wool yarn, rayon ribbon
L. 54.8 cm. D. 3 cm.
Princess Ka'iulani Collection, 1911 (10,386)
Color Plates XXXII and XXXIII

The neatly made fringed yarn terminus found on some 19th-century *lei* provides a handy method of finishing the *lei* and concealing the feather shafts and bindings at the working end. Particularly common in the Ka'iulani Collection, the technique probably marks the work of a single feather artist.

182. Feather Lei, *lei paukū*

Black 'ō'ō, red 'i'iwi and Vini kuhli feathers, cordage, thread, wool yarn, rayon ribbon.
L. 53.2 cm. D. 1.8 cm.
Princess Ka'iulani Collection, 1911 (10,385)
Color Plate XXXII

183. Feather Lei, *lei kāmoe*

Yellow 'ō'ō, red 'i'iwi, green Vini kuhli feathers, cordage, thread, satin ribbon
L. 63 cm. D. 1.8 cm.
Acquired before 1892 (2824)
Color Plate XXXII

Lei with the feathers tightly folded together were likened to a rope and called *kāmoe* from the word *moe*, meaning "to sleep."

184. Feather Hat Lei, *lei papa*

> *Dyed yellow rooster feathers, paper, cotton, thread, glue*
> *L. 58.7 cm. W. 10 cm.*
> *Acquired before 1892 (5099)*
> *Color Plate XXXV*

When the wearing of European style hats made of plaited coconut leaf and other materials became popular in the mid-19th century, feather *lei* were "flattened" out and adapted for use as colorful hat bands. This early example still retains a fullness reminiscent of the traditional circular variety, although the feathers are sewn to only one side of a flat paper and cloth backing, rather than tied around a sturdy fiber core.

185. Feather Hat Lei, *lei papa*

> *Peacock feathers, wool, thread*
> *L. 64 cm. W. 5.7 cm.*
> *Bequest of Helen Irwin Fagan, 1967 (HH 1961)*
> *Color Plate XXXVI*

This is a fine example of overlap patterning that can be achieved by careful placement of individual feather elements—in this case the central iridescent "eyes" of peacock tail feathers.

186. Feather Hat Lei, *lei papa*

> *Ringneck pheasant feathers, wool, thread*
> *L. 66.5 cm. W. 4.6 cm.*
> *Bequest of Helen Irwin Fagan, 1967 (HH 1972)*
> *Color Plate XXXVII*

187. Feather Hat Lei, *lei papa*

> *Ringneck pheasant feathers, wool, thread*
> *L. 65.5 cm. W. 3.4 cm.*
> *Bequest of Helen Irwin Fagan, 1967 (HH 1965)*
> *Color Plate XXXVIII, top*

188. Feather Hat Lei, *lei papa*

> *Ringneck pheasant feathers, wool, thread*
> *L. 66.5 cm. W. 3.2 cm*
> *Bequest of Helen Irwin Fagan, 1967 (HH 1955)*
> *Color Plate XXXVIII, center*

189. Feather Hat Lei, *lei papa*

> *Ringneck pheasant feathers, wool, thread*
> *L. 65 cm. W. 3 cm.*
> *Gift of Jon and Howard C. Wiig in memory of Howard E. Wiig, 1975 (1975.265)*
> *Color Plate XXXVIII, bottom*

"God created beautiful birds for a purpose and why not make use of them?" Johanna Cluney (1895-1978) once asked rhetorically in summing up her long career as a feather artist. In this *lei*, she used the iridescent blue-green neck feathers of some 150 to 200 birds, accented with six tiny bands or "points" of white.

A part-Hawaiian herself, she learned the art in the 1930's from an elderly Hawaiian lady who taught her to select, wash, and dry feathers of many different kinds. "I tell a story with my needle and thread," Cluney told a reporter for the *Honolulu Advertiser* (February 22, 1978) shortly before her death. "The feather leis that I make are the symbols of the expert toil of people of long ago, of leis that decorated chiefess's heads, of magnificent cloaks and helmets that warrior chiefs wore into battle." Johanna Cluney is regarded by many as the savior of the once nearly extinct art of feather *lei* making.

190. Mounted 'I'iwi

> *L. 14 cm. female*
> *Collected by A. Koeble, 1894 (BBM 7214-A)*
> *Not illustrated*

191. Mounted 'Ō'o

> *L. 32 cm.*
> *Collected by James D. Mills, c. 1859 (BBM-5)*
> *Not illustrated*

One of four species of *'o'o* known in the Hawaiian chain, this species from Hawai'i island is thought to have become extinct just after the turn of the present century. Even though Kamehameha I is reputed to have advocated their conservation—"The feathers belong to me, but the birds themselves belong to my heirs"—they fell victim to a combination of introduced pests and excessive hunting (Berger, 1972, p. 119).

192. Kāhili, with Stand

> *Ostrich and tropic bird feathers, turtle shell, walrus ivory, wood, olonā cordage, wooden splints, string, satin ribbon (modern)*
> *H. 278 cm. D. 54 cm.*
> *Queen Emma Collection, 1886 (30)*
> *Not illustrated*

Important *kāhili* were named, and many came in pairs. This and a mate, also made of imported ostrich feathers in somber 19th-century funerary black, are named Kaleoaloha, "The-Voice-of-Aloha." The shaft is made in the traditional manner of alternating segments of ivory and thin turtle shell disks slipped over a supple wooden pole. The *kāhili* was apparently assembled for Queen Emma's funeral in May, 1885.

193. Kāhili, with Stand

> *Albatross, tropic bird, and dyed red rooster feathers, ash, brass, tin, olonā cordage, wooden splints, satin (modern)*
> *H. 275 cm. D. 40 cm.*
> *Acquired before 1892 (9)*
> *Not illustrated*

Ka'ulaho'anolani, "The-Red-Awe-of-Heaven," was given by the *hapa haole*, or half castes, of Honolulu to the Prince of Hawai'i to celebrate his birth on May 20, 1858 (see Nos. 233 and 234). The imported wood shaft is sheathed in alternating metal sections to represent silver and gold, befitting the status of the only son of Queen Emma and King Kamehameha IV. When the original crown of imported red feathers disintegrated, the *kāhili* was refurbished with albatross feathers from the guano islands in the Leeward Hawaiian chain so it could be presented to Bishop Museum.

194 a, b. Pair of Hand Kāhili

Ringneck pheasant, dyed red and white duck feathers, wood, walrus ivory, cardboard, wire, thread, wooden splints, seized cotton, red paint.
a: L. 117 cm. D. 20 cm. (63)
b: L. 113 cm. D. 20 cm. (64)
Acquired before 1892

Hand *kāhili* were in constant use in aristocratic households—originally as fly-flaps to stir the air, but by the 19th century to signify the presence of royalty. This pair has matching handles of turned native woods tipped with ivory, an innovation by late 19th-century cabinet makers. The white and dyed red duck feathers are pasted to cloth-covered cardboard cones and tops in patterns reminiscent of older feather capes and cloaks.

195. Hand Kāhili

Black 'ō'ō, white goose and dyed duck feathers, turtle shell, walrus ivory, wood, cardboard, seized cotton, wooden splints, wire, thread, satin ribbon (modern)
H. 122 cm. D. 30 cm.
Acquired before 1892 (55)
Not illustrated

Retaining the traditional ivory and turtle shell handle, this *kāhili* has an inner core of white goose feathers skillfully arranged to conceal the lashings of the branched and layered feather stalks forming the crown. Brightly dyed feathers glued in geometric patterns to the cone and cap are a distinctive Victorian feature of many late 19th-century *kāhili*.

196. Hand Kāhili

Tern, yellow and black feathers, gold, ivory, wood, onyx, thread, silk ribbon
H. 85 cm.
Gift of Lili'uokalani Estate, 1924 (B.7544)

Split and curled feathers, black on one side and white on the other, give this small hand *kāhili* a supple and delicate appearance. The riding crop handle bears a likeness of the Hawaiian crown over the word Dominis, Lili'uokalani's married name. She married John O. Dominis, son of a Croatian sea captain and Bostonian mother, in 1862.

Chiefly Ornaments

Hawaiians possessed a richer variety of adornments for the body than other Polynesians. Besides facial and body tattoo, they wore ornaments of feathers, ivory, teeth, bone, seeds, and shells—not to mention numerous *lei* strung or woven from flowers and fragrant leaves for festive occasions. After European contact, wealthy Hawaiians added trade beads to their stock of personal ornaments, in time adopting the full assortment of precious and semiprecious gems and metals so highly prized by Westerners.

The most valuable ornament was and still is the *lei niho palaoa*, a hook-shaped pendant traditionally worn by men and women of chiefly rank. Sometimes likened to a tongue—or an extension of the chin-mouth-tongue configuration rendered in abstract sculpture—prototypes of the *niho palaoa* were probably introduced by early immigrants from Polynesia, where whale tooth pendants of one form or another were widely distributed throughout the ancestral homeland.

Early versions of the Hawaiian hook pendant exist in coral, shell, calcite, and other substances, but the preferred material was whale ivory. The scarce resource was obtained from the teeth (*niho*) of beached sperm whales (*palaoa*), which were claimed by chiefs on whose beaches they occasionally foundered. As Hawaiians ventured into colder northern waters on whaling vessels in the late 18th century, they encountered the walrus, adding its previously unknown tusks to their scant reserves of whale ivory. With more dependable sources of raw material, the small pendants that formerly averaged no more than two or three inches long soon developed into the larger version familiar today. The trend toward "gigantism," abetted by technological improvements and introduced metal tools, helped create and sustain a market for the distinctive ornament. The standardized form that evolved by the early 19th century became an object for exchange to visiting Europeans, as well as a status symbol aspired to by Hawaiians of all classes.

The symbolism conveyed by the *niho palaoa* has long been a source of debate. Lucia Jensen (1977), historian for the Hale Nauā III Society of Hawaiian Artists, suggests: "They represent the embryonic form, shaped in a crescent, the ho'aka (crescent), which again symbolized the vessel of mana. Those who ruled wore the lei niho palaoa in remembrance of their solemn birthright. The crescent is turned upwards, allowing the imaginary continuing line of the design to create a complete circle with the downward crescent of the helmet or top of the head. Within this circle or vessel is contained the mana and aura, the essence of the ali'i."

Whatever interpretation one chooses, the *niho palaoa* persists as a symbol of birthright for the Hawaiian people. "We still possess the blood that allows us and only us the possession of the lei niho palaoa" Jensen continues. "We are not dead, our culture is not dead."

197. Hook Pendant on Human Hair Necklace, *lei niho palaoa*

Walrus ivory, human hair, olonā cordage
H. 9.3 cm. W. 3.2 cm. Th. 5.6 cm. (hook)
Gift of Lili'uokalani, 1910 (1910.18.09)
Color Plate XXXIX

The usual method of wearing the *niho palaoa* in the early 19th century was suspended from thick coils of braided human hair. Consisting of more than 300 strands of eight-ply square braid, this typical example averages 50 to 90 hairs per strand. Relatively few strands pass through the perforated shank, the remainder forming continuous loops held together by partly concealed *olona* cords that emerge from the top to form the ties. The pendant is walrus ivory, recognizable by its characteristic mottled and slightly crystalline core.

198. Hook Pendant, *niho palaoa*

Fossilized rock oyster
H. 4.8 cm. W. 1.7 cm. Th. 2.9 cm.
Bellows Air Force Base Collection, 1967 (1967.302.02)

Excavated from an early site at Bellows Beach, O'ahu, this *niho palaoa* is believed to be about 1,000 years old, if the stratigraphic evidence has been accurately interpreted. Lacking the suspension hole, it appears to be unfinished, even though the form itself is otherwise remarkably similar to the *niho palaoa* of the late 18th century. Before this site was excavated, the classic *niho palaoa* shape was considered a relatively late development in Hawaiian culture.

199. Hook Pendant, *niho palaoa*

Elephant ivory
H. 16.2 cm. W. 6.4 cm. Th. 9.3 cm.
Hawaiian National Museum Collection, 1891 (1287)
Color Plate XL

More than three times the size of the average pre-European *niho palaoa*, this unusual example was no doubt a special presentation piece. Elephant ivory was unknown until trade with the Orient developed toward the end of the 18th century, and the few pieces that managed to reach Hawai'i were evidently very highly regarded. Taking advantage of imported steel tools, the artist has copied the form and proportions of the smaller pieces with unsurpassed skill. Note that the circular suspension hole has been drilled with a metal bit.

200. Hook Pendant, *niho palaoa*

Whale ivory, velvet
H. 3.5 cm. W. 1.6 cm Th. 2.0 cm. (hook)
Gift of Mrs. R. G. Peterson, in memory of her mother, Louise King Dods, 1969 (1969.67.05)

The small size and rectangular perforation suggest pre-European manufacture for this whale tooth pendant. Like many heirloom *niho palaoa*, it has been refitted for use in the 20th century, in this case with a velvet ribbon tie.

201. Hook Pendant, *niho palaoa*

Whale ivory, turtle shell, wood or metal pins
H. 6.5 cm. W. 2.2 cm. Th. 3.8 cm.
Acquired before 1892 (4925)

Very few composite *niho palaoa* are known, even though Hawaiian craftsmen were expert at laminating turtle shell and ivory rings for *kāhili* handles, bracelets, and similar objects. Apparently they encountered difficulty in pegging diverse materials that could not be slipped over a wooden core or held with cordage. Since the "tongue" of this example is slightly larger than the shaft at the joint of juncture, it may have been fitted to a broken pendant.

202. Hook Pendant, *niho palaoa*

Wood
H. 5 cm. W. 1.4 cm. Th. 2.5 cm.
Kapi'olani-Kalaniana'ole Collection, 1923 (B.6988)

Although pendants were occasionally made of wood, the material was never so highly valued as ivory and fell into disuse as imported walrus tusks became plentiful. When King Kalākaua attempted to revive elements of traditional material culture in the 1880's, however, ivory had become so scarce that wood was once again an acceptable substitute. Literally dozens of wooden pendants were manufactured in a somewhat simplified version of the classic *niho palaoa* shape, many being acquired by members of the King's Hale Naua Society.

203. Hook Pendant on Bead Necklace, *lei niho palaoa*

Walrus and whale ivory, glass, cotton string
H. 7.9 cm. W. 3 cm. Th. 4.6 cm. (hook)
Lucy K. Peabody, Kalani and Edgar Henriques Collection, 1932 (C.5825)
Color Plate XLI

Ivory beads were made in pre-European Hawai'i, but their manufacture was greatly stimulated by introduced European drills and cutting implements. This necklace combines four faceted beads drilled with metal tools, 16 trade beads, and a walrus ivory pendant that has the traditional rectangular perforation. Necklaces with trade beads were prized by early 19th-century chiefly women who had the means to obtain them.

204. Hook Pendant on Bead Necklace, *lei niho palaoa*

Whale and walrus ivory, glass, cotton string
H. 8.5 cm. W. 3.5 cm. Th. 4.8 cm. (hook)
Gift of Ruth Ellen Patton Totten, 1959 (D.2162)
Not illustrated

According to the donor, "This lei palaoa was given to my Mother, Beatrice Ayer Patton, by Emma Ahuena Taylor, in 1937, after her book *Blood of the Shark* was published. She said, 'It is the symbol of the tongue and I am giving it to you because you have spoken for my people.'" The beads are drilled with a metal bit, but the whale ivory pendant has the square perforation indicative of earlier manufacture.

205. Ivory Necklace, *lei palaoa*

Walrus and whale ivory, olonā *cordage*
H. 4.3 cm. W. 4.2 cm. Th. 2.9 cm. (kupe'e)
Bequest of Lili'uokalani, 1921 (D.2774)

206. Boar Tusk Bracelet, *kūpe'e ho'okalakala*

H. 8.2 cm. D. 12.7 cm.
Purchase from William Wagner, 1907 (9076)

Bracelets made from boar tusks, matched according to size and strung with their tips pointing in one direction, were collected by Cook's men in 1778-1779, but few were to be seen by 19th-century voyagers. They were presumably worn exclusively by men, since pig flesh itself was forbidden to women before the *kapu* system was overthrown in 1819. This bracelet comes from the same burial chamber that yielded two of the wooden images displayed in this exhibition (see also Nos. 29 and 30).

207. Boar Tusk Anklet, *kūpe'e hoaka*

H. 2.1 cm. D. 7.2 cm.
Bellows Air Force Base Collection, 1967 (1967.302.01)

Although it resembles an ordinary bracelet of trimmed and shaped boar tusks, this object was excavated from a burial at Bellows Beach, O'ahu, believed to date to A.D. 800-1000. It was found around the articulated left lower leg of an individual tentatively regarded as female and about 9 years of age. Similar ornaments of turtle shell, ivory, and boar tusk were still being worn on the arm when Cook visited in 1778-1779. (See also No. 198.)

208. Turtle Shell Bracelet, *kūpe'e 'ea*

Turtle shell, boar tusk, bone, olonā *cordage, coconut sennit (modern)*
H. 6.3 cm. D. 10 cm.
Bernice Pauahi Bishop Collection, 1884 (1304)
Color Plate XLII

One of a pair presumed to have descended in the Kamehameha family, this is undoubtedly one of the most remarkable Hawaiian ornaments in existence. It possesses an elegance of proportion and harmony of color surpassed only by the maker's sense of imagination. The projecting skull-like figures have mischievous, almost whimsical expressions that remind one of the support figures carved on certain wooden bowls.

209. Ivory Wristlet, *kūpe'e palaoa*

Walrus ivory
H. 6.7 cm. W. 4.3 cm. Th. 1.9 cm.
Bequest of Lili'uokalani, 1921 (1921.14.14)

A much more common variety of wrist ornament was made from small or leftover pieces of whale tooth and walrus tusk. Carved into eliptical or oval shapes of various size, they were tied over the wrist by means of braided cords, bark cloth, or ribbons drawn through paired holes on the underside. Popular throughout the

19th century, such ornaments were prized for their rich golden color and intricate grain as much as for their imaginative shape. The color was often achieved or enhanced artifically—in one method by steaming over pieces of sugar cane on a fire of coals (Buck, 1957, p. 553).

210. Ivory Wristlet, *kūpe'e palaoa*

Walrus ivory
H. 2.6 cm. W. 1.7 cm. Th. 1.4 cm.
Kapi'olani-Kalaniana'ole Collection, 1923 (B.6769)
Color Plate XLIII

Occasionally ivory wristlets were carved to imitate the *Nerita polita* marine shell, which Hawaiians called *pipipi*. This particularly realistic example even has the small spiral whorl carved on the correct side of the shell. It would have been threaded on a ribbon or other appropriate band and worn on the outer wrist.

211. Basalt Mirror, *kilo pōhaku*

D. 8.9 cm. Th. 1 cm.
Gift of Lili'uokalani, 1910 (1910.18.13)

When moistened or placed under water in a coconut cup or other shallow vessel, polished basalt disks served as mirrors. Some with rim perforations may also have been suspended from a cord and worn around the neck as ornaments. According to Lili'uokalani, this one is said to have belonged to Keawe, a late 17th-century paramount chief of Hawai'i, from whom all 19th-century kings of the Kamehameha and Kalākaua dynasties claimed descent.

212. Mirror, *aniani kilohi*

Walrus ivory, mirror glass, paper, glue
H. 5.8 cm. W. 10.8 cm. Th. 2 cm.
Gift of Lili'uokalani, 1910 (1910.18.15)

Among the first items to be obtained in trade from visiting Europeans, glass mirrors were immensely popular possessions. Ordinary glass or shards of broken mirrors were sometimes mounted in carved wood or ivory frames, often with perforated lugs for wearing around the neck. This distinctive example is said by Lili'uokalani to have belonged to Keōpūolani, wife of Kamehameha I and the mother of Kings Kamehameha II and Kamehameha III.

213. Comb, *kahi*

Whale ivory
H. 8.6 cm. W. 3.5 cm. Th. 3.6 cm.
Purchase from Helen Street Ranney, 1945 (C.9646)

While combs in Polynesia were ordinarily made from dried pieces of coconut leaflet or some other similar material, Hawaiians occasionally carved more elegant ones from ivory. Given to missionary Dr. Rufus Anderson in 1863, this comb is clearly patterned after the *niho palaoa* ornament, much as the lugs and handles on certain Hawaiian calabashes have been fashioned.

The Kamehameha Dynasty

Kamehameha the Great was a remarkable man, by any standard of history. Born about 1758, he was already an experienced and ambitious warrior when Cook met him briefly in 1779. Described as arrogant and "savage looking" (his hair was coated with brownish paste), yet good natured, well built, and possessing a sense of humor, "The Lonely One" was still a subordinate chief facing an uncertain future. Some 20 years of military conquest lay ahead of him before he would emerge a living legend in the Pacific as unifier of the islands under one government. Shrewd and autocratic, he refused to depart from the traditions and religion of his ancestors, even though painfully aware that the dynasty he had established must eventually face the political and economic realities of contact with the Western world.

Kamehameha the Great died on May 8, 1819, and within months the old religion was overthrown, ushering in a new era. The government passed to his son Liholiho (Kamehameha II), a weak and ineffective man who died in London in 1824 before facing the challenge of rule. His younger brother succeeded to the throne a minor, biding his time under the firm regency of high chiefess Ka'ahumanu until taking full control of the government in 1833. Twenty-one years of progressive rule followed—first a period of benevolent autocracy leading to the first Constitution of 1840, then gradual development of monarchical government culminating in a new and liberalized Constitution in 1852. Land reforms occurred too, and in the Great *Mahele* or "Division" of 1848, the Kingdom was apportioned into unequal tracts for the chiefs, King, government, and, finally, commoners.

Kamehameha IV succeeded to the throne in 1855, enchanted with the institutions and ceremony of English monarchy. Disillusioned with rigid Protestant mores that had dominated Hawaiian affairs since the 1820's, he introduced the Anglican religion and sought to limit the influence of American missionaries in government. His more assertive brother Kamehameha V refused to swear allegiance to the Constitution of 1850 on ascending the throne, and within a year promulgated his own. The Constitution of 1864 greatly strengthened the Monarchy—bolstering the prerogatives of the King and his Cabinet while curtailing the powers of the Privy Council and Legislature.

The Kingdom underwent economic transformation as well. Most significant was the decline of whaling and its replacement by sugar, which created new demands for labor and land. As the Hawaiian population plummeted to a third, and then a quarter, of its precontact level, indentured immigrants were sought world wide to work the plantations. First came the Chinese in the 1850's, followed in 1868 by the first Japanese, who set off a massive influx when new labor treaties were signed in 1886.

The dynasty founded by Kamehameha the Great came to an end in 1872, when Kamehameha V died without issue and without naming a successor. Although the new King, Lunalilo, was a distant relative, he came to the throne by popular election and remained apart from the aloof Kamehamehas. After 13 months of rule, he died in 1874 and the Kingdom passed on to the Kalākaua dynasty.

The symbols of sovereignty also changed, as the Hawaiian government evolved from a loose confederacy of fractious chiefdoms to a full-fledged constitutional monarchy. The featherwork and ivory ornaments valued as symbols of rank and authority by the first Kamehameha and his predecessors gave way to new symbols, added to by succeeding kings of the Kamehameha dynasty. Although many elements of traditional culture persisted, Western symbols came to dominate court life, the final trappings of European monarchy being introduced by King David Kalākaua in the 1880's.

214. King Kamehameha I, unknown artist

Oil on fabric
56 × 44.5 cm.
Gift of Mrs. Frances B. Pearce, 1976
Color Plate XLIV

The only known paintings from life of Kamehameha I were made on November 24, 1816, by Louis Choris, draftsman with the Russian von Kotzebue expedition. The King first sat in native dress, then to Choris's surprise appeared of his own accord in European clothing. Choris made an unknown number of watercolor sketches differing slightly in detail, from which at least six versions in oil were copied later by unknown artists. The rendering of Kamehameha in a red vest seems to have been his favorite, becoming in time a kind of symbol of kingly office.

Kamehameha is said to have given this painting to Captain Nathaniel Pearce (1770-1851), a ship's master from Rhode Island, whose son William died in 1839 and is buried on O'ahu.

215. King Kamehameha II, unknown artist

Watercolor, mounted on paper
52.5 × 42.4 cm.
Color Plate XLV

The sacred child of Kamehameha I and Keōpūolani, Liholiho succeeded his father as Kamehameha II in May, 1819, charged with the unwanted duty of leading his nation into a new era. Pampered, overly fond of alcohol, unstable, and dissolute in habits, the young King offered few objections when one of his father's widows, the powerful Ka'ahumanu, assumed the role of *kuhina nui* and ruled virtually as vice-king.

Leaving the government in her hands, Liholiho and a party of chiefs departed for England on November 27, 1823, intent on gratifying their curiosity and learning more of foreigners, who were now arriving in ever-increasing numbers. More important, the royal visitors sought useful political and commercial information, and an audience with King George IV to negotiate a limited protectorate over the islands. Arriving in mid-May, 1824, the uninvited guests were royally entertained and escorted to the city's leading sights. Before measles suddenly halted all further activity, several of their party found time to have their portraits painted (see Nos. 165 and 216). This unsigned watercolor of Kamehameha II is believed to be copied from a lithograph produced by John Hayter in 1824.

216. "Tamehamalu Queen of the Sandwich Islands Aged 22 Years, From a drawing made by the express desire of her Majesty," unknown artist

Engraving, mounted on paper watermarked: J. Whatman 1824
23.9 × 31.1 cm. 47.7 × 34.5 cm. (larger sheet)
"This likeness was drawn by the express desire of Captain Valentine Starbuck and by an artist that he engaged."
Inscribed on verso in same hand is an historical account of the royal visit to London
Gift of Evangeline Priscilla Starbuck, 1927

Kamehameha II had five wives, but it was Queen Kamāmalu, his half-sister and favorite, who accompanied the royal party to England. Described by contemporary Londoners as a "tall, fine, masculine figure" (Daws, 1968, p. 73), the Queen, who had arrived unprepared in matters of dress, was quietly outfitted in fashionable clothing before having her portrait made. Having no immunization to Western childhood diseases, she succumbed to a severe case of the measles not long afterward and died of complications, July 8, 1824. Grief-stricken and barely recovering from the same disease himself, Kamehameha II sank into a decline and followed her in death six days later.

Signed "H," this portrait was probably done by John Hayter, who is well known for another, similar view of Queen Kamāmalu.

217. "Their Majesties King Rheo Rhio; Queen Tamehamalu; Madame Poki; of the Sandwich Islands, and Suite. As they appeared at the Theatre Royal, Drury Lane, June 4th 1824," by John William Gear (1806-1866)

Lithograph, handcolored
Published 1824
31.3 × 34.5 cm.
Gift of Mrs. A. W. F. Fuller, 1964

During a happier moment in London, the royal party was escorted to the new Theatre Royal to see a performance of "Zoroaster." Curious theater goers, glimpsing the

party in the royal box, later were able to purchase mementos of the occasion "drawn from life" by John Gear, an English artist who specialized in theatrical portraits. This was only one of many prints of the Hawaiian visitors created for sale in bookshops and store windows throughout London during the course of their stay.

218. Engraved Design for Casket Plaque of Kamehameha II

Engraved border with holograph writing in Hawaiian and English. Watermarked: Cansell 1821
40.2 × 30.2 cm.(plate mk.) 47.5 × 38.2 cm. (sheet)
Inscribed on verso in same handwriting is a similar text to that described in item 216
Gift of Evangeline Priscilla Starbuck, 1927
Not illustrated

Before his death, Kamehameha II requested that his and Kamāmalu's bodies be taken home for burial. While arrangements were being made for the return voyage, their magnificent coffins of mahogany and oak covered in light crimson velvet were placed under guard at historic St. Martin's Church. On each were engraved plaques, that of the King's reading, in part:

Tamehameha 2nd King of the Sandwich Islands died July 14th 1824 in London in the 28th year of his age—may we ever remember our beloved King Iolani

219. Miniature Bust of King Kamehameha II

Wax, wood, velvet (modern)
H. 46 cm. W. 41 cm. Th. 11.7 cm.
Gift of Mrs. E. K. Pratt, 1897 (8052)
Color Plate XLVI

Commanded by Lord George Byron, cousin of the poet, H.M.S. *Blonde* sailed from England in late September, 1824, with instructions to return the royal party to Hawai'i as a courtesy of the British government. Along with the bodies of Kamehameha II and Kamāmalu, the *Blonde* carried gifts for several of the most important Hawaiian chiefs. The day after reaching Honolulu, expedition artist Robert Dampier described their presentation to the royal court assembled in the grass house of high chief Kalanimoku, May 7, 1825:

The presents were then brought forward . . . The widow of Riho Riho [Kīna'u, one of Kamehameha II's other wives] was then presented with a likeness of her deceased husband, engraved upon wax and encased in a gold frame. I narrowly watched Karaimoku, as he examined this picture. He seemed somewhat moved when contemplating it, and as it was handed to the disconsolate widow her feelings were also excited at the resemblance. As however she had lately married a young chief of the first rank, her grief very soon subsided, and in a few minutes more, she appeared as Gay as usual (Dampier, 1971, p 36).

220. Silver Teapot Given to Ka'ahumanu in 1825

Sterling, ivory
Hallmarked: Robert Hennell, London, 1824-1825
L. 25.5 cm. D. 15.7 cm. H. 13.0 cm.
Bernice Pauahi Bishop Collection, 1884 (6889)
Color Plate XLVII

The *Blonde's* gift to Ka'ahumanu was a silver teapot engraved with the British coat of arms, an intimate reminder in heraldic symbolism of Britain's paternalism toward the young Kingdom.

The next present was to Kahumanu. It consisted of a beautifully embossed silver teapot, with the Arms of England engraved upon one side, and on the opposite, her own name: this present seemed to give her the greatest satisfaction. It is rather surprising, that at this moment a rage prevails for possessing teapots, the whole Nation of Islanders, wishing to become determined Tea-drinkers (Dampier, 1971, pp. 36-37).

221. King Kamehameha III, unknown artist

Oil on fabric. Painted in Boston from a photograph
76 × 63 cm.
Color Plate XLVIII

Kauikeaouli was confirmed by a national council of chiefs as King Kamehameha III on June 6, 1825, about a month after the *Blonde* returned the bodies of the former King and Queen for burial. A boy of about ten years, Kamehameha III grew into a tall and handsome man of amiable disposition and reigned for some 30 years, longer than any other Hawaiian monarch. Shrewd and strong willed, yet sound in judgment, he presided over a kingdom that was transformed during his lifetime from an autocratic, oppressive chiefdom to a constitutional monarchy able to command the attention and respect of leading world powers. A foremost Hawaiian historian has said of him: "Few kings have in their lifetime more clearly won the affection of their people, or deserved more to be held in grateful remembrance by their own and later generations" (Kuykendall, 1938, p. 427).

222. "Assemblée des Chefs des Iles Sandwich en conférence avec le Commandant de la Vénus," by Louis-Jules Masselot

Lithograph
33.9 × 53.5 cm. (sheet)
Published in Atlas Pittoresque *accompanying Du Petit-Thouars'* Voyage autour du monde . . . pendant les années 1836-1839 . . . (Paris: Gide, 1840-1864)
Gov. G. R. Carter Collection, 1959

Kamehameha III's early reign was beset with all the difficulties that characterized rapidly changing societies in the Pacific: lawlessness, violence, alcoholism, disease, troubles with foreigners, property disputes, religious persecution, and so on. In this scene, recorded on or about July 20, 1837, Captain Du Petit-Thouars is ascertaining the rights of French priests to practice Catholicism, while Captain Edward Belcher of the British warship *Sulphur* looks on. In the center, before a group of female chiefs reclining on mats, Kamehameha III

listens to advice from his prime minister, the high chiefess Kīna'u, whom the French accused of taking instructions from Hiram Bingham (center), head of the Protestant mission. In the end, the French were accorded most favored nation status and allowed to come and go freely, the two governments pledging "perpetual peace and friendship."

The conference lasted several days and took place at Halekauwila Palace, a one-room thatched structure about 40 by 60 feet, which could be divided into apartments by movable screens. Located adjacent to Honolulu Fort, it had come into occasional use as the royal palace the year before. It was so named because of the *kauila* timber framework Ka'ahumanu had taken from the royal mausoleum at Hale-o-Keawe in 1830 (see Nos. 31 and 32).

223. Throne of Kamehameha III

Koa wood, silk brocade (1979 reupholstery based on 1899 restoration)
H. 173.5 cm. W. 89 cm.
Gift of the Republic of Hawai'i, 1898 (8114)
Color Plate XLIX

In July, 1844, the capital moved permanently to Honolulu, and a one-story brick and coral structure just completed by O'ahu Governor Kekūanao'a for his daughter, Princess Victoria Kamāmalu, became the first 'Iolani Palace. Realizing the necessity of carrying on the business of government with etiquette befitting his court's growing dignity, the King commissioned a local German cabinetmaker named Christian LaFrenz to make a state chair of native *koa* wood for the new palace. It was surmounted by a likeness of the Hawaiian crown, which had come into general use the year before as a symbol of office. Ready by November, 1847, for $138.00 (which included a matching footstool, now lost), the first Hawaiian throne was used by succeeding monarchs until King Kalākaua had a gilded pair of Gothic design made in Boston in 1882 for the second 'Iolani Palace.

224. Clock of Kamehameha III

Koa wood, glass, metal, marble, ormolu
H. 91 cm. W. 49 cm. Th. 26 cm. (case)
Clock marked: "Brothers Melly"
Bernice Pauahi Bishop Collection, 1884

This clock case is thought to have been part of the royal household possessions transferred to Honolulu from the old capital at Lahaina, Maui. The *Polynesian* for February 15, 1845, called attention to such a carved clock case, reflecting "much credit upon the makers, Halstead & Hoyt, of Lahaina . . . worthy of the examination of the curious . . . We need not look abroad for superior cabinet-work hereafter, while the country can produce such excellent specimens, both of work and woods." Decorated with a simplified "K III" monogram, red and white bunting, and other heraldic devices, the ornate case was for a clock presented to Kamehameha III in the 1840's.

225 a,b. "Kamehameha III" and "H. Kalama," by August Plum (1815-1876)

Pencil and watercolor, 1846
Signed by the King and Queen
a: 20.6 × 27.2 cm.
b: 22.8 × 29.1 cm.
Purchase from August E. Plum, 1927

This pair of unfinished portraits shows the King and Queen in November, 1846, as they appeared to an artist aboard the Danish corvette *Galathea*. In the course of negotiating a friendship treaty with Denmark, Captain Steen Bille was presented to the royal couple at 'Iolani Palace:

In the audience room which took up the entire right half of the palace, I found the King standing at the end of the room surrounded by his Ministers . . . The King was a tall, rather handsome man, with a heavy beard, and a kindly but rather weak expression . . . The Queen was a very obese lady with a good-humoured, kindly face . . . said to be an excellent person, exceedingly godfearing and charitable. She spends the greater part of her day in company with some other ladies making feather ornaments or sewing clothes for the poor. She is said to be an excellent needle-woman, and usually she sews her own dresses. It was generally regretted that she was not of noble lineage. The aristocracy in this part of the world is as proud and prejudiced as anywhere else. We were informed that several chiefs did not even show her the least courtesy (Translated from Bille, 1849-1851, pp. 35, 39).

226. King Kamehameha III, unknown photographer

Daguerreotype, gold highlights, c. 1848
9.9 × 7.6 cm.
Gift of Mrs. Henry Waterhouse, 1904 (1904.22.01)
Not illustrated

This likeness of Kamehameha III, taken toward the end of his life, is the source of several engravings and other representations, including the oil portrait, No. 221.

227. Queen Kalama, unknown photographer

Daguerreotype, gold highlights, c. 1848
9.9 × 7.6 cm.
Gift of Mrs. Henry Waterhouse, 1904 (1904.22.02)
Not illustrated

In his youth, Kamehameha III married his younger sister, Nāhi'ena'ena. A match of mutual affection that caused no end of consternation to the missionaries, it was also one of the last attempts to maintain an ancient chiefly custom encouraging brother-sister marriage in order to produce heirs of high birth. Torn between two cultures, Nāhi'ena'ena died in 1836, about 20 years old.

Acceding to missionary pressure and his own laws to increase the race, the grief-stricken King married Kalama Kapakuhaili in February, 1837. Although the King hoped she would provide a royal heir, their only two children died in infancy. On his own death in 1854, according to historian Kamakau (1961, p. 422), "For a year or more she wept aloud, longer than was known of any other queen for a royal husband, even those who wear black in sign

of mourning but seldom shed real tears, and after a few months turn to idle and foolish romances."

228. The Kamehameha Royal Family, unknown photographer

Daguerreotype, gold highlights, c. 1852
7.5 × 9.7 cm.
Gift of C. P. Iaukea, 1922 (1922.94.03)
Color Plate L

Posed in this rare image are one reigning and two future kings of the Kamehameha dynasty. Left to right are Victoria Kamāmalu, Lot Kamehameha, King Kamehameha III, Alexander Liholiho, Queen Kalama.

Having failed to produce a royal heir of his own, Kamehameha III adopted as his son and successor Prince Alexander Liholiho, who became Kamehameha IV in 1855. Liholiho's older brother, Prince Lot, succeeded to the throne in 1863 as Kamehameha V, the last in the Kamehameha line of succession. Both were the sons of Mataio Kekūanao'a and Kīna'u, the half-sister of Kamehameha III. Their only daughter, Princess Victoria Kamāmalu, was named heir apparent by Kamehameha V, but died in 1866 at age 28.

229. Prince Lot Kamehameha, Dr. Judd, and Prince Alexander Liholiho on a Diplomatic Mission, unknown photographer

Daguerreotype, Boston, May 23, 1850
21.6 × 16.4 cm.
Gift of A. F. Judd III, 1978 (1978.176)

In 1849-1850, the two royal Princes accompanied Dr. Gerrit P. Judd to Europe and America. Kamehameha III had appointed Judd Special Commissioner and Plenipotentiary Extraordinary to negotiate serious disputes with France, and the two youths were to further their education by a year of foreign travel. Judd's mission accomplished little, but 16-year-old Prince Alexander Liholiho filled a diary with experiences that profoundly influenced his later attitudes. Boarding a train in Washington, D.C., for example, he was asked to change carriages because of his dark skin: "The first time that I ever received such treatment, not in England or France, or anywhere else. But in this country I must be treated like a dog to go & come at an American's bidding" (Adler, 1967, p. 108). Coupled with highly favorable impressions of England, such episodes were to help shape the course of Hawaiian politics for the next 25 years.

230. "Iles Sandwich.—Funérailles du roi de l'Archipel, à Honolulu.—le cortége [sic] funéraire quittant le palais royal d'Yolani," attributed to Mesnard

Woodcut, c. 1870
17.2 × 49 cm.
Gov. George R. Carter Collection, 1959

Kamehameha III died on December 15, 1854, and his funeral was held January 10th. This woodcut, based on sketches by M. Marinetti, who was attached to the

French consulate in Honolulu between 1867 and 1870, is believed to have been adapted from a sketch by Paul Emmert of the funeral procession of Kamehameha III. Marinetti's view shows the procession leaving 'Iolani Palace for the Royal Mausoleum in Nu'uanu Valley. According to the *Polynesian* for January 13, 1855:

> The procession was by far the most imposing ever witnessed in the Islands, it extended upwards of half a mile . . . It was forty minutes in passing one point and could not have contained less that 5000 persons. The inhabitants of this and other Islands were assembled in great numbers and must have exceeded twelve or fifteen thousand. There was no disturbance, no noise. Everything passed off with the greatest quietness. Thus was Kamehameha the III carried out to his last Home.

231. King Kamehameha IV, by William Cogswell (1819-1903)

Oil on fabric, 1879. Painted from a photograph by H. L. Chase, c. 1862
117.5 × 91.5 cm.
Color Plate LI

Kamehameha IV succeeded his uncle to the throne on January 11, 1855. Aristocratic and intensely pro-British, he brought a touch of elegance and formality to the Kamehameha court inspired by his visit to the courts of England and France as a young Prince.

Despite his good qualities, his personal life was filled with tragedy. Highly emotional, he suffered from fits of melancholy complicated by a nervous disorder and asthma. After a bout of drinking one week in September, 1858, he shot his friend and personal secretary, Henry A. Neilson, whom he suspected of having an affair with his wife. The suspicion proved groundless, but the King was filled with remorse as Neilson lingered on for two and a half years before dying. When his only son died in 1862, Kamehameha IV sank into intense desolation and died on November 30, 1863, an old man of 29 years.

232. Queen Emma, by William Cogswell (1819-1903)

Oil on fabric, 1890. Painted from a photograph
142.5 × 101.5 cm.
Not illustrated

Kamehameha IV came to the throne a 21-year-old bachelor, and on June 19, 1856, married his childhood sweetheart, Emma Naea Rooke. Great-granddaughter of one of Kamehameha I's brothers, and granddaughter of John Young, Emma personified English ancestry and descent from a long line of illustrious chiefs. She was adopted in infancy by Dr. T. C. B. Rooke, an English physician who had married her mother's sister. Well educated, regal, and charming, Emma was a near perfect consort for the new king. Later in her life, she sought the throne for herself but retired from active politics on losing to David Kalākaua in 1874. Embittered, she devoted her remaining years to charitable works, especially the Queen's Hospital and the Anglican Church in Hawai'i, both of which she and Kamehameha IV helped establish.

233. The Prince of Hawai'i, by Enoch Wood Perry (1831-1915)

Oil on fabric, c. 1864. Painted from a photograph
76.7 × 64.1 cm.
Color Plate LII

After two years of marriage, Queen Emma bore a son on May 20, 1858—a joyous event heralded as the symbolic rebirth of the Hawaiian race. Christened Albert Edward Kauikeaouli Leiopapa o Kamehameha, the sturdy little Prince was the doting parents' pride and joy. Once while the King was traveling, Emma wrote him affectionately of Baby taking his nap, "with one of your patent leather boots hugged fast in his arms" (Kuykendall, 1953, p. 84).

Hopes for the Kamehameha line were suddenly extinguished when the Prince of Hawai'i fell mysteriously ill. Some said it was "brain fever," others sunstroke, but the King blamed himself for having doused the little boy with cold water in a fit of irritation over something he had done. He died within a few days, August 27, 1862, at age four, the last child born to a Hawaiian monarch.

234. Silver Christening Cup of the Prince of Hawai'i

Sterling, wood
Made by Robert Garrard
H. 78.7 cm. W. 37.5 cm. Th. 23.5 cm.
Loaned by Daughters of Hawai'i, Queen Emma Summer Palace
Color Plates LIII and LIV

Wishing to strengthen ties with England, Emma and Kamehameha IV named their son Albert in honor of Queen Victoria's consort, whom the King had met in 1850. Pleased, the English Queen consented to be godmother and ordered a costly silver cup as a christening gift. Unable to attend herself, she designated as proxy Mrs. William Synge, wife of the new British commissioner and consul general to Hawai'i. Arriving August 22, 1862, they found the Prince gravely ill, with little hope of recovering. Next morning, Anglican baptismal ceremonies were hastily performed in 'Iolani Palace as the little boy lay in bed. Four days later he was dead, with him the hopes of the nation shattered.

235 a,b. Holy Bible and The Book of Common Prayer, presented to the Prince of Hawai'i

Published in 1860 by Oxford University Press, this matched set was bound in morocco by Rivington, Waterloo Place. Upper boards have sunken oval panel with carved ivory cross. Edges are brass bound and clasps engraved and stamped
Kapi'olani-Kalaniana'ole Collection, 1923
Not illustrated.

Queen Emma's deep commitment to the Anglican Church is poignantly reflected in this matching Bible and prayer book, inscribed "His Royal Highness The Prince of Hawaii with the affectionate good wishes of Lady Franklin August 1862." The widow of the celebrated Arctic explorer, Lady Jane Franklin had visited Hawai'i in

1861, where she became friendly with Emma and later invited her to England.

Emma did make the journey in 1865. After a short stay with Lady Franklin, she was entertained by Queen Victoria at Windsor Castle, then by Emperor Napoleon III and Empress Eugénie in Paris. Returning in 1866, Queen Emma stopped briefly in the United States at the request of King Kamehameha V, who feared her British leanings might otherwise alarm Americans living in Hawai'i. She was welcomed with honors and formally received by President Andrew Johnson in Washington, D.C.

236. King Kamehameha IV as a Young Man, unknown photographer

Daguerreotype, tinted. c. 1849
8.3 × 7 cm.
Gift of Mrs. Randolph Charles Walker, 1937
(1937.53.02)
Not illustrated

This early daguerreotype shows Kamehameha IV as a teenager, about 15 years old. He is wearing a *lei* of *maile* leaves, a sweet-scented vine in great favor then as now for festive decorations and garlands. *Maile* is traditionally associated with Laka, patron of the *hula*.

237. King Kamehameha IV, unknown photographer

Ambrotype, c. 1860
10.8 × 8.1 cm.
Gift of Doak C. Cox, 1964 (1964.149)

This image was taken about three years before Kamehameha IV's death in 1863. He is about 26 years old.

238. Queen Emma, by Joseph W. King (fl. 1858-1870)

Ambrotype, c. 1860
10.6 × 8.1 cm.
Case marked: "Littlefield, Parsons, & Co. patented Oct. 14, 1856 & April 21, 1857"
Gift of Doak C. Cox, 1964 (1964.149)

Emma is depicted here as a robust young woman about 24 years old, two or three years before the deaths, in quick succession, of her only son and husband. To commemorate her losses, she took the epithetic name Kaleleonālani, "The-flight-of-the-heavenly-chiefs."

239. Queen Emma's Silver Bracelet

H. 2.9 cm. D. 6.9 cm.
Lucy K. Peabody, Kalani and Edgar Henriques Collection, 1932 (HH 143)

A precursor of Hawaiian heirloom jewelry, this simple band of silver bears Queen Emma's monogram—an intwined double "E" over a representation of the Hawaiian crown. The bracelet is inscribed "ALOHA IA KA HEIHEIMALIE," a token of remembrance possibly for an elderly high chiefess who died in 1877. The name also belonged to Hoapili-wahine (see No. 69), Kamehameha IV's maternal grandmother.

240. State Sword of Kamehameha IV

Brass, steel, glass, felt
Blade marked: "Baldwin & Co. Newark."
L. 88.5 cm.
Kapi'olani-Kalaniana'ole Collection, 1923 (B.6642)
Color Plate LV

The King may have obtained this sword in America or Europe while traveling with Dr. Judd and his older brother in 1849-1850, since it is depicted in a daguerreotype taken about five years later. The hilt, sheath, and blade are decorated with symbolic devices of the Monarchy, including a crown set with paste jewels, an ornate "K," taro leaves, and different versions of the royal coat of arms. Succeeding Hawaiian kings used the sword as an emblem of state until Kalākaua acquired a new one of his own (No. 254) for the Coronation of 1883.

241. King Kamehameha V, by William Cogswell (1819-1903)

Oil on fabric, 1879. Painted from a photograph by Charles Leander Weed, 1865
128.2 × 103.5 cm.
Color Plate LVI

Lot Kamehameha succeeded his younger brother on November 30, 1863, and reigned for slightly more than nine years. Although lacking his brother's grace and refinement, Kamehameha V possessed an autocratic strength of character that reminded many older subjects of his grandfather, Kamehameha I.

The nation faced a crisis of succession when the King's sister, Princess Victoria Kamāmalu, died in 1866. Although the portly bachelor had been frequently urged to marry and produce an heir, he was said to be in love with the widowed Queen Emma and would accept no other woman when she rejected his proposal out of devotion to her late husband. Superstitious, he also refused to name another successor until he lay on his death bed, at the last moment asking Princess Bernice Pauahi Bishop to succeed him as the best choice for the nation. She declined, suggesting her cousin Princess Ruta Ke'elikōlani or Queen Emma instead. Lapsing into unconsciousness before the matter could be settled, the King died about an hour later—on his 43rd birthday, December 11, 1872. It signaled the end of the Kamehameha line of succession.

242. Princess Ke'elikōlani with Featherwork, by Menzies Dickson (c. 1840-1891)

Albumen print, c. 1880
24.8 × 20.2 cm.

Despite her high birth—she was half-sister to Kamehameha IV and Kamehameha V—Ke'elikōlani was considered unfit for the throne. Aloof, suspicious of foreigners, and devoted completely to Hawaiian ways, she was misunderstood and feared by many who did not know her well. Standing six feet tall and weighing more than 400 pounds, she had suffered an accident in her 30's that left her face cruelly disfigured. Governess of Hawai'i for a number of years, Ke'elikōlani amassed through inheritance and occasional business ventures vast land holdings that made her the richest woman in the islands. On her death in 1883, her estate passed to Princess Bernice Pauahi Bishop, her closest surviving relative.

243. Keōua Hale, Home of Princess Ke'elikōlani, unknown photographer

Albumen print, c. 1883
17.5 × 23.3 cm.
Gift of Miss Lucille Christy, 1971 (1971.343)

Not to be outdone by an upstart, Princess Ke'elikōlani built this elegant Victorian mansion to match in grandeur King Kalākaua's new Palace (No. 270). She timed the housewarming to coincide with his Coronation, February 12, 1883, and invited 1,000 guests to a grand *lū'au*, where more than 200 hogs and 20 bullocks were consumed, along with immense quantities of *poi*, sweet potatoes, and other foods. Destined never to occupy her costly mansion, Ke'elikōlani fell ill the next day and sailed off to Kailua for rest, dying there a few weeks later in a simple grass house built in the style of her ancestors. Her Honolulu mansion, whose name means ''Rainy Cloud'' (after the father of Kamehameha I), was inherited by Princess Bernice Pauahi Bishop, who lived there barely a year before her own death. It was demolished in the 1920's to make way for a new schoolbuilding.

244. Princess Ke'elikōlani's Grass House in Kailua, Hawai'i, unknown photographer

Albumen print, c. 1883
18 × 23 cm.

Princess Ke'elikōlani died in this house on May 24, 1883, a few steps from where Kamehameha I died in 1819. It was situated on the grounds of her residence at Hulihe'e Palace, which is now restored as a museum. In the background rises the steeple of historic Moku'aikaua Church, finished in January, 1837, under the direction of Rev. Asa Thurston.

245. Shell Bracelet

Cowrie shells, silk ribbon, thread, metal hook and eye
H. 1.3 cm. D. 7 cm.
Princess Ruta Ke'elikōlani Collection, 1883 (2252)
Not illustrated

Regardless of her wealth and taste for fine clothing and luxuries, Ke'elikōlani remained staunchly Hawaiian in her views and sentiments. Her bracelet of deep yellow ''money'' cowries is much like ones worn by Hawaiian women of earlier decades, except that velvet ribbon has replaced the traditional fibers holding the shells together.

246. Mr. and Mrs. Charles Reed Bishop, unknown photographer

Ambrotypes, c. 1857
8.2 × 7 cm.
Gift of Gorham D. Gilman (1979.464)

A great-granddaughter of Kamehameha I, Princess Bernice Pauahi steadfastly refused the throne, even after Kamehameha V specifically designated her his successor. Married in 1850 to Charles Reed Bishop, a New Yorker who had settled in Hawai'i four years earlier, she preferred instead to live quietly as the last of the Kamehamehas. On her death, October 16, 1884, the vast estate she had inherited from Princess Ke'elikōlani was placed in trust for the education of Hawaiian youth. The Kamehameha Schools were established to fulfill the terms of her will. Independently, Mr. Bishop founded the Bernice Pauahi Bishop Museum in 1889 to collect and preserve the vanishing relics of Hawai'i in her memory.

247. Gold and Coral Jewelry Set

Necklace, brooch, earrings, bracelet
Gift of Dr. and Mrs. George F. Mainwaring, 1969
(1969.162.02a-d)
Color Plate LVII

Mrs. Bishop is said to have worn this ensemble when presented to Queen Victoria in May, 1876, during a tour of Europe and the United States, which included the American Centennial in Philadelphia.

248. King Lunalilo as a Young Man, unknown artist

Oil on fabric
92 × 69.2 cm.
Color Plate LVIII

William Charles Lunalilo was the first Hawaiian monarch elected to the throne. Distantly related to the Kamehameha line of succession, Lunalilo pressed his claims as closest and rightful heir and by popular acclaim was elected to office on January 8, 1873, winning almost unanimously over his closest rival, David Kalākaua. Well educated and devoted to music and English literature, he was ill-suited to office. In poor health and addicted to alcohol, he lacked practical experience as well as administrative skills, his financial affairs having been managed by guardians most of his life. Reigning one year and 25 days, he succumbed to pulmonary tuberculosis on February 3, 1874, three days after his 39th birthday. He was respected and admired as a ''people's king,'' and left the bulk of his estate to establish the Lunalilo Home for the poor, destitute, infirm, and elderly of Hawaiian extraction.

249. Bust of King Lunalilo, by Allen Hutchinson
(1855-1929)

Plaster, koa *wood. Nov., 1890*
H. 47.5 cm.
Gift of John F. Colburn, 1895 (1895.05)

Modeled from photographs taken in later life, this is one
of several busts and bas-reliefs created by an itinerant
British sculptor who worked in Honolulu between 1888
and 1897. Like the painter William Cogswell, Hutchinson
was commissioned by royalty and leading families to
record for posterity the images of Hawaiian dignitaries of
the late Victorian era, who were slowly but inevitably
passing from the scene.

250. Lunalilo as a Young Boy, attributed to A. T. Agate
(1812-1846)

Pencil and watercolor
Watermark: 1831
22.3 × 18.2 cm.
Acquired by 1892

Lunalilo was five years old when an artist with the
United States Exploring Expedition produced this sketch,
sometime between September, 1840, and April, 1841. The
expedition commander, Lieutenant Charles Wilkes,
stayed in the home of Miriam Kekāuluohi, the boy's
doting mother. The sensitive princeling was a pupil at the
Chiefs' Children's School (later called the Royal School),
which was founded by the chiefs in 1839 and directed by
the Protestant mission to educate young chiefs of rank.

The Kalākaua Dynasty

King Kalākaua was elected to the throne by a special session of the Legislature, February 12, 1874, and
hastily sworn in to office next day as backers of dowager Queen Emma, his rival candidate, rioted in the
streets. It was an inauspicious beginning for a reign
that came to be noted for its pomp and ceremony,
rivaling foreign courts in elegance and lavish entertainment and earning for Kalākaua the dubious
nickname The Merry Monarch.

Kalākaua no doubt resented his unceremonious
accession to the Hawaiian throne. Comparing notes
with fellow royalty during a trip around the world in
1881, he determined to stage a Coronation befitting his
kingly dignity, arranging the belated ceremony for
February 12, 1883, the ninth anniversary of his accession. His numerous critics—especially the foreign
taxpayers who had to foot the bill (in excess of
$50,000)—ridiculed the two-week extravaganza as a
foolish waste of the Kingdom's limited resources.
Others, not least his sister Lili'uokalani, considered it
an occasion of serious national importance. Fully

aware that not all Hawaiians conceded their family's
genealogical title to the throne, she rationalized that it
would also confirm that right: "the direct line of the
'Kamehamehas' having become extinct, it was succeeded by the 'Keawe-a-Heulu' line, its founder having been first cousin to the father of Kamehameha I. It
was wise and patriotic to spend money to awaken in
the people a national pride. Naturally, those among us
who did not desire to have Hawaii remain a nation
would look on an expenditure of this kind as worse
than wasted" (Lili'uokalani, 1898, p. 105).

Throughout his reign, Kalākaua strived to achieve
for his subjects a sense of pride in their Hawaiian
heritage. Unfortunately, he proved to be a capricious
ruler, too frequently relying upon the questionable
advice of those near him. His friendship with Claus
Spreckles, the wealthy California sugar magnate,
nearly brought the Kingdom to financial ruin. Walter
Murray Gibson, his Minister of Foreign Affairs and
virtual head of government from 1882 to 1887, was
thoroughly disliked and mistrusted by a large and
influential segment of the population. Kalākaua also
sought to expand his influence throughout the Pacific,
hoping to establish a Polynesian confederation with
himself as head. Prompted by Gibson, Kalākaua went
so far as to commission a miniature navy and send a
diplomatic envoy to Samoa, a move that soon
threatened to embroil the Kingdom in a war with
Germany, England, and the United States over the
international balance of power in the Pacific. The mission was withdrawn at the last minute, but too late to
avert a revolution at home. Gibson was ousted in July,
1887, and the King forced to sign a new Constitution—at gunpoint, some maintained—that greatly
limited his powers.

Chastened, Kalākaua reigned until his death on
January 20, 1891, little more than a figurehead. His
sister Lili'uokalani, heir apparent since the death of
their brother Prince Leleiohoku in 1877, became
Queen and immediately made it clear that she intended to rule rather than reign in a ceremonial vac-
uum. Naming and replacing cabinets almost at will,
she brought her Kingdom to the brink of armed revolt
while attempting to replace the hated Bayonet Constitution of 1887 with one of her own choosing. She
was deposed on January 17, 1893, bringing an end to
the Kalākaua dynasty as ruling monarchs of Hawai'i.
All attempts to restore her Kingdom through interces-
sion with the United States ended in failure. Hawai'i
became an American Territory in 1900 and a State in
1959.

251. King David Kalākaua, by William Cogswell
(1819-1903)

Oil on fabric, 1878
129 × 102 cm.
Color Plate LIX

Courtly and refined, Kalākaua came to the throne experienced in royal etiquette and matters of state. Born in 1836 and educated at the Chiefs' Children's School, he became an aide to Kamehameha IV at the age of 16, a member of the Privy Council at 19, and Chamberlain to Kamehameha V at 28. In 1863, the same year he was named Postmaster General, he married the granddaughter of King Kaumuali'i of Kaua'i, a retiring but prestigious woman who shared his reign as Queen Kapi'olani.

Kalākaua was an impressive man, thickset, with black kinky hair, long sideburns, a drooping mustache, and skin said to be slightly darker than average for Hawaiians. Of the numerous photographs and portraits of him, few capture his regal dignity so well as the one by William Cogswell, an American artist commissioned to paint portraits of Hawaiian royalty in 1878-1879 and again in 1890. Kalākaua may have become familiar with Cogswell's famous portrait of Abraham Lincoln while visiting the White House in December, 1874, the first reigning monarch in history, incidentally, to tour the United States.

252. Crown of Hawai'i

Gold, diamonds, opals, emeralds, rubies, pearls,
carbuncle, enamel, kukui nut, velvet, silk
H. 20.5 cm. D. 25 cm.
Gift of the Republic of Hawai'i, 1898 (HH 101)
Frontispiece

The Coronation regalia of King Kalākaua and Queen Kapi'olani combined European insignia with ancient symbols of Hawaiian royalty. The Crowns, ordered from England in 1882 for £1,000 (plus £3 3/extra for silk and velvet linings), were described with appropriate splendor by the *Pacific Commercial Advertiser* in its famous account of the Coronation:

The Crown is composed of a fillet or band of gold one inch in width, set, on each edge, with 192 small diamonds. Midway in the fillet are set 20 opals, alternating with 8 emeralds and as many rubies, save at the back, where there are set in the place of the emeralds and rubies 6 *kukui* nut jewels of a deep reddish black, highly polished.
At the front and back, and on each side, the fillet is surmounted by a golden Maltese cross, in the arms of which are set forty-eight diamonds, each arm having three. In the center of the cross in front of the crown is a magnificent diamond of about six carats' weight, and on the sides others a little smaller. A splendid carbuncle glows in the center of the cross at the back. Between the crosses are short curved bars forming twelve points, from which spring taro leaves in frosted gold, beautifully veined, and each one holding a diamond in its center. Between the points are set twelve other fine diamonds. Springing from the fillet, over the crimson velvet cap of maintenance, are eight bars of gold, whose surfaces are studded with half-round knobs, as in the crown of France. These eight bars diminish in width, and finally unite at the base of a globe of dark red enamel. These

eight bars are emblematical of the union of the islands of the group under one rule. The globe that they uphold is banded horizontally with a circle of pearls, and another like band passes over the upper half of the globe. Surmounting the whole is a golden Maltese cross, in which is set four brilliant diamonds . . . Each crown contains 521 diamonds, 20 opals, 8 emeralds, 1 large carbuncle, and 6 *kukui* jewels.

The Coronation proper was held just before noon, February 12, 1883, in a special pavilion erected in front of 'Iolani Palace and surrounded by a temporary amphitheater. As the choir sang "Almighty Father! We Do Bring Gold and Gems for the King," Prince Kawānanakoa, the King's nephew, advanced with the Crowns while thousands of spectators looked on. The King awaited, robed in the ancient feather cloak of Kamehameha I, the coronation "Ensign of Knowledge and Wisdom." Raising a Crown for the multitudes to see, the President of the Legislative Assembly passed it to the Chancellor of the Kingdom, who handed it to the King saying, "Receive this Crown of pure gold to adorn the high station wherein thou hast been placed." Crowning himself, the King lifted up the other, turned, and spoke to his Queen: "I place this Crown upon your head, to share the honors of my throne." Just then, it is said, the sun broke through the leaden skies, and a moment later the choir burst forth with the anthem, "Cry Out O Isles with Joy!" After a prayer and salute from warships in the harbor, the King and Queen marched back into the Palace to the strains of Mayerbeer's "Coronation March," played by the Royal Hawaiian Band (Kuykendall, 1967, p. 263).
The Crown exhibited here is Queen Kapi'olani's. The King's Crown was pillaged by vandals breaking into 'Iolani Palace in 1893, later recovered, then forgotten until 1925 when the Legislature appropriated $350 for its restoration, using synthetic materials.

253. Royal Scepter

Silver, gilt, velvet
L. 93.5 cm.
Gift of the Republic of Hawai'i, 1898 (8118)
Color Plates LX and LXI

Part of the Coronation regalia ordered from England, the royal Scepter was described in these words in the *Advertiser's* account of the ceremony:

The Sceptre, the Ensign of Kingly Power and Justice, is of gold, about 2 feet 4 inches in length, divided by the design into three parts. The base and shaft are shaped as an Ionic column, bound around with the Roman fillet. The shaft of the column has the laurel leaf entwined about its polished surface, and the capital is finished with three rams' heads, symbols of strength. The central part, by which the sceptre is held, is covered with imperial velvet, and the third, or upper part of the shaft, is surmounted by a Globe on which is perched a dove with out-stretched wings, the emblem of Peace.

According to contemporary records, the Scepter cost £12 12/ plus an additional £ 1 5/ for preparing the design and drawing.

254. Sword of State

Brass, steel, velvet, wood, ray skin, silver, gold, silk, leather
Marked: "Robt. Mole & Sons Makers Birmingham" and "Proof"
L. 102 cm.
Gift of the Republic of Hawai'i, 1898 (8119)
Color Plate LXII

The sword of state replaced another that had been used since the time of King Kamehameha IV. It was a somewhat more ornate version of a new design adopted by the Kalākaua court for full dress occasions, but owing to an oversight had the first word of the national motto misspelled. According to the *Advertiser* account of the Coronation:

The sword of State placed in the King's hands as the ensign of Justice and Mercy, is an exact counterpart of that of England. It has a straight blade of fine Damascus steel inlaid in gold with the Hawaiian coat of arms surmounted by the crown and bearing the motto of the realm. The hilt, guard and cord and tassels are of gold, the hilt and guard beautifully engraved, as are the gold mountings of the purple velvet sheath.

255. Ring of State

Gold, carnelian, diamonds
H. 2.7 cm. D. 2.8 cm.
Gift of the Territory of Hawai'i and Prince Jonah Kūhiō Kalaniana'ole, 1918 (1918.09.09)
Color Plate LXIII

The *Advertiser's* contemporary description of the Coronation regalia states:

The Ring, the ensign of kingly dignity, is of Etruscan gold, massive—weighing nearly an ounce—and bears on its broad surfaces a shield in which is set a carnelian, engraved—*intaglio*—with the Hawaiian coat of arms. The seal is surmounted with the crown, and below is a ribbon bearing the legend *Ua mau ka ea o ka aina i ka pono*, with the star of the crown of Hawaii pendent. On each side of the shield are the two supporters, two Hawaiian chiefs, carved in full relief, bearing spears. Outside of each supporter is a solitaire diamond of one carat weight.

King Kalākaua placed high symbolic value on his Ring of State, which cost the treasury £25 in 1882. Five years after the Coronation, he sealed it up with a bundle of bones he had obtained from a secret cave on Hawai'i—a royal mark certifying his conviction that they were the bones of Kamehameha I. In 1918 the Ring was retrieved by the King's nephew, Prince Kūhiō, who had it put away for safekeeping. It is reunited here with the Coronation Scepter, Sword, and Crown for the first time in almost a century.

256. Hawaiian Coat of Arms, artist unknown

Oil and gilt on glass c. 1882
61 × 61 cm.
Color Plate LXIV

The royal Coat of Arms came into existence when Rev. William Richards, adviser to Kamehameha III, and

Timothy Ha'alilio, private secretary, were sent to America, France, and Great Britain in 1842 to negotiate treaties guaranteeing the continued independence of Hawai'i. Commissioned also to seek help with a royal seal or crest, the delegation consulted with professionals in Brussels and Paris before settling on a design suggested by Ha'alilio and prepared by the Herald's College, London. The design finally adopted for use in 1845 served, with minor modifications, throughout the Monarchy and is the basis for the present Great Seal of the State of Hawai'i.

This version, incorporating the Crown of Hawai'i, the initials "K.R." for Kalākaua Rex, and a representation of the Order of Kamehameha (bottom) was prepared just before the Coronation of 1883. The quartered shield bears red, white, and blue stripes representing the eight inhabited islands, and two *pūlo'ulo'u* staves or emblems of taboo (see No. 45). The triangular flag and crossed spears forming the central escutcheon are ancient chiefly insignia, while the supporters, holding a *kāhili* and spear, are the chiefly twins Kameeiamoku and Kamanaawa. They are dressed in feather cloaks and helmets allegedly copied from actual specimens collected by Captain Cook in 1778-1779. The scroll bears an early version of the national motto, the third word not yet having changed from *ka* to *ke* for grammatical euphony. Completing the Hawaiian symbolism, the background is an open feather cloak, whose crossing lines represent the undernetting to which the feathers are attached.

257. Royal Order of Kamehameha I, Knights Commander Class (in Brilliants)

Silver gilt, gold, enamel, paste, brass
H. 11 cm. W. 6 cm.
Kapi'olani-Kalaniana'ole Collection, 1923 (B.7259)
Color Plate LXV

The first Hawaiian royal order was established by King Kamehameha V on April 11, 1865, to commemorate his grandfather, Kamehameha the Great. It was bestowed on Hawaiian subjects and foreigners as an award of merit or for service to the Kingdom, and came in three classes—Knights Grand Cross, Knights Commander, and Knights Companion. Of some 140 conferred, one insignia is known in brilliants, which King Kalākaua seems to have bestowed upon himself.

As early as 1848 the Privy Council had discussed the institution of a series of orders to honor distinguished subjects and to confer on foreign officials friendly to the Hawaiian Kingdom. Although the proposal lapsed until authorized by the Constitution of 1864, five orders were eventually created, four by Kalākaua between 1875 and 1886. Records are incomplete, but of the 833 known awards, all but 57 were bestowed by Kalākaua or his sister. Of these, well over half were to reciprocate or to encourage the exchange of coveted foreign orders. Frequently criticized but pervasive symbols of the Kalākaua era, they caused no small drain on the royal treasury, contributing in their own fashion to the eventual collapse of the Monarchy.

258. Royal Order of Kalākaua I, Knights Grand Cross

Silver, gold, enamel
Made by Kretly, Paris
D. 9.3 cm.
Gift of Lili'uokalani Estate, 1923 (1923.129.05)

King Kalākaua created this order on September 28, 1875, to commemorate his election to the throne. Divided into four classes—Knights Grand Cross, Knights Grand Officer, Knights Commander, and Knights Companion—it was the King's favorite order, at least 254 having been awarded. The design incorporates the *kāhili* and *pulo'ulo'u*, or taboo staff, as symbolic devices.

259. Royal Order of Kapi'olani, Grand Cross, Commander and Cordon (in Brilliants)

Silver, gold, silver gilt, enamel, paste, silk (replaced)
Made by Kretly, Paris
D. (of badge) 8.9 cm.
Kapi'olani-Kalaniana'ole Collection, 1923 (B.7274)

This order was created by Kalākaua on August 30, 1880, to memorialize Kapi'olani the Great, an early convert who defied the Goddess Pele and thus helped establish Christianity in Hawai'i. In eight classes, it was awarded for contributions to the arts and sciences, charity, and service to the Kingdom. The insignia bears a small medallion of Queen Kapi'olani and her motto, *Kūlia i ka nu'u*, translated either as "strive to the summit" or "Julia to the throne," Julia being her given name. The Grand Cross and Commander pendant was awarded at least once in brilliants, this example to Queen Kapi'olani herself.

260. Royal Order of the Crown of Hawai'i, Grand Cross

Silver, silver gilt, gold, enamel
Made by Kretly, Paris
H. 9 cm. W. 9 cm.
Princess Ka'iulani Collection, 1911 (10,262)

Anticipating his forthcoming Coronation, Kalākaua established this order on September 12, 1882. It is divided into seven classes and bears a likeness of the Hawaiian crown, the inscription translating "Crown of Hawaii."

261. Royal Order of the Star of Oceania, Grand Officer

Silver, silver gilt, enamel
D. 10 cm.
Princess Ka'iulani Collection, 1911 (10,263)

To honor those who helped promote Hawai'i throughout the Pacific and neighboring countries, Kalākaua created his last order on December 16, 1886. Based on a design by Isobel Strong, daughter of Robert Louis Stevenson's wife, it portrays Hawai'i as a beacon of light rising from the sea, encircled by the order's Hawaiian title. Unpopular after the ignominious defeat of Kalākaua's mission to Samoa in 1887, the order was conferred on only 25 persons.

262. Supreme Order of the Chrysanthemum

Silver, enamel, cabochon
D. 8.6 cm.
Kapi'olani-Kalaniana'ole Collection, 1923 (B.7279)
Not illustrated

Established in 1877, the Supreme Order of the Chrysanthemum was Japan's highest order when Emperor Mutsuhito presented it to King Kalākaua on March 14, 1881. In return, the King conferred on the Emperor the Grand Cross of the Order of Kamehameha (later regretting that his own Kingdom had so few orders to bestow). It was the King's first stop, after leaving San Francisco, on his trip around the world. Impressed by the potentials of political alliance between their two nations, Kalākaua also proposed marriage of his niece, the five-year old Princess Ka'iulani, to Prince Komatsu; betrothed already, he politely declined. The royal visit helped clear the way for new labor treaties in 1886, leading to massive immigration of Japanese laborers to the Hawaiian Islands.

This is one of the three foreign orders Kalākaua wore during his Coronation, prized among the dozens he eventually acquired.

263. Kalākaua Election Medal

Silver, gold, silk, enamel
H. 11.2 cm. W. 4.6 cm.
Kapi'olani-Kalaniana'ole Collection, 1923 (B.7261)
Illustrated with No. 268

Besides royal orders, a number of commemorative medals were created during the reign of Kalākaua to publicize significant events or achievements. The Mō'ī, meaning "King," medal was awarded on February 16, 1874, to friends and officials who had helped elect Kalākaua to the throne. It bears David Kalākaua's initials on a gold heart—the device used on his ballot—and the date of the election, February 12, 1874. Hastily made in Honolulu, it is considered rare today.

264. Kalākaua and Kapi'olani Anniversary Medal

Silver, silk
H. 7.4 cm. W. 3.9 cm. D. 3.1 cm.
Lucy K. Peabody, Kalani and Edgar Henriques Collection, 1932 (HH 1953)

A medal showing the King and Queen facing left was issued to commemorate the 10th anniversary of Kalākaua's accession to the throne, February 12, 1884.

265. King Kalākaua Jubilee Medal

Silver, silk
H. 7.2 cm. W. 3.9 cm. D. 3.1 cm.
Kapi'olani-Kalaniana'ole Collection, 1923 (B.7304)
Illustrated with No. 264

This medal was presented to Hawaiian military and government officials, and later sold to the public. It commemorated King Kalākaua's 50th birthday on November 16, 1886, a two-week Jubilee that included fireworks, receptions, a regatta with aquatic sports, a historical procession, a grand *luʻau* and *hula* program, a birthday ball in ʻIolani Palace, competitive athletic games and military drill, a historical tableaux, and finally a state dinner.

266. Coat of Arms Medal

Gold, brass
H. 5.8 cm. W. 5.5 cm.
Kapiʻiolani-Kalanianaʻole Collection, 1923 (B.7293)

The circumstances behind this medal are unknown, but it memorializes the royal Hawaiian Coat of Arms, a symbol that was extensively used during the reign of King Kalākaua.

267. Hail! Kalākaua Medal

Gold
H. 5 cm. W. 3.5 cm.
Kapiʻolani-Kalanianaʻole Collection, 1923 (B.7309)
Illustrated with No. 266

A posthumous medal inscribed in Latin, this seems to have been an unofficial sentimental commemoration of the 10th anniversary of King Kalākaua's Coronation. One side is engraved "Ave Kalakaua 1883 Rex Hawaii" and the other "Ave Kalakaua 1893 Polunesiae."

268. World Tour Medal

Stainless steel, ceramic, silk
H. 11.5 cm. W. 5.3 cm.
Kapiʻolani-Kalanianaʻole Collection, 1923 (B.7258)

The revolving globe suspended in a cross attached to a banner dated 1874-1881 was prepared to publicize Kalākaua's seven-year reign and world tour in 1881. He was the first monarch in the history of any nation to encircle the globe, leaving Honolulu January 20, 1881, and returning October 29. During the trip, the King and his suite made official visits to Japan, China, Hong Kong, Siam, Singapore, Johore, Malacca, Burma, India, Egypt, Italy, the Vatican, England, Scotland, Belgium, Germany, Austria, France, Spain, Portugal, and the United States. Ostensibly, the purpose was to seek and attract new sources of immigrant labor to the islands, but the tour served more as a good will and sightseeing mission.

269. King Kalākaua in Hong Kong, unknown photographer

Albumen print, 1881
22 × 28.5 cm.
Elizabeth Kalanianaʻole Woods Estate, 1935
Not illustrated

Kalākaua reached Hong Kong on April 12, 1881, during his world tour and was entertained in the name of the British Queen by Sir John Pope Hennessey, the Colonial Governor. The whirlwind visit lasted about four days, in which the King was honored at two state banquets plus formal luncheons and receptions.

Seated front row center in this photograph (sixth from left), the King seems to be enjoying the lavish attention bestowed on him. According to William Nevins Armstrong (ninth from left) in his book *Around the World with a King*, Kalākaua impressed the Colonial Governor by his bearing and conduct, which "could not be excelled by any sovereign" (Armstrong 1904, p. 114).

270. ʻIolani Palace, unknown photographer

Albumen print, c. 1885
17.2 × 23.1 cm.
Gift of Miss Lucille Christy, 1971 (1971.343)

Two or three years after coming to the throne, Kalākaua announced his desire for a new palace to match his dignity as King of the Hawaiian Islands. The first ʻIolani Palace, which had served since the 1840's, was razed, and on Queen Kapiʻolani's birthday, December 31, 1879, the cornerstone for the second ʻIolani Palace was laid with elaborate Masonic ceremony. After three years of construction, the new building was inaugurated with a formal banquet for the Masonic fraternity on December 27, 1882, followed by a grand opening during the Coronation festivities six weeks later. Cost of the magnificent structure exceeded $350,000—well over the initial estimate of $65,000—but the King and Queen preferred to spend their private hours in Kīnaʻu Hale, a wooden bungalow built in 1844. It is visible just to the left of the Palace, with Princess Keʻelikōlani's mansion rising above the trees in the far distance (see No. 243).

271. King Kalākaua and Staff on ʻIolani Palace Steps, by J. J. Williams (1853-1926)

Albumen print, c. 1886
17.1 × 24.1 cm.
Not illustrated

Left to Right: James Boyd, Curtis P. Iaukea, Charles H. Judd, E. W. Purvis, King Kalākaua, George W. Macfarlane, Governor John O. Dominis, A. B. Haley, John D. Holt, Jr., Antone Rosa.

272. Queen Kapiʻolani and Princess Liliʻuokalani at Rackheath Hall, unknown photographer

Albumen print, 1887
26.8 × 35.6 cm.

Standing, left to right: George Macfarlane, C. P. Iaukea, unknown man, Captain William J. Steward, unknown man, James Boyd, John Holt, Jr., unknown man. Seated in chairs, left to right: unknown woman, Mrs. William J. Steward, Queen Kapiʻolani, Princess Liliʻuokalani, unknown woman, unknown woman. Seated on ground, left to right: unknown man, son of Captain and Mrs. Steward, unknown man.

Kapiʻolani remained at home while her husband toured the world in 1881, but was able to visit the United States and England as head of the Hawaiian delegation to Queen Victoria's Golden Jubilee in 1887. Unaccustomed to speaking English, she was accompanied by her sister-in-law, Princess Liliʻuokalani, and several members of the Hawaiian court. Arriving in England on June 2, 1887, the royal party spent their first few days as guests of Captain and Mrs. William J. Steward at Rackheath Hall, a grand country estate near Norwich. After the Jubilee festivities, news reached England of political unrest at home, and the party was forced to cancel any plans they may have had for touring the Continent.

273. Court Uniform of Colonel Curtis P. Iaukea

Wool, cotton, silk, silver braid, brass
Coat: L. 98 cm. Shoulder width 39 cm.
Trousers: L. 100 cm. Waist 87 cm.
James W. Robertson Estate, 1919 (B.1818)
Color Plate LXVI

Having served as special representative to the coronation of Czar Alexander III of Russia in 1883, Colonel Curtis P. Iaukea, the King's Chamberlain, was a seasoned diplomat and well able to carry out his mission in 1887 as Envoy Extraordinary and Minister Plenipotentiary to the Court of St. James. His uniform, made in London while attending Queen Victoria's Jubilee, conforms to the British style generally favored by the Kalākaua court for formal diplomatic occasions. Although the fern and taro leaf decoration originated as part of the Kamehameha court symbolism, it was extensively used throughout the Kalākaua era, adding a dazzling touch of elegance to court functions whether at home or abroad.

274. David Kalākaua in Youth, unknown photographer

Daguerreotype; tinted, gold highlights, c. 1850
10.7 × 8 cm.
Kapi'olani-Kalaniana'ole Collection, 1923 (1971.179.19)

During his reign, Kalākaua was a favorite subject of photographers around the world, but few images depict him in earlier life. About 16 years old in this daguerreotype, Kalākaua already reflects the jaunty confidence and social ease that impressed most people who knew him in his maturity.

275. King Kalākaua and Robert Louis Stevenson at Waikīkī Beach, 1889, unknown photographer

Silver print by Gurrey, c. 1910
26.1 × 19.6 cm.
Not illustrated

Among the eminent visitors who found Hawai'i an idyllic haven during the Kalākaua era was Robert Louis Stevenson. Hoping to gain some relief from tuberculosis, the renowned author passed through Honolulu in 1888 during a yachting cruise of the Pacific and returned the following year. Stevenson settled for about six months, living mostly at Waikīkī, where he finished a novel, *The Master of Ballantrae*. During this pleasant interlude, Kalākaua and Stevenson became friends, frequently hosting *lū'au* and informal parties for one another. Stevenson returned in 1893 after the fall of the Monarchy but stayed only five weeks before going back home to Samoa, where he died a year later.

276. King Kalākaua Lying in State, by J. J. Williams (1853-1926)

Albumen print, 1891
Verso autographed "Kapiolani"
17.7 × 23.2 cm.

Ailing and tired, Kalākaua went to California toward the end of November, 1890, hoping that the invigorating climate would restore him to health. Temporarily revived after a warm welcome and a round of receptions and banquets, the King went to Mexico and on the return suffered a mild stroke at Santa Barbara. Proceeding to San Francisco to recuperate, he steadily worsened and succumbed to Bright's disease at the Palace Hotel on January 20, 1891—the second Hawaiian King to die abroad.

His body was returned to Honolulu nine days later and lay in state in the Throne Room of 'Iolani Palace until the funeral took place on February 15. Surrounded by towering *kāhili*, the coffin draped in ancient featherwork, Queen Kapi'olani kneels in silent grief as a lady-in-waiting looks on. Kapi'olani followed him in death nine years later, June 24, 1899.

277. Queen Lili'uokalani, unknown photographer

Albumen print, 1892
50 × 44.2 cm.
Charles R. Bishop Collection, 1893 (1893.10.190)

Lili'uokalani succeeded her brother to the throne on January 29, 1891, destined to rule a few days short of two years before the Monarchy was overthrown. Coming to power a mature woman of 52 years, Lili'uokalani was already well known to her subjects, having ruled as Princess Regent during Kalākaua's absence from the Kingdom on three previous occasions. Stubborn, aristocratic, and proud, she believed in the absolute authority of the ruling class and was determined to restore some of the prerogatives Kalākaua had been forced to relinquish as a consequence of the revolution of 1887. When it became known that she intended to abrogate the "Bayonet Constitution" of 1887 and substitute her own, alarm spread through the foreign business community. The Queen was forced to resign, under pressure, on January 17, 1893. Although she hoped eventually to be restored to the throne, as was Kamehameha III when he ceded his Kingdom to Britain in 1843, events proved otherwise. Embittered, she could do nothing, as the Provisional Government that replaced her became a Republic on July 4, 1894, and finally a Territory of the United States.

Imperious and regal, Queen Lili'uokalani is posed in this photograph with one of the symbols of her office—the feather cloak of Kamehameha the Great.

278. Princess Lili'uokalani's Coronation Ball Gown

Silk, velvet, glass and metalic beads
Skirt L. 96.5 cm. Waist 91.5 cm. Jacket L. 48.3 cm.
Circumference of hem 238 cm.
Gift of Lili'uokalani Estate, 1917 (1917.19.01)
Color Plate LXVII

Preparing for her brother's Coronation on Feburary 12, 1883, Princess Lili'uokalani ordered "two elegant dresses" from a Parisian dressmaker, willing to pay up to $200 each for something "very handsome." The gown of "Royal Purple satin and trimmings to match according to the best of your judgment" was intended for the royal soirée on the evening of the Coronation. Both were furnished with two bodices, one sleeveless and the other with sleeves and high neck, "that these dresses might also be worn at dinners." Giving her waist measurement at 32 inches, the Princess made a practical request: "In cutting out these dresses, I hope you will make some allowances in the seams, for in case I should grow any stouter I could let the seams out." Pleased with the results, Lili'uokalani wrote later in her autobiography (1898, p. 101): "each costume was perfect in itself, the lesser details being in harmony with the dress; both were heavily embroidered, and were generally considered to have been the most elegant productions of Parisian art ever seen in Hawaii on this or any other state occasion."

Note: Exhibited at Bishop Museum only.

279. Princess Lili'uokalani, unknown photographer

Daguerreotype, c. 1853
8.3 × 7 cm.
Loaned by Hawaii State Archives
Not illustrated

Born September 2, 1838, a descendant of chiefly families from Maui and Hawai'i, Lili'uokalani grew up with her foster sister, Princess Bernice Pauahi. She was educated at the Chiefs' Children's School and very early demonstrated a natural talent in music, which alone would have insured her fame or enduring respect. She is shown in this early daguerreotype as a teenager, about age 15, several years before her marriage on September 16, 1862, to John O. Dominis, a childhood friend of European and American parentage.

280. "Aloha Oe Farewell to Thee" by Princess Lili'uokalani (1838-1917)

Score, published as sheet music by John Worley, Boston, c. 1884
34.6 × 26.7 cm.
Inscribed: "Me ke Aloha Pumehana C. P. Iaukea"
Gift of Curtis P. Iaukea, 1933
Not illustrated

Aloha 'Oe was inspired by a weekend trip Lili'uokalani made on horseback to the ranch of her brother's chamberlain, Edwin Boyd, in 1878. Taking leave the last day, she chanced to see one of her companions receive a *lei* from a Hawaiian girl, and touched by the tender parting, began to hum during the long ride home. Next day she set to paper the words and music of this love song, her most famous composition.

The song is intensely original in sentiment (even though the melodic line is adapted from Charles Crozat Converse's 1857 ballad, "The Rocks Beside the Sea," and the chorus perhaps from George Frederick Root's "There's Music in the Air"). *Aloha 'Oe* still arouses a sense of longing wherever it is heard in parting. Hardly a person alive has not at one time or another felt the pain of a last kiss, or a last embrace:

Farewell to thee, farewell to thee
Thou charming one who dwells among the bowers.
One fond embrace before I now depart
Until we meet again.

281. "Aloha" Bracelet

Human hair, gilt, pearl, glass, ? bone and horn
D. 8.6 cm. H. 3.6 cm.
Gift of Lili'uokalani, 1910 (1910.18.29)

Princess Bernice Pauahi Bishop gave Lili'uokalani this treasured keepsake, made from the hair of her own father, who was also Lili'uokalani's foster father. Victorian in style, yet deeply Hawaiian in sentiment, it is a reminder of the attachment Lili'uokalani retained throughout her life for her ancestral heritage.

282. Hook Pendant on Bead Necklace, *lei palaoa*

Whale bone, walrus and whale ivory, silk ribbon
H. 7.1 cm. W. 2.1 cm. Th. 4.4 cm. (hook)
Bequest of Lili'uokalani, 1921 (1921.14.146)
Not illustrated

Lili'uokalani's respect for ancestral traditions extended to the sacred symbols of her forebears. This *lei palaoa*, still an insignia of chiefs in the days of her youth, was found among her possessions after her death in 1917.

283. Shell Choker

Nerita shells, silk ribbon, thread, metal hook
L. 45.6 cm. W. 2.1 cm.
Bequest of Lili'uokalani, 1921 (1921.14.151)
Not illustrated

This necklace was also found among Lili'uokalani's possessions after her death. The *kūpe'e* shells, often beautifully and subtly colored, were fondly regarded by women of an earlier age. Sewn to velvet or silk ribbon, they were equally admired during the late Victorian era, not only as pleasant reminders of the past, but also as symbols of the natural beauty of the land, or *'āina*—to all Hawaiians the source of spiritual rebirth.

284. Hawaii's Story by Hawaii's Queen, by Lili'uokalani, Queen of Hawai'i (1838-1917)

Octavo; standard cloth cased binding; gold stamped on upper board and spine
Boston: Lothrop, Lee & Shepard Co., c. 1898
Gift of Mrs. Katharine F. Johnson, 1954
Not illustrated

Largely autobiographical, Lili'uokalani's book was an attempt to give her version of the end of the Monarchy. Controversial as soon as it appeared, the book prompted many Hawaiians to denounce her for denigrating the memory of Queen Emma, and for tampering with chiefly genealogies in order to prove herself of royal descent. William N. Armstrong, who had accompanied King Kalākaua around the world in 1881, published a contemporary review in the *Hawaiian Gazette* for March 11, 1898, epitomizing the prevailing European point of view:

In summing up the story told in this book, we believe that it is just that this woman should be judged not by "foreign" but largely by Polynesian standards . . . Compared with many other female sovereigns, she is perhaps equal to the average of them. Like them, she was not selected by the people as a leader, but became so by the accident of her birth. She is obstinate, and suspicious. She never had the sense to seek the advice of honest and capable men. She possessed a pretty little Kingdom, an ideal affair in the singular harmony that existed between the natives and the whites. She had abundant income from it. The whites did not stand aloof . . . All that was demanded of her was decent government. She did not have sense enough to see it. In this she shared, by inheritance the defects of her brother's character. She went too far. The whites demanded, absolutely, stable government. In her book she gives the best and most powerful reasons for her overthrow . . . She has driven the last nail into her political coffin.

285. Great Seal of the Republic of Hawai'i

Bronze, koa wood
H. 50 cm. W. 50 cm. D. (of seal) 31.8 cm.
Purchase from Eugene Buffandeau, 1933 (1933.46)

The revolutionaries who forced Lili'uokalani to resign on January 17, 1893, organized a Provisional Government with Sanford B. Dole, a missionary descendant, as its head. One of the first acts of the new regime was to outlaw and remove from use the Crown and other insignia of the Monarchy.

Unable to achieve immediate annexation to the United States as expected, the embarrassed government had little recourse but to proclaim itself the Republic of Hawai'i on July 4, 1894, with Dole its first President. As a symbol of office the old royal Coat of Arms was modified and converted to the Great Seal of the Republic of Hawai'i by eliminating all symbols offensive to the new government. Among the changes, the Crown was replaced by a rising sun, symbol of a new era, and the pendant royal order became a phoenix rising in triumphant rejuvenation from the ashes of Monarchy. The supporters, the chiefly twins dressed in Hawaiian featherwork on the royal Coat of Arms, were replaced by a likeness of the statue of

Kamehameha the Great, and the Goddess of Liberty. Thus was represented the old and the new, the fusion of two races.

286. "Another Shotgun Wedding, with *Neither* Party Willing," by Charles Jay Taylor (1855-1929)

Cartoon cover for Puck, December 1, 1897, published by Keppler & Schwarzmann
32.7 × 23.2 cm.

Annexation to the United States had been discussed seriously as early as the 1850's and was close to becoming a reality when the death of Kamehameha III intervened in 1855. The new King, Kamehameha IV, promptly put an end to negotiations, no doubt in part because of the negative views he had formed while visiting America five years earlier. The issue came up again during the reign of Lunalilo but was temporarily resolved early in Kalākaua's reign by a Reciprocity Treaty that brought commercial advantages to the Kingdom in the form of reduced tariffs on sugar exported to the United States. When the McKinley Tariff Act of 1891 negated these advantages, annexation again came to the forefront, substantially contributing to Lili'uokalani's overthrow in 1893. Almost immediately the Provisional Government presented a treaty for consideration by the U. S. Congress, but President Cleveland, installed in office in March, 1893, withdrew it and ordered an investigation of the Hawaiian situation. President McKinley returned to power four years later and presented a similar annexation treaty to the U. S. Senate on June 16, 1897, prompting this political cartoon. When the importance of Pearl Harbor as a strategic outpost in the Pacific became apparent with the outbreak of war in the Philippines, the annexation treaty was hastily signed, July 7, 1898. Once administrative matters were worked out, Hawai'i became a U. S. Territory on June 14, 1900.

287. The Hawaiian and American Flags in Union

Silk, thread
H. 76 cm. W. 60 cm.
Gift of John and Gertrude Lombard, 1974 (1942.11.05)
Not illustrated

Many Hawaiians were deeply saddened or bitter about annexation but could do little more than accept the situation. Others welcomed the new union with bursts of patriotic enthusiasm. When these flags came to Bishop Museum in 1942 they were carefully wrapped around the handle of a *kāhili*, the symbolic union of two nations and two cultures. The Hawaiian and 46-star American flag, dating between 1907 and 1912, belonged to the family of anti-Americanist William Cornwell, who served briefly as Queen Lili'uokalani's Minister of Finance in 1892, and again in January, 1893, at the moment of her overthrow.

288. Hawaiian Flag Quilt

Cotton
L. 214 cm. W. 214 cm.
Gift of Mrs. Agusta Suder, in memory of Lucy Wilcox,
1970 (1970.53)

After annexation, many Hawaiians continued to revere the old symbols of monarchy, including the Hawaiian flag—a compromise by Kamehameha I between the British Union Jack and the Stars and Stripes. The flag quilt became a popular favorite, this one incorporating an unusually detailed representation of the royal Coat of Arms with the legend, "Kuuhae Hawaii," My Beloved Flag. Stories still circulate of one prominent turn-of-the-century family who boasted how their children were all born under the Hawaiian flag—a flag quilt on the canopy of their four-poster bed.

289. Hawaiian Coin Belt

Silver, enamel
L. 78 cm. W. 4 cm.
Anonymous gift (1980.74)

Hawaiian silver coins, which King Kalākaua issued in 1883 with much political and financial stress on the Kingdom, ceased to be legal tender in 1904 once Hawai'i became a functioning Territory. Many coins that had not been redeemed were converted to jewelry or other sentimental items to evoke and preserve the spirit of the monarchy. This belt, one of the more unusual creations, contains 54 Hawaiian dimes and a silver dollar buckle, enameled to accent the royal Coat of Arms.

290. Selection of Coat of Arms Jewelry

Color Plate LXVIII

Upper left: Brooch

Sterling, enamel. Marked "W"
H. 2.9 cm. W. 5.1 cm.
Inscribed "M.I.S. Aug. 3, 1904"
The inscription is the birthday of Mary Isabel Salter, and the date she moved from Honolulu.
Gift of Mary Salter Braams, 1958 (HH 630)

Upper right: Pendant

Sterling, enamel. Made by H. W. Foster & Co.
H. 5 cm. W. 4 cm.
Inscribed "Miss J. P. Aloha Oe to J. P. H."
John P. Helelio was a member of the Royal Hawaiian Band, who died in 1928.
Gift of Selma Allen Zucke, 1958 (HH 1936)

Lower right: Brooch

1883 silver dollar, enamel
D. 3.8 cm.
Gift of Mrs. Walter C. Miller, in memory of Evangeline Midler, 1975 (1975.250)

Lower left: Brooch

Silver, enamel
H. 3.9 cm. W. 3 cm.
Anonymous gift (HH 1943)

Center, clockwise starting at top: Watch Fob

Sterling, enamel. Made by H. Culman & Co., Honolulu
H. 2.4 cm. W. 2.3 cm.
Gift of Mary Salter Braams, 1958 (HH 631)

Pair of Cufflinks

Gilt sterling, enamel. Made by H. Culman & Co., Honolulu
H. 1.7 cm. W. 1.5 cm.
Gift of Mrs. Morris C. Augur, 1962 (HH 1937)

Pin

Sterling, enamel
H. 1.2 cm. W. 2.7 cm.
Gift of Mary Salter Braams, 1958 (HH 632)

Tie Pin

Gold, enamel
H. 5.7 cm. W. 1.5 cm.
Gift of Mrs. Morris C. Augur, 1962 (HH 1938)

Watch Fob

1883 silver quarter, enamel
D. 2.4 cm.
Lucy K. Peabody, Kalani and Edgar Henriques Collection, 1946 (HH 343)

291a-c. Funeral of Queen Lili'uokalani, unknown photographer(s)

Silver prints, 1917
10 × 15 cm.
a: Lying in State, Kawaiaha'o Church
b: Bier Leaving 'Iolani Palace
c: Funeral Procession to the Royal Mausoleum
Not illustrated

Lili'uokalani died at her home, Washington Place, on November 11, 1917, at age 79. Regarded with affection and deep respect in her later years, the last Queen of Hawai'i was laid to rest with all the dignity and honor of a bygone era. Her funeral procession through the streets of Honolulu on November 18 was the last sad *aloha* of the Monarchy—the final Farewell to Thee.

Contemporary Reflections of the Past

Attempting to revive and preserve the eroding cultural heritage of Hawai'i, King David Kalākaua founded a semisecret oranization in the fall of 1886, called the Hale Nauā Society, or "Temple of Science." According to Article I of its constitution, "The object of this Society is the revival of Ancient Science of Hawaii in combination with the promotion and advancement of Modern Sciences, Art, Literature, and Philanthropy" (Kuykendall, 1967, p. 345). It was patterned vaguely after an older manifestation of the same name that, among other things, sought to prevent strife and bloodshed by uniting chiefly families through bonds of kinship and rank, and by verifying the genealogies of affiliates to ruling dynasties.

The Society met regularly for a number of years and espoused many practical as well as purely ceremonial objectives. By working through the Hale Nauā, Kalākaua was able to record and print a creation chant called the Kumulipo, collect genealogies, protect the bones and relics of revered ancestors, legitimize native medical practitioners, and much more. Perhaps most important, the Hale Nauā inculcated in its members a much needed sense of pride in being Hawaiian.

Unfortunately, the Society's political and ritual activities were poorly understood or feared by many Europeans and Americans. Pious-minded critics maligned the Society as "a retrograde step" and gossiped about supposed illicit sexual adventures. Because material revivalism and ritual manipulation of objects of material culture—including fishhooks, cordage, bark cloth, and wooden and stone images—also figured prominently in the Society's Masonic-like ritual (Kalākaua was a 33rd degree Mason), many people simply dismissed the Hale Nauā as the "Ball of Twine Society." The Hale Nauā disintegrated after Kalākaua's death in 1891, and had disappeared by the turn of the century.

In 1975 Rocky Ka'iouliokahihikolo'ehu Jensen founded Hale Nauā III, a Society of Hawaiian Artists, to carry out some of the unfinished objectives of Kalākaua's 19th-century forerunner. Directed to young artists of Hawaiian descent, the Society's primary goal is to stress and maintain "Hawaiianness" in the arts. By studying language, genealogy, history, herbal medicine, religion, and other forms of traditional knowledge practiced by their *kupuna*, or ancestors, Society members strive to reveal ancient learning in contemporary art. According to Director Rocky Jensen, Hale Nauā III provides Hawaiian artists with the chance to address a continuing need, felt throughout the Pacific, for art that springs from indigenous sources:

Culture is a living entity which should grow and change with time. Therefore, to understand what we are today, we must first know and understand our past, for the solution to today's problems lies therein. The form which culture takes today must have its roots in what has come before. The remolding of an "injured" culture is a slow ongoing task. It must begin with the gathering of material about the past. Only then can we give new meanings to the culture of the present and insure the security of OUR FUTURE.

292. Memorial Bust of King Kalākaua, by Allen Hutchinson (1855-1929)

Bronze, c. 1896
H. 73 cm. W. 61 cm.
Allen Hutchinson Collection, 1897 (1897.04.02)

The memorial bust of King David Kalākaua dressed in a stylized feather robe reflects a lesser known side of his character—that of a man intent upon preserving the traditions of his ancestors. The bust was commissioned by the Kalākaua Monument Association and exhibited by the Kilohana Art League in 1896, shortly before the Association dissolved and the bust was forgotten. During his residence in Honolulu between 1888 and 1897, the itinerant British sculptor, Allen Hutchinson, had modeled other busts of the King, but it was this likeness the Monument Association chose—not the more familiar one of Kalākaua dressed in court attire, resplendent with royal orders and decorations.

293. The Legends and Myths of Hawaii. The Fables and Folk-Lore of a Strange People, by His Hawaiian Majesty King David Kalākaua (1836-1891)

Published by Charles L. Webster & Co., New York , 1888
A. W. F. Fuller Collection, 1964
Not illustrated

Kalākaua was regarded by many contemporaries as one of the best versed men in the lore of his forefathers. To lend substance to the Hawaiian Renaissance he sought to achieve, Kalākaua published a collection of legends and semihistorical narratives, drawing freely upon the works of such noted authorities as Abraham Fornander, W. D. Alexander, Emma Nākuina Beckley, and others. Although written in florid Victorian prose and with occasional lapses of accuracy, the book is still regarded as an early and significant contribution to Hawaiian oral literature. The need for such a book is made clear in the lengthy introduction by Rollin M. Daggett, the U.S. Minister to Hawai'i. Daggett gloomily foresaw the Hawaiian race "slowly sinking . . . their footprints will grow more dim . . . until finally their voices will be heard no more for ever" (p. 64).

294. "Meeting Place of an Ancient Secret Society," by
Robert C. Barnfield (1855-1893)

Watercolor
31 × 46.5 cm.
Inscribed "From an Old Print R. C. Barnfield 1886"
Kapiʻolani-Kalanianaʻole Collection, 1923

Kalākaua seems to have been deeply affected by this
view. He used a detail for the cover of *Legends and Myths
of Hawaii* and a lithograph in the introduction,
suggestively titled to establish legitimacy and lend
precedence to his own Hale Naua Society. The scene
actually depicts the Royal Mausoleum at Hale-o-Keawe
(see No. 31), which Surgeon William Ellis visited in 1779,
later publishing an amateur sketch in *An Authentic
Narrative of a Voyage Performed by Captain Cook and Captain
Clerke* in 1782. Barnfield's rather grotesque copy is one of
several works Kalākaua commissioned the English artist
to reproduce from late 18th- and early 19th-century
historic voyages during his eight-year residence in
Honolulu. Kalākaua hung some of the works, including
this one, in ʻIolani Palace, exhibiting eleven others of
similar nature at the Paris *Exposition Universelle* of 1889.

295. "Hawaiian godess [*sic*]—Kiha wahine or Lailai,"
by Robert C. Barnfield (1855-1893)

Watercolor
22.9 × 16.9 cm.
*Pencil notes: "Carved in Kou wood" "Found in 1885 by
natives of Waimanu."*
"This drawing is about ⅓ of real size. R. C. Barnfield."
*"The back of the head is hollow for decorating with
feathers or hair–and the eyes were of pearl shell. Human
teeth in mouth."*

An avid collector himself, Kalākaua became friendly with
a bacteriologist and amateur ethnologist, Dr. Eduard
Arning, who visited Hawaiʻi between 1883 and 1886 to
study leprosy under the auspices of the government's
Board of Health. During his travels throughout the island
group, Arning assembled a large ethnographic collection,
obtaining this wooden image from a site near
Laupāhoehoe, Hawaiʻi. Kalākaua had this watercolor and
several plaster replicas made before Arning took the
original to the Berlin Museum für Völkerkunde.
Kiha-wahine is the name of a powerful lizard goddess,
and Laʻilaʻi is the legendary first woman, ancestress of
the Hawaiian race. Both names were apparently supplied
at the time of the image's discovery.

296. Post Image

Wood, black pigment
H. 192 cm. D. 10 cm.
Gift of Princess Kawānanakoa, 1920 (B. 2140)
Not illustrated

Hearing of a mysterious cave high on the slopes of Mt.
Hualālai on Hawaiʻi, King Kalākaua sent a party to
investigate toward the end of September, 1885. According
to Dr. Eduard Arning and Joseph S. Emerson, two other
collectors who explored the cave about the same time, it
contained about two dozen roughly carved wooden posts
arranged in two semicircles around an "altar"—that is, a
stone-lined fire pit with a shell trumpet concealed in a
small cavity (Arning, 1931; Eichhorn, 1929; Rose, n.d.).
Isolated, and unknown to the nearest modern
inhabitants, the cave was interpreted as a secret place of
worship—perhaps used by one of the revivalist cults that
had sprung up after abrogation of the *kapu* system in
1819. Kalākaua had a number of the post images
removed, and this is one of at least five (out of 12
surviving) that appear to have descended through the
Hale Naua Society. Bearing uncanny resemblance to
Barnfield's watercolor, "Meeting Place of an Ancient
Secret Society" (No. 294), the so-called "Cave of Images"
undoubtedly figured heavily in the King's founding of
the Hale Naua Society a year later.

297. Stone Image, *kiʻi pohaku*

Vesicular basalt
H. 26 cm. W. 22.5 cm. Th. 14 cm.
Kapiʻolani-Kalanianaʻole Collection, 1923 (B. 7224)
Not illustrated

From King Kalākaua's collection, this stone image of late
19th-century manufacture is one of several presumed to
have been used by the Hale Naua Society. From time to
time, the Society arranged special exhibits for public
enlightenment, both in Hawaiʻi and abroad, including a
traveling exhibit of some 130 curios sent to Sydney and
on to Melbourne for the Australian Centennial
International Exhibition of 1888. The Hale Naua display
proved so popular that it was sent to the Paris *Exposition
Universelle* the following year, then on to a Colonial
Exhibition in Bremen, Germany, in 1890.

298. Covered Container of the Hale Naua Society

Kou wood, with varied contents
H. 25 cm. D. 15.2 cm.
Purchase from Grace Chapman, 1902 (5822)

Turned wooden containers like this were used by
members of King Kalākaua's semisecret Society to hold
ethnographic items of ritual importance. This one, used
by a woman, originally contained two stone adz blades,
two *ʻulu maika* or circular gamestones, an imitation shark
tooth weapon carved from bone, a piece of *kauila* wood
used for medicine, one fragmentary and three complete
fishhooks, a miniature *niho palaoa* of walrus ivory, two
pieces of bark cloth, a fragment of netting, a maroon and
gold ribbon in the colors of the Society, five photographs
of "idols," and a ball of twine—the last said to be the
Society's most important symbol. Most other Hale Naua
containers, the contents of which have survived, offer a
similar range of materials, but little is known about their
actual ceremonial uses.

299. Cloth Cape of the Hale Nauā Society

Cotton, silk, thread
L. 67 cm. W. 47 cm.
Purchase from Grace Chapman, 1902 (5859)

Used by a man, this yellow cloth cape ornamented with one black and two red crescents, and two black half-crescents, formed part of the regalia of the Hale Nauā Society. In design, color, and size, it is a faithful reproduction of 19th-century feather capes.

300. Imitation Feather Cloak

Crepe paper, cotton, thread
L. 118 cm. W. 284 cm.
Elizabeth Kalaniana'ole Woods Estate, 1935 (HH 743)

For 200 years, feather cloaks and capes have played a major symbolic role, whether as chiefly insignia of rank, items of court display, or costumes for modern parades and historic pageants. As cloaks and capes of indigenous feathers became increasingly rare, or inappropriate for one reason or another, substitutes were made in a variety of materials. This one, probably created in the early 20th century, is an exceptionally fine and intricate example showing the high degree of skill and patience lavished on cloaks and capes of "base" materials. Although its exact function has been lost, it descended in the Kalākaua family through the King's nephew, Prince Jonah Kūhio Kalaniana'ole and his widow, Mrs. Woods.

301. Feather Cape, *'ahu'ula*

Dyed duck feathers, cotton shrimp net, thread
L. 47.0 cm. W. 65.5 cm.
Loaned by Dennis Kana'e Keawe
Not illustrated

Purposefully left unfinished by the maker, Dennis Kana'e Keawe, this cape can perhaps be regarded as symbolic of the future of Hawaiian featherwork. The black semicrescent on a yellow background accented with red, triangular-like motifs reflect the traditional past, but the dyed duck feathers on shrimp netting are 20th-century adaptations. Such capes promise a vital future for one of the most distinctive art traditions of Hawai'i and the Pacific.

302. Coconut Dance Rattle, *'uli'uli*, by Kukui'ola
(1939-   )

Coconut shell, hemp, muslin, chicken and pheasant feathers
H. 30 cm. L. 52 cm. W. 36 cm.
Loaned by Hale Nauā III Society of Hawaiian Artists

Dance rattles persist as an important part of contemporary *hula*, having remained in use since first observed by Captain Cook more than 200 years ago. Besides serving a musical function (see No. 153), they have also entered the domain of symbolic art. This example is modeled after one seen in a *hula* performance

and sketched by Louis Choris while visiting Hawai'i with the Russian expedition under Otto von Kotzebue late in 1816.

303. "Hula Ku'i," by A. C. Kahekiliuila Lagunero
(1945-   )

Charcoal, 1979
63 × 47 cm.
Loaned by Hale Nauā III Society of Hawaiian Artists

Ku'i means to join. Hula Ku'i, the name of a *hula* danced since the days of King Kalākaua's Jubilee in 1886, is here the joining of old steps with the new.

304. "Kihanuilulumoku, the Dragon That Shook the Island," by Rocky Ka'iouliokahihikolo'ehu Jensen
(1944-   )

Wood, human hair, bark cloth, cordage
H. 68.5 cm.
Loaned by Hale Nauā III Society of Hawaiian Artists
Not illustrated

Legend states that Kihanuilulumoku was a powerful dragon who guarded the portals of Pali-uli, the legendary homeland, by alighting atop *'ohi'a* trees and pouncing on trespassers. Kihanuilulumoku was also a great chief of Waipi'o Valley, Hawai'i, and father of the renowned Līloa. This statue represents an *'aumakua*, or ancestral image of a departed great one.

305. "Wailua A'u (My Two Souls)," by Rocky Ka'iouliokahihikolo'ehu Jensen (1944-   ).

Koa wood, brass
H. 66 cm. W. 38.5 cm. Th. 28 cm.
Loaned by Hale Nauā III Society of Hawaiian Artists

Ancient Hawaiians, according to the artist, believed that our subconscious (*'unihipili*) must be influenced by the superior conscious soul (*'uhane*) in order to achieve success on this earthly plane. In this sculpture, the face with round eyes represents 'Uhane, "The Soul That Persistently Returns to Me," or "The Enlightened One." The face with squinting eyes is 'Unihipili, "My Fragile Soul That Clings," or "The One Who Is Enlightened."

Kings and Queens of Hawai'i

	Reign
King Kamehameha I (?1758-1819)	-1819
King Kamehameha II (Liholiho, c. 1797-1824) Queen Kamāmalu (c. 1800-1824)	1819-1824
King Kamehameha III (Kauikeaouli, 1813-1854) Queen Kalama (1817-1870)	1825-1854
King Kamehameha IV (Alexander Liholiho, 1834-1863) Queen Emma (1836-1885)	1855-1863
King Kamehameha V (Lot Kamehameha, 1830-1872)	1863-1872
King Lunalilo (William Charles Lunalilo, 1835-1874)	1873-1874
King Kalākaua (David Kalākaua, 1836-1891) Queen Kapi'olani (1834-1899)	1874-1891
Queen Lili'uokalani (Lydia Kamaka'eha Dominis, 1838-1917) Prince Consort John Owen Dominis (1832-1891)	1891-1893

Provisional Government of Hawai'i
1893-1894

Republic of Hawai'i
1894-1900

Territory of Hawai'i
1900-1959

State of Hawai'i
1959

Glossary

Hawaiian, English, and Scientific Names of Native Plants and Animals Used in the Manufacture of Hawaiian Artifacts

ali'ipoe	wind canna seeds	*Canna indica*
'apapane	Hawaiian honey creeper (bird)	*Himatione sanguinea*
'ie'ie	aerial rootlet of a vine	*Freycinetia arborea*
'i'iwi	Hawaiian honey creeper	*Vestiaria coccinea*
ipu	Hawaiian bottle gourd	*Lagenaria siceraria*
'iwa	fern	*Asplenium horridum*
kalo	taro	*Colocasia esculenta*
kauila	tree	*Alphitonia ponderosa*
ki	ti plant	*Cordyline terminalis*
koa	tree	*Acacia koa*
kou	tree	*Cordia subcordata*
kūkae pua'a	grass	*Digitaria pruriens*
kukui	tree	*Aleurites moluccana*
mamo	Hawaiian honey creeper	*Drepanis pacifica*
'ōhelo	berry-bearing shrub	*Vaccinium reticulatum*
olonā	cordage	*Touchardia latifolia*
'ō'ō	Hawaiian honey eater (bird)	*Moho* spp.
pueo	Hawaiian short-eared owl	*Asio flammeus sandwichensis*
wauke	paper mulberry	*Broussonetia papyrifera*

Bibliography

Adler, Jacob (Editor)
1967. *The Journal of Prince Alexander Liholiho: The Voyages Made to the United States, England, and France in 1849-1850.* Honolulu: Univ. Hawaii Press.

Alexander, Mary Charlotte, and Charlotte Peabody Dodge
1941. *Punahou 1841-1941.* Berkeley and Los Angeles: Univ. California Press.

Arago, Jacques Etienne Victor
1823. *Narrative of a Voyage round the World . . . during the Years 1817-20 . . .* London: Treuttel.

Armstrong, William Nevins
1904. *Around the World with a King.* New York: Stokes.

Arning, Eduard
1931. Ethnographische Notizen aus Hawaii 1883-86. *Mitt. Mus. Völkerkunde Hamburg* 16. (Trans. by Michael Mueller-Ali, 1974. Bishop Mus. Library MS.)

Barrère, Dorothy B., Mary Kawena Pukui, and Marion Kelly
1980. *Hula: Historical Perspectives.* Pacific Anthropological Rec. 30. Dept. Anthropology, Bishop Mus.

Barrot, Theodore-Adolphe
1978. *Unless Haste Is Made.* Kailua: Press Pacifica.

Beaglehole, J. C.
1955-1967. *The Journals of Captain James Cook on His Voyages of Discovery.* 3 vols. Cambridge.

Beckwith, Martha Warren
1970. *Hawaiian Mythology.* Honolulu: Univ. Hawaii Press.
1972. *The Kumulipo: A Hawaiian Creation Chant.* Honolulu: Univ. Press Hawaii.

Bell, Edward
1929-1930. The Log of the Chatham. *Honolulu Mercury* 1(4):7-26; 1(5):55-69; 1(6):76-90; 2(1):80-91; 2(2):119-129.

Berger, Andrew J.
1972. *Hawaiian Birdlife.* Honolulu: Univ. Press Hawaii.

Bille, Steen
1849-1851. *Beretning om Corvetten Galathea's Reise omkring Jorden 1845, 46 og 47.* Deel 1-3. Copenhagen: Reitzel. (Trans. by the Misses Hedemann, 1931. Bishop Mus. Library MS.)

Blonde
1826. *Voyage of the H.M.S. Blonde to the Sandwich Islands in the Years 1824-1825.* London: Murray.

Bloxam, Andrew
1925. *Diary of Andrew Bloxam, Naturalist of the "Blonde," on Her Trip to the Hawaiian Islands from England, 1824-25.* B. P. Bishop Mus. Spec. Publ. 10. Honolulu.

Brigham, William Tufts
1906. Old Hawaiian Carvings. *Mem. B. P. Bishop Mus.* 2(2):173-184.
1908. The Ancient Hawaiian House. *Mem. B. P. Bishop Mus.* 2(3):185-378.

Buck, Peter H. (Te Rangi Hiroa)
1957. *Arts and Crafts of Hawaii.* B. P. Bishop Mus. Spec. Publ. 45. Honolulu.

Cook, James, and James King
1784. *A Voyage to the Pacific Ocean . . . for Making Discoveries in the Northern Hemisphere . . . In the Years 1776, 1777, 1778, 1779, and 1780.* London: W. and A. Strahan for G. Nicol and T. Cadell.

Dampier, Robert
1971. *To the Sandwich Islands on H.M.S. Blonde.* Pauline King Joerger (ed.). Honolulu: Univ. Press Hawaii.

Daws, Gavan
1968. *Shoal of Time: A History of the Hawaiian Islands.* New York: Macmillan.
1973. *Holy Man: Father Damien of Molokai.* New York: Harper and Row.

Du Petit-Thouars, Abel Aubert
1840-1864. *Voyage autour du monde sur la frégate la Vénus, pendant les années 1836-1839 . . .* Paris: Gide.

Eichhorn, Aug.
1929. Alt-Hawaiische Kultobjekte und Kultgeräte. *Baessler Archiv,* Band XIII, Heft 1. Berlin.

Elwes, Robert
1854. *A Sketcher's Tour round the World.* London: Hurst and Blackett.

Emerson, Joseph S.
n.d. Catalog of Hawaiian Curios, No. 1. Div. Ethnology, Bishop Mus. MS. Honolulu.

Emory, Kenneth P.
1928. *Archaeology of Nihoa and Necker Islands.* B. P. Bishop Mus. Bull. 53. Honolulu.

Feher, Joseph
1969. *Hawaii: A Pictoral History.* B. P. Bishop Mus. Spec. Publ. 58. Honolulu.

Fornander, Abraham
  1916. Hawaiian Antiquities and Folk-Lore. *Mem. B. P. Bishop Mus.* 4(1-3): 1-662.

Handy, E. S. Craighill, and Mary Kawena Pukui
  1958. *The Polynesian Family System in Ka-'u, Hawai'i.* Wellington, New Zealand: Polynesian Soc.

Henshaw, Henry Wetherbee
  1920. Autobiographical Notes. *Condor,* May.

Jarves, James Jackson
  1843. *History of the Hawaiian or Sandwich Islands.* London: Moxon.

Jensen, Lucia Tarallo
  1977. Background of Ornament. Letters to the Editor, *Honolulu Advertiser,* October 21.

Johnson, Rubellite Kawena
  1979. Can the Humanities Help the Search for Traditional Hawaiian Values? *Hawaii Comm. for Humanities Newsletter,* May, pp. 1, 7-8.

Jones, Stella M.
  1973. *Hawaiian Quilts.* Honolulu: Daughters of Hawaii, Honolulu Acad. Arts, and Mission Houses Mus. First published 1930.

Kalakaua, David
  1888. *The Legends and Myths of Hawaii: The Fables and Folk-Lore of a Strange People.* R. M. Daggett (ed.). New York: Webster.

Kamakau, Samuel M.
  1961. *Ruling Chiefs of Hawaii.* Honolulu: Kamehameha Schools Press.

  1976. *The Works of the People of Old: Na Hana a ka Po'e Kahiko.* Dorothy B. Barrère (ed.), Mary Kawena Pukui (trans.). B. P. Bishop Spec. Publ. 61. Honolulu.

Kanahele, George S. (Editor)
  1979. *Hawaiian Music and Musicians: An Illustrated History.* Honolulu: Univ. Press Hawaii

Kent, Harold Winfield
  1965. *Charles Reed Bishop: Man of Hawaii.* Palo Alto: Pacific Books.

Kotzebue, Otto von
  1830. *A New Voyage Round the World, in the Years 1823 . . . 1826.* London: Colburn and Bentley.

Kuykendall, Ralph S.
  1938, 1953, 1967. *The Hawaiian Kingdom.* Vol. I, 1778-1854, *Foundation and Transformation.* Vol. II, 1854-1874, *Twenty Critical Years.* Vol. III, 1874-1893, *The Kalakaua Dynasty.* Honolulu: Univ. Hawaii Press.

Liliuokalani
  1898. *Hawaii's Story by Hawaii's Queen.* Boston: Lee and Shepard.

Malo, David
  1951. *Hawaiian Antiquities (Moolelo Hawaii).* Nathaniel B. Emerson (Trans.). B. P. Bishop Mus. Spec. Publ. 2. 2nd ed. Honolulu.

Pukui, Mary Kawena, and Samuel H. Elbert
  1971. *Hawaiian Dictionary.* Honolulu: Univ. Hawaii Press.

Roberts, Helen H.
  1926. *Ancient Hawaiian Music.* B. P. Bishop Mus. Bull. 29. Honolulu.

Rose, Roger G.
  1978a. Reconstructing the Art and Religion of Hawaii. Review of *Hawaiian Sculpture,* by J. Halley Cox and William H. Davenport. *J. Polynesian Soc.* 87(3): 267-278.

  1978b. *Symbols of Sovereignty: Feather Girdles of Tahiti and Hawai'i.* Pacific Anthropological Rec. 28. Dept. Anthropology, Bishop Mus. Honolulu.

  n.d. The Cave of Images: "New" Discoveries in Hawaiian Art. Paper read at Second International Symposium on the Art of Oceania, Wellington, New Zealand, Feb. 1-8, 1978.

Sinclair, Marjorie
  1976. *Nāhi'ena'ena: Sacred Daughter of Hawai'i.* Honolulu: Univ. Press Hawaii.

Stewart, C. S.
  1828. *Journal of a Residence in the Sandwich Islands,during the Years 1823, 1824, and 1825 . . .* London: Fisher.

Wilkes, Charles
  1845. *Narrative of the United States Exploring Expedition, during the Years 1838 . . . 1842.* Philadelphia: Lea and Blanchard. (First edition published 1844 by C. Sherman.)

Wiswell, Ella (Trans.)
  1978. *Hawaii in 1819: A Narrative Account by Louis Claude de Saulses de Freycinet.* Notes and Comments by Marion Kelly. Pacific Anthropological Rec. 26. Dept. Anthropology, Bishop Mus. Honolulu.

Photo Credits

Seth Joel

(color) 1, 16, 24, 25, 26, 27, 29, 30, 37, 65, 91, 101, 119, 122, 123, 140, 150, 153, 161, 164, 165, 168, 170, 173, 174, 177, (178-183) 179, 181, 184, 185, 186 (187-189) 197, 199, 203, 208, 210, 214, 215, 219, 220, 221, 223, 231, 233, 234, 234 detail, 240, 241, 247, 248, 251, 252, 253, 253 detail, 254, 255, 256, 257, 273, 278, 290.

(b/w) 32, 36, 39, 40, 43, 76, 77, 79, 81, 84, 85, 86, 88, 89, (90, 92, 93, 94) 98, 99, 100, 103, 104, 105, 106, 107, 108, 109, 110, 111, 112, 113, 114, 115, 117, 118, 120, 121, 125, 128, 129a, 129b, 130, 131, 132, 147, 148, 149, 162, 169, 175, 194, 198, 200, 201, 202, 205, 206, 207, 209, 211, 212, 213, 224, 239, 249, 259, 260, 261 (263 & 268) (264 & 265) (266 & 267) 281, 285, 288, 289, 292, 298, 300, 302, 303, 305.

Bishop Museum Photographer, Ben Patnoi

28, 33, 35, 38, 41, 42, 54, 78, 80, 82, 83, 87, 95a, 95b, 97a-c (102, 133, 134) (134, 135) 151, 160, 152 (154, 157, 158, 159) (155, 156) 163, 176, 196, 258, 299.

(color) 171

Bishop Museum Photo Archives

2, 3, 4, 5, 6, 7a, 7b, 8a, 8b, 9, 10, 11, 12, 14, 15, 23, 31, 46, 47, 50, 52, 53, 56, 57, 58, 59, 62, 66, 67, 68, 69a, 69b, 73, 74, 75, 136, 137, 138, 141, 143, 144, 146, 216, 217, 222, 225a, 225b, 229, 230, 237, 238, 242, 243, 244, 246, 250, 270, 272, 274, 276, 277, 286, 294, 295.

(color) 13, 22, 49, 167, 228